OPERATIONAL ANALYSIS OF REGIONAL RURAL BANKS

OPERATIONAL ANALYSIS OF REGIONAL RURAL BANKS

Dr. Shyama Charan Acharya
Dr. Ashok Kumar Mohanty

Publications

KALPAZ PUBLICATIONS
DELHI-110 052

Operational Analysis of Regional Rural Banks

Rs. 690

ISBN : 81-7835-412-8

Published in 2006 in India by
Kalpaz Publications,
C-30, Satyawati Nagar,
Delhi-110 052
Email : kalpaz@hotmail.com

Lasertype Setting by: Tact Computer Graphics, Delhi
Printed at: Salasar Imaging System, Delhi

Contents

	Preface	7
1.	Introduction	9
2.	Significance and Sources of Rural Credit and Emerging Scenario of Rural Banking in India	21
3.	Evolution, Growth and Development of RRBs at the All-India Level	49
4.	Socio-Economic Background of and Imperatives for RRBs in Orissa	87
5.	Analysis of the Progress and Performance of RRBs in Orissa (Total Sample)	121
6.	Analysis of the progress and performance of RRBs in Orissa (Variable wise)	185
7.	Summary of the findings and conclusions	245
	Annexure-I	275
	Annexure-II	277
	Bibliography	279
	Index	287

Preface

Rural Banking is an important dimension of rural economy which essentially caters to the growing credit needs of rural areas. Development of rural economy holds the key to natural development. Needless to emphasize that credit is a vital input for the development of the rural economy for financing agriculture and allied activities, rural infrastructure and poverty alleviation programme meant for the weaker sections of the rural population. Rural Banking system is the institutional mechanism which brings credit to those who need it Rural Banking System in India is comprised of Co-operatives, the rural branches of Commercial Banks and Regional Rural Banks. While Co-operation credit institutions have completed almost a century, the commercial Banks and century, the commercial Banks and Regional Rural Banks have been in the rural credit scene for almost 36 and 30 years respectively. These rural credit institutions have undoubtedly broadened the much needed rural banking infrastructure in the country through branch expansion deposit mobilization and credit dispensation.

Regional Rural Banks (RRBs) which form an integrate part of the rural banking system, came into existence in 1975. The uniqueness of RRBs lies in the harmonious blending of low-cost profile and local feel of Co-operative credit system and modernized on look and professional management of Commercial Banks. They were created exclusively for catering to the credit requirements of the rural poor.

The role of these rural banks is more relevant in a State like Orissa Which has been designated as the poorest State in India, according to the latest estimates of the Planning Commission. The incidence of poverty is more in rural areas with 48 per cent of the rural population in the State living below poverty line. More strikingly, in no other States in the country, the density of rural population is so high as that (nearly

87 per cent) in Orissa. Agriculture is the dominant sector of the State's economy contributions nearly 40 per cent of the NSDP. Further, 66 per cent of its total work force depends directly or indirectly on agriculture for their livelihood. In view of these reasons, the present work bears added significance, as the RRBs assume a very crucial role as a rural financial intermediary for the upliftment of the rural poor.

The RRB system in India, ever since its inception in 1975, grew very rapidly. The number of these banks reached to 196 caring 492 districts with a branch network of 14517. It accounts for nearly 66 per cent of all Rural Financial Institutions in the country. The advent of RRBs made it possible to achieve the bank population ratio of 1:15000 by the end of March 2000 in the country. Despite these commendable performances, in course of time, strained viability, directed lending programmes, weak recycling of credits due to poor recovery, cutthroat competition in the make of liberalization and globalisation initiated in the economy are some of the emerging challenges facing RRBs in the country of late, a proposal for merger of RRBs with their sponsoring bank has been mooted by the Govt. More importantly, the banking sector reforms initiated in the early kinetics have made ranging implications on the performance of RRBs. Against this back drop, a modest attempt has been made in this book to cover all these issues at length and also to assess the quantitative and qualitative impact of the reform measures on the performance of RRBs. Such a study is expected to bring to the fore the strength and weaknesses of RRBs so that appropriate corrective measures can be taken for the rectification of the weaknesses to make them organizationally vibrant operationally sound and socially relevant.

Dr. S. C. Acharya
Dr. A. K. Mohanty

1
Introduction

1.1.1. Agriculture and rural development form integral part of India's development strategy even in the days of electronic and telecommunication revolution that is having an edge over other development instruments. Rural development has been *sine qua non* in the process of accelerating pace of economic development and significantly improving the standard and quality of living of rural households. Needless to emphasise that credit is a vital input for accelerating the pace of development of the rural economy through financing of agriculture and allied activities, rural infrastructure and poverty alleviation programme meant for the weaker sections of the rural population. In the context of the magnitude of future rural credit requirements, the Washington based Food Policy Research Institute has drawn the attention of the policy makers in India. The Institute has categorically pointed out that demand for food in India will be far more than its supply by the year 2020.[1] Keeping in view the need for doubling country's food production, NABARD has estimated the production as well as investment credit requirements for the period from 1998-99 to 2007-08. Accordingly, average annual disbursements of Rs. 1281.76 billion of production credit and Rs. 328.66 billion of investment credit to the rural and farm sector will have to be made as against Rs. 107.45 billion and Rs. 62.68 billion per annum respectively already made on the basis of average annual disbursement during the past 14 years' period.[2] Besides, the data show that by the end of the year 1999-2000, the various rural credit institutions in India were managing an annual credit flow to the tune of Rs. 41,800 Crore which was expected to reach a level of Rs. 51,500 Crore by the end of the year 2000-2001.[3] These figures of the present and future credit requirements call for the need to suitably reorient the farm development policy in particular and the rural credit policy in general.

1.1.2. Rural Banking System is the institutional mechanism which brings rural credit to those who need it. Rural Banking System in India is comprised of cooperatives, the rural branches of commercial banks (CBs) and Regional Rural Banks (RRBs). While cooperative credit institutions have completed 95 years, the CBs and RRBs have been for almost 31 and 25 years respectively. In fact, the structure has been very unique in India as compared to any other country in the world. It serves around 120 million rural households residing in about 7 lakh villages through a large number of cooperative outlets and rural branches of CBs and RRBs.[4] These rural credit institutions have undoubtedly broadened the much needed rural banking infrastructure in the country through branch expansion, deposit mobilisation and credit dispensation.

1.1.3. Regional Rural Banks (RRBs) which form an integral part of the rural banking system, came into existence in 1975 and have been working along with the cooperatives and CBs in meeting the increasing credit requirements in rural area. The uniqueness of RRBs lies in the harmonious blending of low-cost profile and local feel of cooperative credit system and modernised outlook and professional management of CBs. It was created exclusively for catering to the credit requirements of the rural poor. The RRB system in India ever since their inception in 1975 grew very rapidly. The number of these banks reached to 196 covering 492 districts with a branch network of 14517 by March 2000. RRBs account for nearly 66 per cent of all rural financial institutions in the country. The per capita lending by the RRBs is about Rs. 8100 with more than 124 lakh borrowal accounts and per account deposit is Rs. 5300 with above 440 lakh deposit accounts. It is with the advent of RRBs that the bank population ratio of 1:15000 could be achieved by the end of March 2000 in the country. Despite these commendable performances, in course of time the RRB system has become financially weak/ unviable and is facing several pernicious problems. The net impact of this has been manifested in the form of huge accumulated losses of RRBs to the tune of nearly Rs. 3000 crore as on 31 March, 2000. Out of 196 RRBs in the country, 140 are in an unviable condition and have become a prime cause of concern for all concerned.[5]

Significance of the Study

1.2.1. The study entitled "Operational Analysis of Regional Rural Banks in Orissa" is undertaken in appraising the performance of RRBs in a State like Orissa which has been designated as the poorest State in the country, according to the latest estimates of the Planning Commission.[6] Agriculture contributes 40 per cent of the State's Net Domestic Product (NSDP) and provides employment opportunities to nearly 66 per cent of the total workforce directly or indirectly. More strikingly, 86.6 per cent of State's population live in rural areas of which nearly 48 per cent live below poverty line. In no other State of India the density of rural population is higher than Orissa. Thus, the economy of Orissa is rural and agricultural in character with high incidence of poverty. The State is highly prone to natural calamities like flood, cyclone and drought which further compound the problem of underdevelopment in the State. In addition to the facts given above, even after so much of efforts to expand the base of institutional rural finance, 60 per cent of rural credit is still provided by non-institutional agencies viz. village moneylenders, friends and relatives in the State. In view of the reasons stated above, the RRBs assume a very crucial role as a rural financial intermediary for the upliftment of rural poor in the State. Hence, the establishment of RRBs began in 1976 and by now there are 9 RRBs with 843 branches operating in the State. In collaboration with Central and State Government, they have been actively participating in the rural development of Orissa through deposit mobilisation, credit deployment and financing of anti-poverty programmes like IRDP, RLEGP, ERRP, JRY etc. While the performance of RRBs in terms of branch expansion, deposit mobilisation, credit deployment etc. are somewhat satisfactory, over the years, they have faced several problems. Strained viability, directed lending programmes, weak recycling of credits due to poor recovery, cut-throat competition in the wake of liberalisation and globalisation drive initiated in the economy are some of the emerging challenges facing RRBs in the State. Four out of the total nine RRBs in Orissa are incurring losses and none of them have yet attained sustainable viability. More importantly, the banking sector reforms initiated in the early nineties, have wide ranging implications on the performance of RRBs in the State as well as in the country. Against this backdrop it is thought expedient to undertake the study of operational analysis of RRBs in the State and to assess the quantitative and qualitative impact of these reform measures on their performance. Such a study is expected to bring to the fore the strengths and weaknesses of the RRBs so that appropriate corrective measures can be taken for the rectification of the weaknesses to make the RRBs organisationally vibrant, operationally sound, financially viable and socially relevant.[7]

Objectives of the Study

1.3.1. The study broadly aims at making an analysis of all the basic operations of RRBs in Orissa and assessing the impact of banking sector reforms on their performance. More specifically, the objectives of the study are :

1. Analysis of the structural growth and geographical coverage of RRBs in Orissa.
2. Trends in resource mobilisation drive of RRBs in the State through own funds, borrowings and deposits.
3. Trends in deployment of credit for both agricultural and non-agricultural operations.
4. Performance appraisal of RRBs in the recovery front.
5. Analysis of operational efficiency of RRBs in terms of eight ratios.
6. Analysis of productivity of RRBs in terms of business per branch and per employee.
7. Profitability analysis.

Sources of Data

1.4.1. The secondary data constitute the major data source for the study. The theoretical background of the study is based on an exhaustive list of research articles and books on the subject compiled by the National Social Science Documentation Centre (NASSDOC), ICSSR, New Delhi. These study materials have been collected from Jawaharlal Nehru Library, University of Bombay, Indira Gandhi Institute of Development Research (IGIDR), Mumbai, Centre for Monitoring Indian Economy (CM1E), Mumbai and EPW Research Foundation Office, Mumbai. The quantitative information such as Statistics on RRBs, other banking statistics and RBI Bulletins, Economic Surveys of Orissa, Statistical Abstracts of Orissa and India, Annual Reports of individual RRBs and other RBI and NABARD publications were collected from NABARD Central Library and RBI, Mumbai, NABARD Regional Office, Bureau of Economics and Statistics, Orissa, State Level Bankers' Committee (SLBC), Bhubaneswar and head offices of the individual RRBs in Orissa.

Selection of Samples

1.5.1. The sample comprises of all the nine RRBs operating in Orissa and hence, represents the whole universe. All these 9 RRBs established during the period from 1976 to 1982, have been in operation till now.

Study Period

1.6.1. The period of the study is confined to 15 years commencing from 1985-86 to 1999-2000. The selection of this period is significant in view of the fact that the process of liberalisation in Indian economy started in mid-eighties and got intensified in 1991 with the enunciation of the New Economic Policy (NEP). The criteria of profitability and viability of rural credit structure get due recognition in this liberalised policy regime even without jeopardising the social objectives of rural banking. Hence the period from 1986 to 2000 has been chosen for the study. The whole period of study is divided into two parts: the pre-reform period consisting of 7 years from 1986 to 1991-92 and post-reform period consisting of 8 years from 1992-93 to 1999-2000. It is worthwhile to mention that the RRBs were adopting the calendar year as the accounting year till 1987. However, from 1988-89 onwards the financial year was adopted as the accounting year by these banks. Therefore, in some tables used in the study, the calendar year 1988 has been replaced by the financial year 1988-89. In that case the year 1988-89 is comprised of a period of 15 months from 1 January 1988 to 31 March 1989. Further, due to non-availability of data, the micro-level analysis covers only the post-reform period, i.e., 1992-93 to 1999-2000. This is not likely to affect the findings of the study, as the data relating to this period are reasonably expected to reflect the impact of reform measures on the performance of the RRBs in Orissa.

Methodology

1.7.1. The study involves the application of accounting and statistical tools like ratios, percentages, arithmetic averages, trends, flow charts, tables and graphs etc. with the help of which the basic operations of RRBs in the State have been critically analysed.

Study Plan

1.8.1. The study is broadly divided into two parts. The first part comprises of the theoretical discussions on the subject. The second part constitutes the core of the study encompassing the empirical analysis of the collected data. In sum the study is dealt in the following seven chapters. The first chapter deals with the introduction, scope, objectives, methodology, sources of data, hypotheses of the study and a brief review of the available literature on the subject. Second chapter covers a theoretical discussion on the significance and sources of rural credit, rural credit policy adopted so far and the emerging scenario of rural banking in India. The third chapter contains an analysis on the evolution, growth and development of RRBs at the all-India level including a brief review of the reports of various committees on RRBs. The fourth chapter highlights the imperatives for RRBs in the sample State of Orissa in the context of its prevailing socio-economic background. The fifth chapter seeks to make an analysis of the progress and performance of the RRBs in Orissa (Total sample). The sixth chapter deals with the variable-wise analysis of the progress and performance of RRBs in the state. The seventh and last chapter contains the summary of the findings and conclusions of the study.

Hypotheses of the Study

1.9.1. The study aims at testing the following hypotheses on the basis of the available data. The test applies only to the region and holds good for the sample to which the study relates. The hypotheses are :

1. Rural credit gets more and more institutionalised with the passage of time.
2. RRBs operate mainly in rural areas. RRBs in Orissa stay ahead of those at the all-India level so far as coverage of rural areas in terms of rural branch network, deposit mobilisation from and credit dispensation in rural areas are concerned.
3. Structural growth of RRBs in terms of branch expansion was concentrated in the eighties (1981 to 1990) whereas, the functional

growth, in terms of deposits, advances or volume of business, was concentrated in the nineties (1991-2000).

4. RRBs in Orissa have depended for their resources much more on deposits than on other resources available to them. Their dependence on borrowing has been gradually declining over the years. Thus, the trend of self-reliance can be looked upon as a welcome sign.
5. Term Deposits constitute the major part of total deposits followed by Savings Bank Deposits and Current Deposits of RRBs in Orissa.
6. In terms of composition of credit structure of RRBs, there is a tendency towards diversification of the credit portfolio with specific emphasis being laid on giving credit support to the non-farm sector in addition to meeting the credit needs of the farm sector.
7. Though RRBs are providing credit to farm and non-farm sector, but are gradually shifting their priorities from farm sector to the non-farm sector lending. They are going away from the professed agenda of working in rural areas for the development of the rural economy in the post-reform period; and
8. The revamping initiatives and other developmental measures taken by NABARD, RBI and GOI on RRBs, have left positive impact on the working and financial health of the RRBs in the State especially towards the latter half of the period from 1992-93 to 1999-2000.

Review of Literature

1.10.1. Ever since the inception of the RRBs in 1975, the RRBs and the various aspects of their performance have attracted the attention of academicians, researchers and policymakers from time to time in the country. The first review of the working of the RRBs was done just two years after their establishment, i.e., in 1977 by the Review Committee headed by Prof. M.L. Dantwala. The Committee was of the view that the superiority of the RRB as an agency of rural credit over the rural branches of commercial banks is derived from its relatively low cost of operation, its simplicity and low profile, local staff and the close association of the district level agricultural and rural development agencies and personnel. The Committee, therefore, liked to suggest the GOl and RBI to take steps to initiate the process of making the RRBs an integral part of the rural credit structure.[8]

1.10.2. A comprehensive case study on the RRBs was conducted by CD. Wadhva in his book entitled *Rural Bank for Rural Development* (1980). The study revealed that the major problem that the RRBs face relates to the degree of their acceptance within the rural environment in terms of the support received from the existing institutional credit agencies and the state government with whom they have to constantly interact and depend on various ways.[9] The author urged the policy makers to reorganise and revitalise the working of these banks for achieving the objectives for which they have been set up.

1.10.3. Professor Patel and Shete of the National Institute of Bank Management (NIBM), Pune have made a useful analysis in the form of regional comparison of performance and prospects of the RRBs in different parts of the country. The authors have also given a comparative picture of the performance in terms of some indicators of the cooperatives and commercial banks (CBs) operating within the jurisdiction of the RRBs.[10] Varde and Singh of the NIBM, Pune have also conducted an analysis of the profitability performance of the RRBs. The authors for this purpose developed their own framework using ten indicators.[11] Shete and Karkal conducted an extensive study on the problems and perspectives of rural credit in the context of RRBs. The authors analysed the purpose and logic of the existing credit institutions providing rural credit, the desirability of and the changing circumstances that necessitated for the setting up of a new institution called RRB. The study also contained an analysis of the business, financial and profitability performance of RRBs in India for the period from 1975 to 1987. They prescribed a specified quantum of business per staff under a given set of conditions to enable the branch to attain viability.[12]

1.10.4. The book entitled *RRBs in Rajasthan* by M.S. Bapna (1989) contains an analysis of the performance of 4 RRBs in Rajasthan for the period from 1975 to 1984. In his work, the author has identified the problems faced by these RRBs and offered suggestions for their solution. He was of the view that the operational strategies for RRBs would call for several policy-changes/policy-shifts, besides the induction of immense political will for their implementation.[13] Sunil

Kumar conducted a case study which was published in 1990, on the working and performance of RRBs in Bihar in which the author has highlighted the achievements and failures of RRBs in the State during the period from 1979 to 1985.[14] B.P. Sinha Roy has made case studies of 8 RRBs in West Bengal during the period from 1976 to 1988-89 in his book entitled *RRBs in West Bengal* (1994). The study contains the findings of an intensive field investigation into the conditions of RRBs in West Bengal. He observed that in spite of shortcomings like declining trend of C-D Ratios and most of the RRBs incurring losses, the RRBs have rendered immeasurable service to the rural economy of the State.[15]

1.10.5. V. Balmohan Das, J.V. Pravakar Rao and P. Hrushikesava Rao have made a critical analysis of the performance of RRBs in the country in their book entitled *Rural Banks and Rural Credit.* The authors have observed that the concentration of RRBs in a few states gives a bad picture about them. They were of the opinion that the state government concerned should provide adequate facilities to RRBs to step up their operations. The RBI should chalk out its branch licensing policy in a manner consistent with the objective of filling the rural credit gap in the backward and hilly regions like North-Eastern Region.[16]

1.10.6. T.K. Velayudham and V. Sankaranarayanan have written an exhaustive article on RRBs covering all important issues including viability, policy matters and the issue of merger of RRBs with their sponsor banks. The paper takes stock of the role and problems of the RRBs in perspectives and draws inferences to aid policy formulation. The authors have observed that RRBs arc not just rural credit agencies. They are more than that: they are a fruitful exercise in bank-led rural growth.[17]

1.10.7. I.N. Rao has conducted a comprehcnsive study on the Role of the RRBs in the Economic Development of Orissa covering all the 9 RRBs in Orissa for the period from 1976 to 1987. In his work, the author has made an in-depth analysis of the sectoral disbursements of credit by RRBs in Orissa. The impact of branch expansion and growth of advances of RRBs on the rural development of the State in terms of food-grains production, per capita income, area sown, gross and net area irrigated, agricultural yield etc. was dealt with in this study.[18]

1.10.8. Baidyanath Mishra has written a useful article on RRBs and Rural development in which he has dealt with the setting up of

RRBs, their characteristics, expansion operation in terms of branch network, deposits and advances and the problems faced by the RRBs in Orissa and at all-India level. He was of the view that the merger of RRBs with their sponsor banks to make them viable would defeat the very purpose of RRBs and the very concept of poor man's bank would vanish in the post-merger scenario.[19]

1.10.9. S.C. Acharya has made an analysis of the contribution of RRBs in terms of financial assistance to and employment generation in the village and cottage industries sector in Orissa. The author is of the view that the rural banks should on one the hand, include a consumption component in the total loans so as not to impair the productive efficiency of the artisans due to lack of maintenance income and ensure proper utilisation of the loans given, on the other.[20]

1.10.10. The review of the foregoing literature, which have thrown light on the wide ranging aspects of RRBs in the State and national level, helped to a considerable extent, in getting the background materials for the present study and also in the designing of its overall framework.

References

1. As quoted in Patel, A.R., "Rural Credit System; Need for Restructuring", *Kurukshetra,* New Delhi, Vol. 49, No. 4, January, 2001, p. 17.
2. *Ibid.*
3. Jain, S.C., "Rural Financing in Transition", *Kurukshetra,* Vol. 49, No. 1, October 2000 (Annual Issue), New Delhi, p. 2.
4. RBI, Banking Statistics, Quarterly Handout, March 2000, Mumbai, p.1.
5. (i) *Ibid.*

   (ii) *Annual Report, 1999-2000,* NABARD, Mumbai, p. 117.
6. "Poverty Estimates for 1999-2000", *Kurukshetra,* Vol. 49(7), April, 2001, New Delhi, IInd Cover Page.
7. Data given in this Paragraph have been collected from the *Economic Survey of Orissa, 2000-2001,* Bureau of Economic and Statistics, Government of Orissa, Bhubaneswar.
8. *Report of the Review Committee on Regional Rural Banks,* Reserve Bank of India, Bombay, 1978, p. 75.
9. C.D. Wadhva, *Rural Banks for Rural Development,* Macmillan Co. of India Ltd., Madras (1980), p. 115.

10. Patel, K.V. and Shete, N.B., "RRBs: Performance and Prospects", *Prajnan*, NIBM, Pune, Jan-Mar., 1980, pp. 1-40.

11. Varde, V. S. and Singh, S.P., "Profitability Performance of Regional Rural Banks", *Prajnan,* NIBM, Pune, Oct-Dec., 1982, pp. 247-56.

12. Shete, N.B. and Karkal. G.L. "RRBs: Problems and Perspectives of Rural Credit", *Prajnan*, 18(2), April-June, 1989, NIBM, Pune, pp. 136-67.

13. Bapna, M.S., *RRBs in Rajastan,* Himalaya Publishing House (1989), p.76.

14. Kumar, S., *RRBs and Rural Development*, Deep and Deep Publications, New Delhi (1990).

15. Sinha Roy, B.P., *RRBs in West Bengal,* Mittal Publications, New Delhi (1994), p. 95.

16. Das, V.B. Rao, J.V.P. and Rao, P.H.K., *Rural Banks and Rural Credit,* Discovery Publishing House, New Delhi, p. 57.

17. Velayudham, T.K. and Sankaranarayanan, V., "RRBs and Rural Credit; Some Issues", *Economic and Political Weekly (EPW),* 22 September, 1990, p. 2157-2164.

18. Rao, I.N., "Role of RRBs in the Economic Development of Orissa (A study between 1976-1987)", Ph.D. Thesis (1991), Berhampur University, Orissa.

19. Mishra, B.N., "RRBs and Rural Development", *Kurukshetra*, Vol. XLIV, No. 10, July 1996, pp. 26-29.

20. Acharya, S.C., "Financing of Village and Cottage Industries by RRBs in Orissa", *The Orissa Journal of Commerce*, Vol. XXIII, No. 2, 1999, pp. 77-82.

2

Significance and Sources of Rural Credit and Emerging Scenario of Rural Banking in India

Introduction

2.1.1. Recognising the fact that farm and rural development have been *sine qua non* in the process of accelerating the pace of economic development and significantly improving the standard of quality of living of rural households, the nationalist government which came to power in 1947, soon embarked on an active and expanding programme of development, giving high priority to the alleviation of acute rural poverty in the country. Therefore, the GOI adopted several measures and policies effective enough to deal not only with the rural debt accumulated over the years but also, more basically, with the current credit requirements of the rural population. The democratic State also took up the mission of peasantising agriculture and ending the exploitative practices of indigenous financiers to liberate the poor masses from the strangulating debts. Apart from legislation, the State also created long-term financial instruments to consolidate the entitlements of the liberated peasantry. The socialist orientation of the State prompted it to issue mandates regarding allocation of credit rates and differentiation of interest rates in favour of loans to be given to Below-Poverty Line (BPL) households under the self-employment programme. "After independence, i.e., in 1950-51, the amount of credit disbursed by the rural credit system for rural development was only Rs.24.2 crore. On the other hand, by the year 1999-2000, the various institutional sources were managing in annual rural credit flow to the tune of Rs. 41,800 crore which was expected to reach a level of Rs.51,500 crore by the end of the year 2000-2001.[1] Apart from such spectacular growth in the volume of rural credit, drastic changes are taking place in the field of rural finance. Against this backdrop, this chapter makes an attempt to discuss the significance and sources of rural credit, the emerging scenario of rural banking in India and the role of institutional agencies in providing credit to the rural sector, etc.

Significance of Rural Credit

Rural Indebtedness

2.2.1. In the pre-independence period, villagers who formed the bulk of the population were almost totally dependent on moneylenders and indigenous bankers for meeting their credit requirements. Table 2.1 shows that nearly 93 per cent of the credit requirements of the farming households were met by the moneylenders and other non-institutional credit agencies. "The available credit was not only inadequate but could be secured only at high rates of interest (ranging from 20 to 50 per cent per annum)".[2] Non-payment of loans at the stipulated time or failure to pay interest regularly, resulted therefore, in cumulative growth of debt and ultimately often in loss of land, gold or whatever other assets they had initially offered as security. "During the depression of the 1930, when agricultural prices had fallen very sharply the world over, most villagers in India had to sell such gold and precious ornaments as they had in order to make ends meet".[3] Massive growth of rural debt and large transfers of such assets as they had were thus an almost permanent feature of the Indian economy. It is in this context that the All India Rural Credit Survey Committee (AIRCSC) (1951) made an assessment of the indebtedness of the rural households in the country. The data given in the Table 2.1 which show the shares of different credit agencies in the cash debt of the cultivating and all rural households, are based on the findings of the AIRCSC in their report published in 1954. The table shows that 7.3 per cent of the farmers' cash borrowing in 1951-52 was from the formal sector. The share of the cooperative sector was only 3.1 per cent and moneylenders provided 69.7 per cent of the cash debt. Total cash debt per cultivator was Rs. 316/-, Cash-Debt to Equity Ratio was only 5.9 per cent. The survey further revealed that 46 per cent of the farmers were reported to be in debt "compared to 36 per cent and 32 per cent of the agricultural labourers and other non-cultivators respectively".[4]

Probably this state of rural indebtedness led the government to follow the policy of enlarging the role of institutional credit agencies and correspondingly to reduce the role of non-institutional credit agencies especially, the private moneylenders. This became the guiding principle for framing the rural credit policy in the post-independence period.

Table 2.1

Average Borrowings from Different Credit Agencies in 1951 (By Cultivators and All Rural Households) (Figures in Percentage)

Sl. No.	*Credit Agencies*	*Proportion of borrowings from each agency to total borrowing of Cultivators*	*of All Rural Households*
1.	Government	3.3	3.1
2.	Cooperatives	3.1	2.9
3.	Commercial Banks	0.9	1.1
(A)	**Total Institutional Borrowings**	**7.3**	**7.1**
4.	Moneylenders	69.7	68.6
5.	Traders and Commission Agents	5.5	6.1
6.	Friends and Relatives	14.2	14.4
7.	Landlords	1.5	2.0
8.	Others	1.8	1.8
(B)	**Total Non-Institutional Borrowings**	**92.7**	**92.9**
(C)	**Total (A+B)**	**100**	**100**
9.	Total Capital Stock in 1951 (Rupee per cultivating household)	5356	–
10.	Total Cash Debt in 1951 (Rupee per cultivating household)	316	–
11.	Cash-Debt to Equity Ratio (in per cent)	5.9	–
12.	Percentage of Farmers in Debt (in per cent)	46	–

Source: All India Rural Credit Severy, *The Survey Report*, Vol. 1, Part-2 (Credit Agenices), p. 3.

Transformation in the Field of Agriculture

2.2.2. With two-thirds of the population dependent on agricultural sector and nearly 73 per cent of the population of the country still living in the rural areas, raising both rural income and farm productivity are important not only from the economic point of view of accelerating growth but also for the implications that they have for human development. The need for sustained and rapid improvement in agricultural performance thus remains critical for India's future growth and poverty reduction. Therefore, for an accelerated growth of agriculture, substantial increase in credit for short-term production purposes as well as for investment became imperative. However, the agricultural and rural scene is changing. Commercial crops including plantation of various types are coming to the fore. Horticulture, floriculture, acquaculture, pisciculture, sericulture, apiculture, poultry farming, dairy farming, rearing of goats and sheep etc. were all emerging as profitable activities. These activities not only provide the rural folk the means of earning income round the year and enable them to raise the standard of their living but also divert surplus labour from agriculture to other productive activities. In addition to this, there has been a lot of transformation in the field of agriculture over the last five decades. "The gross irrigated area increased from 22.56 million hectare in 1950-51 to 83.6 million hectares by the end of the 8th Five Year Plan. Similarly, the total food-grains production which was 58.5 million tonnes in 1950-51 went up to a level of 200.9 million tonnes in 1998-99. There has also been increased adoption of agricultural equipment by farmers. Number of oil engine pumps in use rose from 83,000 in 1950-51 to 1,16,65,000 in 1987. The number of tractors in use also went up from 8,600 in 1950-51 to 9,89,598 in 1997-98. Consumption of fertilisers increased from 0.66 million tonnes in 1950-51 to 18.2 million tonnes in 1998-99".[5] There has been a shift from the traditional methods to scientific methods of cultivation through the adoption of modern technology in agriculture. All these activities in addition to those mentioned above would require credit of a larger magnitude for the rural sector in general and the farm sector in particular. Therefore, credit dispersion was perceived as a major tool to accelerate the pace of agriculture and rural development.

Slowing down of Capital Formation in Agriculture

2.2.3. Notwithstanding serious constraints like the persistence of overwhelming dependence on rain, sizeable proportion of agriculture being in the hands of small farmers and archaic land laws, Indian agriculture has become a dynamic sector in the wake of 'green revolution'. "But the overall annual growth rate of agriculture, which was 5.2 per cent in the 80s, fell to 2.6 per cent in the 90s. It is pertinent to note that between 1992 and 1997 only 8 per cent of the total public investment has gone to agriculture and the actual investment in this sector fell about 40 per cent short of the planned level".[6] The declining level of public investment in agriculture "from the peak of Rs. 1796 crore in 1980-81 to Rs. 1132 crore (at 1980-81 prices) in 1996-97 and its relative share from 38.7 per cent to 16.2 per cent during the same period" [7] has become a cause of concern. This decline has been despite introduction in 1995-96 of the provisions for loans to the state governments for investment in agricultural infrastructure out of Rural Infrastructure Development Fund (RIDF). Similarly, studies have shown that the pace of private capital formation in agriculture has also slowed down markedly since 1980s. For example, "share of bank investment in agriculture has gone down from 17.67 per cent in 1983-84 to 10.69 per cent in 1997-98".[8] Studies have shown that there is high degree of correlation between credit flow and private capital formation and also that public sector investment does induce investments in the private sector.[9] Therefore, the optimism that the corporate sector will, in a liberalised environment, make large investments in agriculture cannot be materialised especially, in the absence of efforts to expand public investment in agriculture. Further, the decline in credit flow to agriculture will contribute to the slowing down of investment in rural areas. Keeping this alarming development in view, the investment in agriculture, both private and public needs to be stepped up.

2.2.4. The farm sector development is only a part of rural development. Rural development in real terms would mean improvement in the quality of the life of the rural society as a whole including the weaker sections in the non-farm sector who need a specific thrust for the development of the rural society. Credit is one of the basic needs for the all round development of the rural sector such as irrigation, marketing, transport, infrastructure, land reforms and development etc.

It is in these contexts that the significance of the rural credit needs to be viewed.

Rural Credit Policy

2.3.1. The role of credit and credit institutions in augmenting production and productivity is well recognised. The main thrust of Indian public policy towards rural credit has, therefore, been to ensure that sufficient and timely credit, at reasonable rate of interest, is made available to a large segment of rural population. "The strategy of developing rural financial services has thus been a three pronged one, consisting of :

(i) Expansion of institutional structure

(ii) Directed lending and

(iii) Concessional or subsidised credit"[10]

This approach has resulted in an impressive growth of rural banking in India over the last five decades in terms of its outreach, credit disbursement and support to the poverty alleviation programmes.

Broadening of Institutional Base

2.3.2. The foundations for the building up of a broad credit infrastructure for rural credit were laid by the Report of the AIRCSC of 1954.[11] The main attempt was to expand rural credit and displace the moneylender. It viewed rural credit in India then as being "inadequate and unsuitable". The chosen institutional vehicles for this purpose have been :

(i) the promotion of cooperatives,

(ii) a concerted push to establish branches in rural areas by commercial banks,

(iii) the creation of a new instrumentality in the form of Regional Rural Banks (RRBs).

Directed Lending

2.3.3. Public intervention in rural credit was considered essential to overcome "hostile factors" which could normally discourage lending to agriculture, such as absence of collateral, particularly among the poorer sections, high cost of servicing, geographically dispersed customers, lack of trained and motivated rural bankers and seasonal nature of agricultural activities. Consequently, special credit programmes were drawn up for channelling subsidised credit to the rural sector.

Priority Sector Lending

2.3.4. The concept of "priority sector" was evolved in the late sixties to focus attention on the credit needs of certain neglected and under-privileged sectors. After an initial experiment with the Preferential Refinance Scheme, the principal instrument chosen for directing the credit flow into the priority sector, including agriculture, was the stipulation of the proportion of the total net bank credit to be deployed in these sectors by specific target dates. Public sector banks were asked to extend credit to the priority sector to the extent of at least one-third of their total credit outstanding by March 1979. The target was raised further by 40 per cent to be achieved by March 1985. It was also stipulated that advances to the weaker sections should reach a level of 25 per cent of the total bank credit outstanding by March 1985. The target for lending for agriculture and allied activities was set at 15 per cent of the total credit to be achieved by March 1985, 16 per cent by March 1987, 17 per cent by March 1989, 18 per cent by March 1990 [of 18 per cent, direct loans 13.5 per cent (minimum) and indirect loans 4.5 per cent (maximum)]. The latest figures show that for meeting the credit needs of agricultural sector, a target of 18 per cent of net bank credit (NBC) in case of 22 public sector banks (PSBs) and SB1 with its 7 Associated Banks has been stipulated. For catering to the credit needs of weaker sections of the society, 10 per cent target of NBC has also been prescribed. Banks also provide huge sum of credit every year to a very large number of poor belonging to weaker sections of the society under government sponsored programmes of poverty alleviation and generation of self-employment. These stipulations are still continuing which is a recognition to the imperfections of the rural credit market.

Concessional or Subsidised Credit

2.3.5. Offering credit at concessional rates has been one of the elements of the strategy for the deployment of rural credit. The principal justification for charging lower interest rates to certain category of borrowers was that farm-based investment activity in the short run does not always yield a return which enables regular servicing of loans and at the same time meet the minimum consumption requirements.[12] Since, concessional lending affects the profitability of the rural financial institutions, a policy of cross-subsidisation and refinance from the Central Bank has to be put in place simultaneously.

Special Role of RBI

2.3.6. A special role was envisaged for the Reserve Bank of India right from the beginning in relation to rural credit. Efforts have been made from the 40s to give refinance to the cooperative banking system. The refinance facility was made available directly by the RBI until the establishment of NABARD in 1982. Since then, the facility has been routed through NABARD. The refinance facility is given both in relation to short-term and long-term credit. The General Line of Credit (GLC) I and II provided to NABARD by the RBI facilitates refinance of short-term credit. The long-term refinance facility was provided by the RBI under two funds namely, National Rural Credit Fund (NRCF) [Long-term operations] and the NRCF [Stabilisation]. Even though these allocations have been stopped now, the capital base of NABARD has been widened from time to time. The capital which is contributed in equal proportion by the GOI and the RBI has been raised from Rs. 100 crores in 1991-92 to Rs. 500 crores in 1995-96. The capital base will be further widened in the coming years.[13]

Emerging Scenario of Rural Banking in India

2.4.1. India may perhaps be one of the very few countries in the world which has during the last five decades introduced several policies in the spheres of agriculture and rural development through assigning the pivotal role to the banking system. In this process, the very structure and texture of the Indian banking has undergone metamorphical change. The central theme of this section has been discussed under three broad headings viz.- early initiatives, evolution of the institutional framework and the new development paradigms in the field of rural banking.

Early Initiatives

2.4.2. For over a hundred years, India has followed a deliberate policy to build and strengthen formal credit institutions. "Initially, under the British Colonial Rules, the Civil Courts strengthen the position of the moneylenders. However, in the late 1800s, moneylenders widely abuse their position, taking advantage of farmers' debts to take over farmers' lands. In 1875, near Poona in today's Maharashtra, rioting farmers evicted moneylenders from their villages (Walker & Rayon, 1990). Following the riots legislation was passed to curb the power of the moneylenders and protect farmers' land."[14]

2.4.3. Efforts to build up the institutional finance system for agriculture in India commenced with the adoption of the Cooperative Societies Act in 1904. "But the cooperative movement came to the limelight in 1915 when the Maclagan Committee on cooperation had recognised the need for provision of capital to agriculture".[15] The Committee advocated for the need to relieve agriculturists from indebtedness to expedite the agricultural growth of the nation. "The Central Banking Enquiry Committee in 1929, after a detailed investigation into the problems of agricultural credit, rural banking and agrarian indebtedness, made suggestions for linking agricultural finance with the central banking functions because it felt that since agricultural activity is an important activity in the national economy, a sound and stable monetary (credit) system could not be expected to operate unless the needs and requirements of this sector are brought within the purview of the central banking system".[16] Thus, in 1935, formal recognition to the agricultural lending was accorded with the establishment of the Reserve Bank of India (RBI) with a separate Agriculture Credit Department (ACD). A special developmental role was envisaged for the RBI in the field of agricultural credit right from its inception.

2.4.4. "Sir Malcolm Darling's Report in 1934 recommended to examine whether commercial banks' (CBs) operations could be coordinated to the advantage of the agriculturists. The Agricultural Finance Subcommittee (Gadgil) examined the question of provision of finance, both short-term and long-term, for agriculture and felt that cooperative financing agencies provided the hot and lasting solution to the problem of rural credit."[17] From the perusal of the above crucial development of the events it is clear that right from the beginning the government made greater attempts to nurture cooperative movement and until 1947, the general thinking was in favour of promoting primary credit cooperative societies in rural areas. "At the instance of the RBI, the Government of India (GOI) appointed the Rural Banking Enquiry Committee in 1949 with wide terms of reference".[18] The Committee headed by Sir Purushottamdas Thakurdas was specially asked to suggest measures for increasing banking facilities in rural areas. The recommendations of the Committee proved to be landmark in the evolution of rural cooperative credit structure to be supported by the RBI.

2.4.5. Notwithstanding the efforts made by the RBI, the share of institutional agencies in rural credit dispersion remained rather meagre (only 7.1 per cent) during the first one-and-a half decade of its operation. Therefore, "RBI convened in 1951, the Informal Conference on Rural Finance of some Co-operators, Economists and Others with Prof. D.R. Gadgil as Chairman, to undertake a review of the RBI's role in the rural finance and to conduct a Rural Credit Survey including all strata of the rural population and covering problems of capital formation in the rural areas as well as the credit requirements of both economic and indigent farmers".[19] A significant outcome of the recommendations of the Informal Conference was the constitution of a "Committee of Direction" headed by A.D. Gorwala to design and advise on the details of the proposed survey. This was the origin and institutional mechanism for the All India Rural Credit Survey (AIRCS) conducted in 1951-52. "It was in turn, the first of several such surveys undertaken to secure the database for framing policies and measures that would make adequate credit available to the rural areas of the country".[20] The general report on the AIRCS was published in 1954. The Committee studied the essential features of the existing credit agencies. The report had an initial 'Statement of Problems' and a concluding 'Integrated Scheme of Rural Credit' with detail recommendations.

Evolution of the Institutional Framework for Rural Credit

2.4.6. The foundations for the building up of a broad credit infrastructure for rural credit were laid by the Report of the AIRCSC of 1954. The main attempt was to expand rural credit and displace the moneylender. It viewed rural credit in India then to be "inadequate and unsuitable".[21] The Committee therefore recommended an integrated scheme of rural credit based on the cooperatives. The Committee envisaged development of cooperative credit system as an exclusive agency for providing agriculture credit supplanting the moneylender. The Committee also urged for a well defined role for CBs in providing credit for agriculture in specialised areas, such as marketing, processing, storage and warehousing. Towards this end, the Committee recommended the establishment of the State Bank of India (SBI) in place of the Imperial Bank of India, with a wide network of branches to undertake rural banking. The All India Rural Credit Review Committee (AIRCRC), 1966 undertook a comprehensive review of the agricultural credit system and recommended for a substantial contribution to come from the commercial banking sector in order to provide credit for both current production and long-term development. The specific recommendation of the Committee was : "the requirements of the agricultural sector were so large and diverse that commercial and cooperative banks can both play a mutually complementary role without getting into conflict with each other".[22]

2.4.7. With the introduction of social control on banks in 1967, the nationalisation of 14 major CBs in 1969 and the subsequent implementation of the Lead Bank Scheme in 1970, branch banking in the rural areas acquired a new momentum. Very soon, the commercial banking system was able to broaden considerably the credit delivery system. Even as this expansion was occurring, Narasimham Working Group (1975) made a recommendation for the setting up of Regional Rural Banks (RRBs) - known as "Small Man's Bank".[23] They were also conceived as low cost institutions, exclusively catering to the credit requirements of the rural poor. There, thus emerged by the end of 1977, three separate institutional arrangements namely the cooperatives, the CBs and the RRBs for providing credit in the rural areas, very often described as the 'Multi-Agency Approach".

2.4.8. To augment long-term lendable resources for investment in agriculture, the Agricultural Refinance Corporation (ARC) was set up in 1963, which was converted into Agricultural Refinance and Development Corporation (ARDC) for providing technical expertise to banks and entrepreneurs willing to invest in agriculture. Since July 1982, ARDC's scope of activities has been expanding to cover entire gamut of activities related to agriculture, tiny/village industries, non-farm sector and rural development and renamed as the National Bank for Agriculture and Rural Development (NABARD) as Apex Bank for the country for the purpose. It took over the functions of the erstwhile Agricultural Credit Department (ACD), Rural Planning and Credit Cell (RPCC) of RBI and ARDC. Its subscribed and paid-up capital has been increased from Rs. 100 crores in 1991-92 to Rs. 500 crores in 1995-96 and is contributed by the GO1 and RBI in equal proportion. NABARD's refinance is available to Stale Land Development Banks (SLDBs), State Cooperative Banks (SCBs), Scheduled CBs and RRBs. While the ultimate beneficiaries of investment credit can be individuals, partnership concerns, companies, state-owned corporations and cooperative societies, production credit is generally given to individuals. NABARD operates throughout the country through its 16 Regional Offices located in the capitals of all the major states and 10 sub-offices.

The New Development Paradigms in the field of Rural Credit

2.4.9. It is worthwhile to mention here the latest development patterns in the field of rural credit. These are micro Finance (mF) Scheme, Rural Infrastructure Development Fund (RIDF) and the Local Area Banks (LABs) in the private sector etc.

Micro Finance (MF)

2.4.10. In the early 90s a tacit consensus appeared to be shaping up among the banking authorities and development professionals that development agencies in the non-governmental sector should be called upon to act as the intermediaries in delivery and management of rural credit. The formal sector took the initiative to develop a supplementary credit delivery system (like NGOs - Non-Governmental Organisations) to act as facilitators or intermediaries. "The beginning was made with NABARD's pilot project in Karnataka (1991-92) of linking Self-Help Groups (SHGs) with formal banks, mediated through the NGO - Mysore Resettlement and Development Agency (MYRADA)".[24] The micro-Finance Projects (mF Projects) were expected to be advantageous to the banking sector from the angles of both fulfilment of its social goals (like reaching out to the poor) and achieving operational efficiency (by externalising the part of the transaction cost). This project also known as Bank - SHG Linkage Project was institutionalised by RBI in 1996 as a normal banking activity of banks under priority sector and service area approach.

Rural-Infrastructure Development Fund (RIDF)

2.4.11. Rural Infrastructure Development Fund (RIDF) was created in 1995-96 by the GOI. RIDF, with NABARD as the nodal agency, gets funds from Indian Scheduled CBs that fail to meet their target of lending at least 18 per cent of net bank credit to agriculture. "The net bank credit of Scheduled CBs hovered around 14 per cent in recent past, i.e., 4 per cent lower than the 18 per cent stipulation under the primary sector lending to agriculture."[25] This is an alternative window which was provided to CBs to contribute to RIDF with a maximum ceiling up to 1.5 per cent of net bank credit, which would be given as loans to the State Governments and other agencies by NABARD for building rural infrastructure. The projects to be funded out of RIDF were identified as the major, medium and minor irrigation projects that are lingering on for years due to paucity of funds at the margin, rural roads and bridges, etc.

Local Area Banks (LABs) in the Private Sector

2.4.12. The RBI announced a set of guidelines on August 24, 1996 for the setting up of Local Area Banks (LABs) in the private sector to promote rural savings and provide credit for viable economic activities in local areas. "As on June 30, 1999, eight LABs have been given approval in principle one each in Maharashtra, Punjab, Andhra Pradesh, Tamil Nadu, Rajasthan and Gujarat and two in Karnataka".[26] The LAB policy gives agriculturists an opportunity to form self-help groups in the form of LABs for their banking needs and to look after the development of their respective areas. This is in line with the multi-agency approach to rural credit. Each banking channel has to meet competition and together they are to meet the growing banking needs of rural India. The capital of LAB has been kept at Rs. 5 crore by the Government.

Non-Banking Financial Companies (NBFCs)

2.4.13. One of the objectives of Rural Credit Policy is to subject the banking system to greater competition and for this purpose introduce new players in the market. "In fact the first Narasimham Committee recommended freedom of entry into the financial system and expressed the view that there was a strong possibility of several new banks with a predominantly local character being set up."[27] In order to realise the above objectives, many NBFCs have come into being in semi-urban and rural areas, catering to the saving and investment requirements of these areas. Though, their present financing is predominantly for consumption purposes, they have the potential to finance rural investment needs. As the agricultural sector further diversifies and its need for different financial services grows, the role of banks and NBFCs would become more and more important.

Kisan Credit Card Scheme

2.4.14. Kisan Credit Card (KCC) Scheme which was operationalised during the year 1998-99, is a landmark in the history of Rural Credit in India. The NABARD in accordance with the announcement in the Union Budget for 1998-99, formulated a model "Kisan Credit Card" Scheme in consultation with the RBI and major banks. The scheme aims at quickening the pace and improving the quality of institutional credit delivery for agricultural purposes and was an innovative attempt at further refining the crop-loan system. "The model scheme was circulated by the RBI to CBs and by the NABARD to Cooperative Banks and RRBs in August 1998. As on 31 March 1999, 22 public sector banks, 81 RRBs and 51 DCCBs (including 2 State Cooperative Banks functioning as Central Financing Agencies) had introduced the Scheme. The public sector banks reported to have issued 6.22 lakh cards with credit facility of Rs. 1473.31 crore (including those issued under their existing similar schemes). The RRBs and the Cooperative Banks have made a beginning during the year, issuing 1.61 lakh cards covering credit facility of Rs. 836.77 crore".[28]

Rural Subsidiaries

2.4.15. The Narasimham Committee at the time of framing its recommendations of Financial Sector Reforms (FSRs) in 1992, had been quite concerned on the issue of Rural Banking. Accordingly, the Committee has come out with a recommendation in the context of making Rural Banking a viable proposition, the Committee has been of the view that "the move should be market driven, based on profitability considerations and brought about through a process of mergers and acquisitions".[29] The Committee felt that the structure of rural credit would have to combine the local character of the RRBs and the resource, skills and organisational/managerial abilities of the commercial banks. With this end in view, the Committee recommended that each public sector bank should set up one or more subsidiaries depending on the size and administrative convenience of each sponsor bank, to take over all the rural branches and where appropriate, swap its rural branches with those of other banks. Such rural banking subsidiaries should be treated at par with RRBs in regard to CRR and SLR requirements and refinance facilities from NABARD and sponsor banks.

2.4.16. Rural banking system in India, today, being the most unparallel in the world has been providing production and investment credit in agriculture sector. Besides, public sector banks also provide credit facilities for a wide range of activities pertaining to socio-economic development of rural population. As the country has been very large along with vast social, economic, cultural and agro-ecological diversities, no straight jacket blueprint of any uniform Rural Banking Model can prove to be flawless to meet area-specific needs and be viable at the same time. However, the search of the GOI, RBI and NABARD for evolving an effective rural banking structure is still going on to make the rural banking institutions financially sound, operationally viable, cost-effective and organisationally most responsive to the changing needs of the rural population.

Sources of Rural Credit

2.5.1. The rural financial system as it has evolved in India, operates through two sets of institutions in the formal and informal sectors (vide Chart - 2.1). The formal sector has adopted a multi-agency approach and includes the cooperatives, public sector CBs and the Regional Rural Banks (RRBs) specially created in 1970s to cater to the rural sector. The institutional arrangements for rural credit in India have been displayed in Chart - 2.2. The informal sector, which operates outside the formal system consists mainly the Rotating Savings and Credit Associations (ROSCA), Traders, Landlords, Merchants, Contractors, Commission Agents, Local Moneylenders etc. The former is governed by the existing rules and regulations in the financial sector, whereas the latter largely functions in an autonomous fashion with its own norms, rules and discipline.

Chart - 2.1
Sources of Rural Credit

Formal Sector	Informal Sector
1. Cooperatives	1. Rotating Savings and Credit Associations
2. Commercial Banks	2. Traders
3. Regional Rural Banks	3. Merchants
	4. Contractors
	5. Commission Agents
	6. Moneylenders

Role of Formal Institutional Agencies in Providing Rural Credit

2.6.1. That the formal institutional agencies play a dominant role in the rural financial market is evident from the fact that the shares of these credit agencies in the cash-debt of rural households have been continuously increasing from 7.1 per cent in 1950-51 to 64 per cent in 1990-91 as per the findings of the AIDISs. But the pace of increase in this share (vide Table 2.3) was the highest during the period in between the late 70s and early 80s. This reflects that the multi-agency system of rural credit, which has been functioning in India since seventies, and has recorded impressive progress during this period. Thus, the frontiers of formal institutional credit in rural areas have been widened to a considerable extent.

Cooperatives: Structure, Spread and Membership

2.6.2. The cooperative credit institutions, both the short and long-term structures (Vide Chart - 2.2), have emerged over the years as the prime institutional agencies for dispersion of rural credit. In terms of network, coverage and outreach, cooperatives (both ST and LT) have sizeable presence as is indicated from the following data. "There were approximately 92,000 primary units (PACS, LAMPS and FSS), 367 District Central Cooperative Banks (DCCBs) and 29 State Cooperative Banks (SCBs) as on 31 March 1999, purveying short-term and medium/long-term agricultural credit covering even the remotest parts of the country. Out of the 29 SCBs, 18 have a 3-tier structure and 11 have

Chart - 2.2

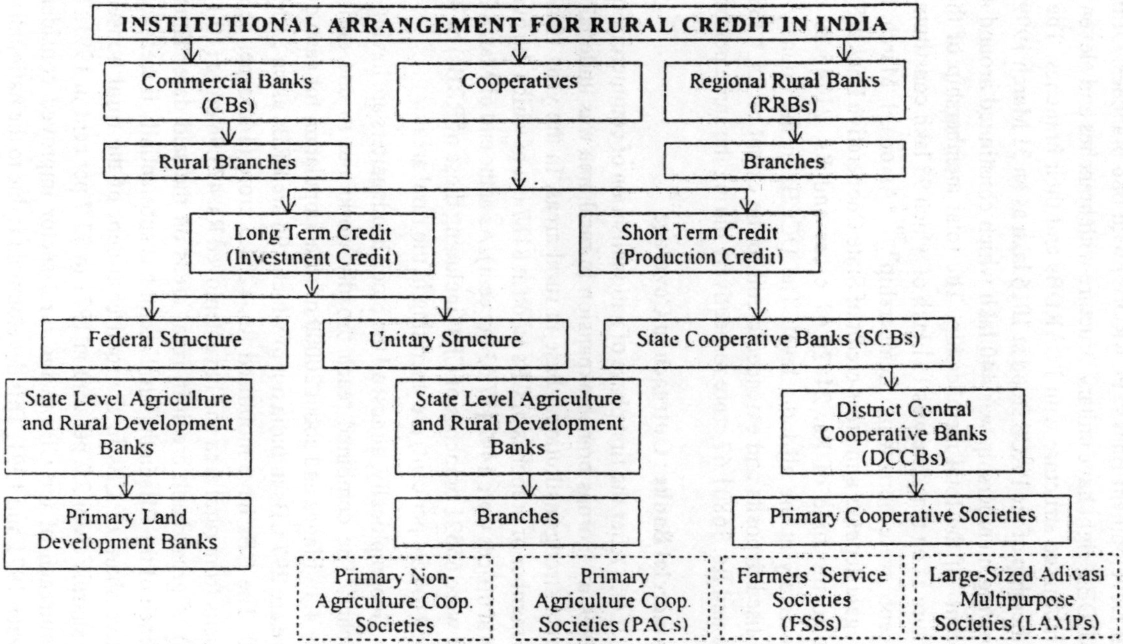

Source: Report of the Review Committee on RRBs (1978), RBI, Bombay, p. 9.

2-tier structure. The long-term credit structure comprises 19 State Cooperative Agriculture and Rural Development Banks (SCARDBs) having 1154 branches and 745 Primary Cooperative Agriculture and Rural Development Banks (PCARDBs) with 686 branches. Of the 19 SCARDBs, eight have unitary structure with branches and eleven have federal/mixed structure with PCARDBs and their branches. The total membership of the PACS stood at 1016 lakh as on 31 March 1999. The borrowing membership was 440 lakh which constituted around 43.31 per cent of the total membership. The total membership of the LT structure as on that date was 131 lakh of which 95 lakh constituting 71 per cent were borrowing membership".[30] "As on 31 March 1999, aggregate deposits and gross credit of State Cooperative Banks (SCBs) were to the tune of Rs. 24826.61 crore and Rs. 21745.29 crore respectively at the all-India level. The DCCBs in the country have mobilised deposits and extended credit to the extent of Rs. 43689.79 crore and Rs. 36801.67 crore respectively during the same period".[31]

Commercial Banks : Outreach in Coverage[32]

2.6.3. After the first phase of nationalisation of commercial banks in 1969, a vigorous branch expansion in rural area was undertaken to create a strong institutional base in rural areas. In the year 1969, the total number of branches of CBs stood at 8187 out of which the number of rural offices were 1443 (17.63 per cent). As at the end of March 2000, there were 65521 branches of CBs (including those of RRBs) of which 32,719 (49.94 per cent) are operating in the rural areas.

Geographically, almost all the block headquarters are having bank branches. The combined reach broadly works out to one outlet for every 4.3 villages and about 20000 of rural population for each outlet. There are 297 CBs in India out of which 196 are RRBs as on 31 March 2000. The CBs have mobilised Rs. 1204.5 crore (14.65 per cent) of deposits from rural area and have deployed Rs. 473.96 crore (10.11 per cent) of gross bank credit in rural areas on the said date. Thus, the outreach of the CBs in the rural sector has substantially increased. The relative share of CBs in the total cash-debt of the rural households rose sharply from 2.2 per cent in 1971 to 33.7 per cent in 1991. Thus, the outreach of the CBs to the rural sector improved considerably between 1971 and 1991. This development is due to the nationalisation of CBs and the emphasis on social banking. CBs usually provide loans for agricultural and non-agricultural sectors which may be classified into: (i) Direct Advances in the form of short, medium-cum-long-term loans, (ii) Indirect Advances routed through such agencies like FSSs, PACSs, LAMPSs, advances to State Electricity Boards, credit to the dealers of fertilisers and advances to cooperative milk societies, sheep-breeders, cooperative societies etc.[33] Apart from these, CBs also provide financial accommodation by participating in various government sponsored anti-poverty programmes.

Ground Level of Credit for Agriculture and Allied Activities

2.6.4. A substantial expansion has taken place in credit flows to the agriculture and allied sectors as is evident from the data given in the Table 2.2. It shows that the total ground level of credit to the farm sector disbursed by all the Scheduled CBs has increased from Rs. 938 crore in 1970-71 to Rs. 41,764 crore in 1999-2000 and is expected to reach a level of Rs. 51,640 crore in 2000-01 recording an overall growth rate of 18 per cent per annum. The amount of loans issued by the cooperatives rose from Rs.743.8 crore during 1970-71 to Rs. 19,093 crore in 1999-2000 and is projected to the level of Rs. 22,706 crore by the end of 2000-01. The cooperative credit institutions accounted for a big share of 44.27 per cent in the total institutional credit to agriculture and allied activities. The proportion of loans extended by RRBs in the total loans issued by all the institutions to this sector has been quite small and it stood around 7 per cent. The loans disbursed by the RRBs have registered a consistent increase in their percentage share and the highest overall annual growth rate during these years. The past three decades have witnessed an impressive growth in the credit disbursed by CBs which amply suggests their extensive participation in the financing of agriculture and allied activities. The amount disbursed by banks rose from a meagre Rs. 184.2 crore in 1970-71 to as high as Rs. 19,755 crore in 1999-2000 and is expected to reach to a level of Rs. 24,693 crore in 1999-2000 at an overall annual growth rate of 16.2 per cent. The CBs accounted for the lion's share of nearly 49 per cent in the total institutional credit to agriculture and allied activities. Thus, the above analysis shows that institutional credit has pierced the stronghold of the informal agencies.

Table 2.2

Bank Credit for Agriculture and Allied Activities (1970-71 and 1997-98 to 2000-01)

(Rs. in Crore)

Sl. No.	*Credit Institutions*	*Years* 1970-71 Amount	1997-98 Amount	1998-99* Amount	1999-00@ Amount	2000-01$ Amount	*Average*
1	2	3	4	5	6	7	8
1.	Cooperatives	743.8	14,085	15,916	19,093	22,706	
			(44.08)	(43.14)	(45.72)	(44.12)	(44.27)
	Growth (per cent)			13.00	19.96	18.92	17.29
2.	RRBs	167.6	2,040	2,538	2,916	4,061	
		[1981-82]	(6.38)	(6.88)	(6.98)	(7.89)	(7.03)
	Growth (per cent)			24.41	14.89	39.27	26.19
3.	Commercial Banks	184.2	15,831	18,443	19,755	24,693	
			(49.54)	(49.98)	(47.30)	(47.99)	(48.70)
	(Growth (per cent))			16.50	7.11	25.00	16.20
4.	Total .	938.0	31,956	36,897	41,764	51,460	
			(100)	(100)	(100)	(100)	(100)
	Growth (per cent)		21	15	13	23	18

* Provisional @ Estimated $ Projections

***Notes*:** (i) In column (3), figures for RRBs relate to the year 1981-82, as RRBs came into existence in 1975. (ii) Figures in brackets refer to the percentage share to the total amount, (iii) Average figures are for the period from 1997-98 to 2000-01. (iv) Growth rate refers to growth rate over previous year.

Sources: NABARD *Annual Report*, 1999-2000, Mumbai, p. 61.

Changes in the Relative Involvement of Various Agencies in the Rural Credit Systemss

2.6.5. During the last five decades of the post-independence era, the rural credit system has undergone a sea-change. The changing and pressing needs of the time and circumstances called for a revolutionary change, the evolution of a multi-institutional approach to ease the problem of the effective demand for credit by rural clientele. The net effect and the impact of this dynamic change in the system has become evident from the data given in the Table 2.3 which reveals the relative position of various agencies involved in rural households' borrowings at four stages 1951, 1961, 1971, 1981 and 1991. The share of institutional agencies in meeting the credit requirements of the rural households have increased from 7.1 per cent in 1951 to 18.4 per cent in 1961, 29.2 per cent in 1971, 61.2 per cent in 1981 and 64.0 per cent in 1991. The institution/agency-wise sharing of cash-debt of rural households has also been exhibited in Fig. 2.1. The performance of the cooperative sector expressed in terms of the percentage distribution of cash debt has improved from 3.1 per cent in 1951 to 28.6 per cent in 1981. But there has been a deterioration in the pace of increase in the outreach of the cooperatives from 28.6 per cent in 1981 to 21.6 per cent in 1991. The table further shows that the outreach of the CBs to the rural sector improved considerably between 1971 and 1991, i.e., from a mere 2.2 per cent in 1971 to 28 per cent in 1981 and to 33.7 per cent in 1991. This is a development which can safely be attributed to bank nationalisation and the consequent stress on social banking. The corresponding decline in the importance of non-institutional sources of credit was anything but dramatic between 1970s and 1980s, i.e., from 70.8 per cent in 1971 to 38.8 per cent in 1981 and has further decreased to 36.0 per cent in 1991.

2.6.6. Thus, the above analysis shows that the indebtedness of the rural households to both banks and cooperatives have increased and the proportion of rural household indebtedness to non-institutional agencies have decreased. The prime objective of rural credit policy, i.e., institutionalisation of rural credit by replacing the non-institutional agencies have been accomplished to a considerable extent in the post-independence era.

Table 2.3
Distribution of Cash Debt of Rural Households by Credit Agencies

Sl. No.	*Credit Agencies*	*1951*	*1961*	*1971*	*1981*	*1991*
	Institutional Agencies	**7.1**	**18.4**	**29.2**	**61.2**	**64.0**
1.	Cooperatives	2.9	-	20.1	28.6	21.6
2.	Commercial Banks	1.1	-	2.2	28.0	33.7
3.	Others	-	-	0.2	0.6	8.7
4.	Government	3.1	-	6.7	4.0	
	Non-Institutional Agencies	**92.9**	**81.6**	**70.8**	**38.8**	**36.0**
5.	Moneylenders	68.6	62.9	36.9	16.9	17.5
6.	Traders and Commission Agents	6.1	7.0	8.7	3.4	2.5
7.	Relatives and Friends	14.4	5.2	13.8	9.0	5.5
8.	Landlords	2.0	-	8.6	4.0	-
9.	Unspecified	-	-	-	-	3.3
10.	Others	1.8	6.5	2.8	5.5	7.2
	All	**100**	**100**	**100**	**100**	**100**

Source : (i) AIRCSC, *The Survey Report,* 1954, Vol. I, Part-2 (Credit Agencies), RBI, Mumbai, p. 3.
(ii) All India Debt and Investment Surveys (AIDIS), 1961, 1971, 1981.
(iii) AIDIS, 1991, Special Features, *RBI Bulletin,* Mumbai, May, 1999.

Summary

2.7.1. Indian economy is rural and agrarian in character since nearly 74 per cent of the population live in rural areas. A large section of the total workforce depend on agriculture for their livelihood. Majority of the farmers in the country belong to the small and marginal category with limited financial means. Thus, agriculture sustains a large section of the community in the country. After the introduction of

Fig. 2.1

Trends of Relative Involvement of Institutional and Non-Institutional Agencies in the Rural Credit System

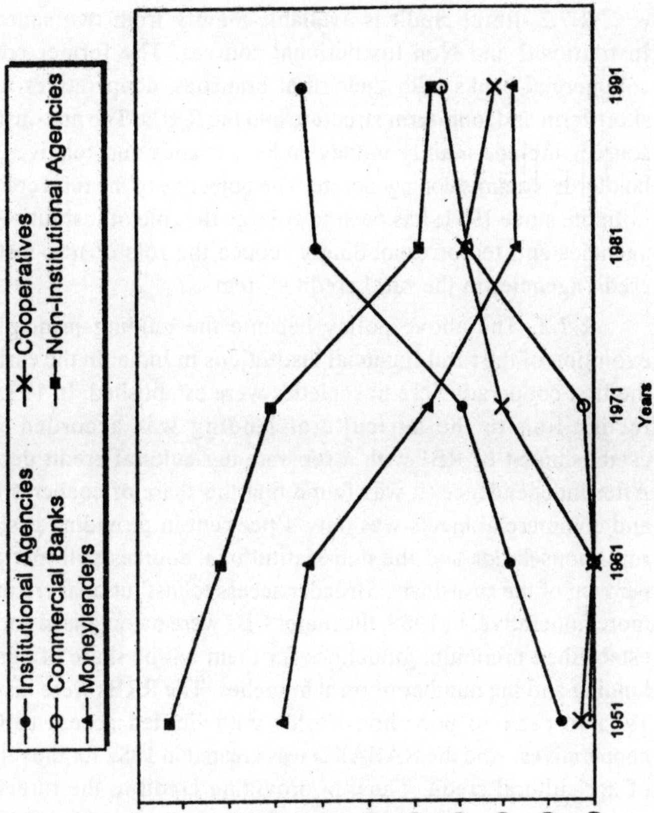

modern technology, agriculture has become a costly proposition. The significance of rural credit needs to be considered in the context of making the rural poor free from their indebtedness to moneylenders, transformation in the field of agriculture and reversing the trend of slowing down of investment in agriculture. Credit is considered as an important instrument for agriculture and rural development.

2.7.2. Rural credit is available mainly from two sources, viz.- Institutional and Non-Institutional sources. The former consists of commercial banks with their rural branches, cooperatives with their short-term and long-term structure and the RRBs. The non-institutional sources include mainly moneylenders, friends and relatives, traders, landlords, commission agents etc. The objective of the rural credit policy in India, since 1951, has been to enlarge the role of institutional credit agencies and to correspondingly reduce the role of non-institutional credit agencies in the rural credit system.

2.7.3. The above policy became the guiding principle in the evolution of the rural financial institutions in India. In the early 1900s, the first cooperative credit societies were established. In 1935, formal recognition to the agricultural lending was accorded with the establishment of RBI with a separate agricultural credit department. After independence, it was found that the share of cooperative sector and commercial banks was only 4 per cent in providing cash-debt of rural households and the non-institutional sources still met about 93 per cent of the cash-loans. Broader access to institutional credit became more imperative. In 1969, the major CBs were nationalised and the RBI established minimum guidelines for them on the share of agricultural lending and the number of rural branches. The RRBs were instituted in 1975 to cater to poor households with limited access to CBs and cooperatives. And the NABARD was created in 1982 for the refinancing of agricultural credit. Thus, in providing credit to the rural sector, a multi-agency approach has been adopted since 1975-76. While the cooperative credit institutions as an integral part of rural credit system in India has completed 95 years, the CBs and RRBs have been for almost 31 years and 25 years respectively. There has been considerable improvement in the involvement of these institutions in the rural credit system.

2.7.4. However, despite their achievement, these banks have not succeeded in abolishing poverty and meeting the growing credit requirements of the agricultural sector and rural poor. Therefore, several innovative schemes have been developed and implemented by the RBI and NABARD in the nineties. The most noteworthy among them are the Bank-Self Help Group Linkage (micro Finance) Scheme, the RIDF, LABs, NBFCs, KCC etc. Under the mF Scheme launched by NABARD in 1992-93, provisions of small credit, savings and other allied activities are made for those who belong to the weaker sections of the population. NGOs play here the role of financial intermediaries by linking the SHGs with the formal banks. It has emerged as a popular means of assisting the poorest among the poor. RIDF started in 1995-96, is made up of contributions from the Indian Scheduled CBs against their shortfall in agriculture target lending up to an extent of 1.5 per cent of net bank credit. The State Governments are provided loans out of this fund to build up infrastructure in rural areas. Local Area Banks (LABs) came into existence since August 1996 and have been established as private enterprises in rural areas for mobilising rural savings and making them available for investment locally. The state-level agricultural development finance companies were also mooted for promoting direct lending to technology and export-oriented new agriculture. And the search of the Indian policymakers is still going on to arrive at a rural banking structure and operational system which will suit the credit and saving needs of agriculturists and the rural population and at the same time improve the economic lot of the rural masses.

References

1. Jain, S.C., "Rural Financing in Transition", *Kurukshetra,* Vol. 49, No. 1, October 2000 (Annual Issue), p. 2.
2. Raj, K.N., "RRBs, Some Issues", *Kurukshetra,* Vol. LXIV, No. 10, July 1996, p. 10.
3. *Op cit.,* p. 10.
4. All India Rural Credit Survey, *The Survey Report,* Vol. I, p. 3.
5. (a) Statistical Abstracts of India, 1997, Central Statistical Organisation, Ministry of Planning and Programme Implementation, GOI, New Delhi; (b) *Annual Report,* 1998-99, NABARD, Mumbai.
6. Thamarajakshi, R., "Agriculture and Economic Reforms", *EPW,* August 14-20, 1999, p. 2293.

7. *Annual Report*, NABARD, 1998-99, p. 33.
8. RBI Basic Statistical Returns, Vol. 26, 27 & 28, March 1996, March 1997 and March 1998.
9. Mishra, S.N. and Chand, R., "Public and Private Capital Formation in Agriculture: Comments on Complementarity Hypothesis and Others", *EPW*, Vol. XXX, No. 5, June 24, 1995.
10. Rangarajan, C., "Some Issues Relating to Rural Finance". Abstract of the First Ram Mathai Memorial Lecture delivered at Ahmedabad on March 8, 1996, *The Banker*, March 1996, p. 15.
11. Reserve Bank of India (1954), AIRCS, *Report of the Committee of Direction*, RBI, Mumbai.
12. Reserve Bank of India (1971), *Report of the Committee on Differential Interest Rates*, RBI, Mumbai.
13. Rangarajan, C., "Rural India: The Role of Credit", Governor, RBI, *The Banker*, 15 March 1996, p. 16.
14. Binswanger, H. and Khandeker, S., "The Impact of Formal Finance on the Rural Economy of India", *Policy Research Working Papers*, The World Bank, August 1992, WPS- 949.
15. Shete, N.B. and Karkal, G.L., "Regional Rural Banks: Problems and Perspectives of Rural Credit", *Prajnan* 18(2), April-June, 1989, p. 132, para 2.
16. *Ibid.*, p. 132.
17. *Ibid.*, p. 133.
18. Patel, A.R., "Rural Credit System—Evolution, Innovation, Progress and Problems", *Kurukshetra*, May 1988, p. 22.
19. "Institutional Development Role of "NABARD" (Year Nil)-A NABARD Publication, p. 4.
20. Raj, K.N., "RRBs: Some Issues", *Kurukshetra*, Vol. XLIV, No. 10, July 1996, pp. 10-11.
21. Reserve Bank of India (1954), AIRCS—Report of the Committtee of Direction, RBI, Mumbai.
22. Reserve Bank of India (1960), *Report of the All India Rural Credit Review Committee*, RBI, Mumbai, p. 999.
23. Government of India (1975), *Report of the Working Group on Rural Banks*, Government of India, New Delhi, pp. 2-3.
24. Nair, T.S., "Rural Financial Intermediation and Commercial Banks: Review of Recent Trends", *Economic and Political Weekly (EPW)*, January 29, 2000, p. 302.
25. Gulati, A., "Agriculture and Rural Development", *EPW*, Vol. XXXV, No. 14, April 2000, p. 1715.

26. [RBI-1999d], quoted in Nair, T.S. "Rural Financial Intermediation and CBs—Review of Recent Trends", *EPW,* 29 January 2000, p. 302.
27. Shivamaggi, H.B., "Reforms in Rural Banking", *EPW,* Vol. XXXV, No. 20, Mumbai, May 13-19, 2000, p. 1718.
28. *Annual Report*, NABARD, 1998-99, Mumbai, p. 45.
29. Patel, A.R., "Rural Credit System: Need for Restructuring", *Kurukshetra*, Vol. 49, No. 4, January, 2001, New Delhi.
30. *Annual Report*, 1999-00, NABARD, Mumbai, p. 105.
31. RBI, *Banking Statistics, Quarterly Handout*, March 2000, Mumbai, p.46.
32. *Ibid.*, pp. 1, 17 & 18.
33. Bramhanand, P.R., "Commerical Banks and Development Agencies" quoted in S.L.N.Sinha (ed.), *Reform of the Indian Banking System*, Madras, 1975, p. 212.

3

Evolution, Growth and Development of RRBs at the All-India Level

Introduction

3.1.1. Agriculture and agro-based activities in rural areas play strategic role in promoting balanced, equitable and self-sustained pattern of development. Hence, the GOI, the RBI and the NABARD have involved themselves in the process of institution building in rural credit. The objective is to ensure such a system of rural credit that serves dual purpose of accelerated growth in production and income and of greater equity in the distribution of credit. Attention has also been given to rectify the structural and organisational deficiencies of the already existing rural credit system and in the process, several institutions catering to the credit requirements of the rural areas have come up in course of time. The present chapter seeks to make an analysis of the purpose and logic of the already existing credit institutions, their strengths and weaknesses in achieving the goals for which they were set up, the changing environment which necessitates the setting up of new institutions called Regional Rural Banks (RRBs) and an analysis of their operations at the all-India level. More specifically, this chapter, divided into eight sections deals with the background of the establishment of RRBs, their evolution, special features they possess as rural credit institution, history of the committees established to probe into the various aspects of their operations, liberalised policy measures exclusively for the RRBs in the wake of the financial sector reforms (FSR) and an analysis of the progress and performance of the RRBs at the all-India level. At the end, the findings of the chapter have been summarised.

The Background of Establishment of RRBs

3.2.1. Rural banking is vital to the Indian social fabric for the simple and cogent reason that it is through such type of banking that the country finds ample opportunities to ameliorate the fate of the rural poor. They can be made an integral part of the national mainstream by creating new opportunities for rural financing and exploiting the existing ones, which may ultimately, lead to the path of better socio-economic transformation. It is in this sense that rural banking had been engaging the attention of the GOI and the RBI from time to time.

A Review of the Rural Credit Scene

3.2.2. There is a widely shared view that in spite of an impressive set-up in the availability of institutional credit to rural areas, it was estimated that on the eve of the establishment of Regional Rural Banks (RRBs) in 1975, the non-institutional credit still accounted for nearly two-thirds of the total agricultural credit in the country. There were still many unbanked areas in the country.[1] Therefore, a more determined effort was needed to speed up the flow of institutional credit, especially to meet the needs of the weaker sections of the rural community. In this context, an attempt has been made in this section to present a brief review of the rural credit scene during the early seventies which paved the way for the establishment of the new institution of rural credit called RRBs in 1975.

Continuing Predominance of Non-Institutional Sources of Rural Credit

3.2.3. (i) The All-India Rural Credit Survey Report (1954) revealed that the share of institutional agencies comprising the government, the cooperatives and the CBs in financing the borrowings of rural households was only 7.1 per cent in 1951-52 whereas the corresponding share of moneylenders was as high as 68.6 per cent. The data provided by the All India Debt and Investment Survey, 1971-72 conducted by the RBI clearly pointed out that even during the period just before the RRBs came into existence, the non-institutional agencies were still providing 70.8 per cent of debts of rural households. Out of this moneylenders accounted for 36.9 per cent.

Table 3.1
Percentage Share of Institutional Credit Agencies
(In the total debt of each category of household as on June 30, 1971)

Figures in per cent

1.	All Rural Households	29.2
2.	Cultivators	31.7
3.	Small Cultivators :	
	Asset Group	
	Rs. 0-500	6.2
	Rs. 500-1000	6.3
	Rs. 1000-2500	10.4
	Rs. 2500-5000	14.5
4.	Agricultural Labourers	4.5
5.	Rural Artisans	4.8
6.	Other non-cultivator households	16.8

Source : All India Debt and Investment Survey, 1971-72; As cited in the *Report of the Review Committee on RRBs* (1978), p. 17.

(ii) Table 3.1 shows the percentage share of the institutional credit agencies in the total debt of each category of rural households as on June 30, 1971. It is evident from the data given in this table that the dependence of the lower asset groups (Rs. 500 and Rs. 500-1000) on non-institutional agencies (which include moneylenders) was much larger than that of the higher asset groups. Similarly, in the case of the agricultural labourers and rural artisans, the principal sources of credit were non-institutional.

Relative Performance of the Existing Credit Institutions

3.2.4. The cooperatives and the branches of the commercial banks were the main institutional agencies catering to the requirements of the rural sector then. Nearly 97 per cent (as on June 1976) of the Indian villages were covered by the cooperatives (PACS) at the grass-root level. Similarly, the CBs were also making concerted efforts towards opening more branches in rural areas in the post-nationalisation period.

Thus, the number of rural branches of all Scheduled CBs (in centres with a population of 10,000 or less) rose from 1832 at the end of June 1969 constituting 22.4 per cent of the total number of branches in the country to 9146 branches at the end of April 1977 which was 37.7 per cent of the total number of branches—representing an increase of nearly 400 per cent in a period of eight years. Whereas, the credit outstanding of all the Scheduled CBs to agriculture (including plantations) accounted for 5.37 per cent of the total credit outstanding of these banks at the end of December 1969, this proportion had risen to 10.44 per cent at the end of 1976.[3] The share of Cooperatives and CBs in the total borrowings of the rural households had grown from 3.1 per cent and 1.1 per cent in 1951 to 20.1 per cent and 2.2 per cent in 1971 respectively.[4]

An Environmental Analysis

3.2.5. While Commercial Banks had started giving a priority treatment to the farm sector, three important aspects of rural environment warranted a fresh thinking about rural banking :

(i) During the 70s the desperation about food production in India was over. After having touched the rock bottom of 72 million tonnes of food grains production in 1965-66, it had exceeded 100 million tonnes in 1970-71.[5] Thus, the farm sector had showed its potential to feed the nation.

(ii) The new technology introduced to Indian agriculture in late 60s, was capital as well as cost intensive. Therefore, it was inclined to favour a better-off section of the farmers in the farm sector. Left to themselves, the weaker sections of the farming community would not be in a position to mobilise enough resources for adopting the new technology and participate in the agricultural development. Given the free option of serving the strong and weak sections of the farming community, it was felt that the bankers would be naturally inclined to opt for the better-off. For instance, our land distribution pattern is such that for covering as much as 22.8 per cent of the total operational area, one has to contact only 2.4 per cent of the farm holders if one prefers to contact only large farmers each having a land holding of

10 hectares and above. On the other hand, dealing with marginal farmers each having a land holding of below one hectare would mean that one has to contact 56.6 per cent of the farmers for covering only 12.1 per cent of the area operated.[6] This would have serious repercussions on the income distribution pattern in the rural area. In addition to this, the farm sector also comprised of the landless labourers. These sections would be naturally left out from the purview of any scheme related to the development of agricultural activities.

(iii) The farm sector development is only a part of rural development. Rural development in real terms would mean improvement in the quality of the life of the rural society as a whole, which includes both the farm and the non-farm sector. The farm sector of the rural areas thus comprises of large farmers, medium farmers, small farmers, marginal farmers and land-less labourers. The non-farm sectors viz., trading class and artisan class. The trading class also consists of two groups viz. who trade in goods of general use and those who trade in farm inputs. In the case of artisans also, there are two groups viz., those who provide general services and those who provide services and inputs to the farm sector proper. From among these constituents of the rural society the large and medium farmers would be direct beneficiaries of new technology. Traders dealing in general goods and the artisan providing general services would be the indirect beneficiaries of the prosperity in rural areas resulting from the development of the farm sector. The small and marginal farmers would benefit from the new technology provided they are given requisite institutional support including financial support. The traders in farm inputs would also be the direct beneficiaries of the advent of new technology and farm development. However, the scale of operation demands that, they operate at the urban or semi-urban centres. The landless labourers would benefit only if the employment opportunities do not shrink on account of techniques of production. The traditional rural artisans dealing with the services and inputs required by the farm sector would be most hard hit due to the change in the technology. The traditional skill of the rural artisans becomes redundant and hence either they are forced to migrate to the urban areas or they have to join the ranks of the unskilled rural labourers.[7] This sort of an environmental analysis justifies the need of a new type of credit institution giving exclusive attention to the credit needs of the weaker sections of the rural areas.

Divergent Views from Different Committees

3.2.6. The various committees set up prior to the establishment of RRBs for looking into the problems of rural credit then were not unanimous in their views in this regard. The Rural Banking Enquiry Committee (Sir Purushottamdas Thakurdas) (1949) found that cooperative infrastructure was quite satisfactory and that CBs had not gone beyond Taluka headquarters and had not shown any appreciable interest in agricultural and rural credit. The All India Rural Credit Survey Committee (AIRCS) (Gorwala) (1954) pointed out that the development of cooperative credit movement has been inadequate in coverage and recommended strengthening of it by developing a three tier cooperative credit structure. The Committee on Cooperative Credit (Mehta) (1960) recommended for development of strong and stable institutional framework for cooperative societies. The National Credit Council Study Group on Organisational Framework for Implementation of Social Objectives (Gadgil) (1968) recommended that the main aim of future national policy should be on involving the commercial banking in providing rural credit. But the All India Rural Credit Review Committee (AIRCRC) (Venkatappiah) (1969) recognised that CBs being essentially urban in origin and conception, they do not have the organisational machinery or the expertise to deal with the rural producers and they do not have any organic link with the rural local institutions or the opportunity to take help of official machinery in the villages. But at the same time the Committee wished that progressive and farsighted banks would boldly enter rural areas providing services of banking and credit.[8] In the midst of such divergent views of different committees, the proposal to set up "rural banks" was first mooted by the Banking Commission (Saraiya) in 1972.

Banking Commission's Proposal

3.2.7. The Banking Commission (Saraiya) was appointed by the GOI in February 1969 with the objective of reviewing the structure and operations of CBs and cooperatives thoroughly in the totality of the working of the existing credit institutions in India and offering suggestions with a view to ensuring a coordinated development of commercial and cooperative banks.[9] After examining the strengths and weaknesses of the CBs and cooperatives, the Banking Commission in its report published in 1972 expressed serious doubts on the capabilities of cooperatives and CBs in catering to the credit needs of the rural sector. In the words of the Commission, in the total scheme of bridging the credit gap in the agricultural sector, the major difficulty is that the cooperative banking sector which has a very wide organisation of the field level, is unable to mobilise deposits, while commercial banks which are able to mobilise deposits in a substantial manner, are unable to provide credit to agriculture owing to their lower coverage of the rural sector and their lack of knowledge of problems of lending to this sector. In this context, it proposed the setting up of a new class of 'rural bank' in areas where cooperative credit structure is generally weak. No action was initiated by the GOI on this proposal.

The Launching of the 20-Point Economic Programme

3.2.8. The need for setting up of some kind of a new institution of 'rural banks' to provide rural credit was again thought of after June 1975. The opportunity for such rethinking was provided after launching of the 20-point Economic Programme of the GOI in 1975. The most important two points of the 20-point programme which had direct bearing on rural credit were liquidation of rural indebtedness, legislation for moratorium on recovery of debts from landless labourers, small farmers and artisans. Accordingly on the basis of directives flown from the Central Government, all the State Governments enacted legislation for a moratorium, discharge and scaling down of debts of rural households from the non-institutional sources. The intention was to create a situation for meeting the production and consumption credit of the weaker sections of the rural areas as the traditional sources of credit would demand unreasonably high rate of interest on loans to cover the risk of non-repayment. Thus, the GOI seriously considered to find out new alternative sources of credit to meet the requirements of the rural poor. In this context, the GOI also felt that it was necessary to establish rural banks as new institutions on the basis of attitudinal and operational ethos entirely different from those obtaining in the public sector banks (PSBs).[11]

3.2.9. This was the background that caused the birth of a new type of credit institution known as Regional Rural Bank (RRB) started in October 1975 with an objective of giving exclusive attention to the credit needs of the weaker sections of the rural/farming society. This institution should not have easy options for operation and showing good performance by dealing with non-rural and non-poor people.

Evolution of RRBs at All India Level

The Logic and Rationale

3.3.1. The idea of setting up of the new institution was two folds:

(a) to provide employment to the rural educated youths who are properly oriented to look after the needs of the rural borrower (unlike the urban oriented personnel who are not able to do this), and

(b) to bring down the cost of rural banking by recruiting staff on the same scale of pay and allowances as for the State Government and local bodies staff.[12] Implicit in the GOI's thinking was an awareness that the weaker sections of the rural society had in general not benefited much from the existing credit institutions and that the new institutions of rural banks must rectify this deficiency and work for furthering the development of the rural poor.

Working Group on Rural Banks, 1975

3.3.2. The GOI thus conceived the idea of establishment of rural banks as part of the New Economic Programme. In order to further rationalise and operationalise this idea, the GOI set up the Working Group on Rural Banks on 4 July 1975 under the Chairmanship of M.Narasimham, the then Secretary of the RBI on deputation with the GOI as Additional Secretary in the Ministry of Finance. The Group submitted its report on 30 July 1975. The main motivation to set up

RRBs was best conveyed in the following observation of the Narasimham Working Group: The main disabilities in the cooperatives in purveying the needed quantum of credit arise from their inability to mobilise adequate deposit resources, their managerial weaknesses and the character of their functioning marked by the dominance of the vested interests which have come in the way of their efficient functioning, specially effective supervision of credit and the inadequate coverage of the small and marginal farmers.... the commercial banks suffered from two basic weaknesses in dispensation of rural credit, i.e., (i) their high cost structure and (ii) their attitudinal character, basically urban oriented.... in a country of the size and regional diversity as India, no single pattern be it commercial banking or cooperative credit can be expected to meet all the emerging requirements in all areas. A degree of adaptation and improvisation is called for and the range of institutional alternatives widened.[13] The Working Group, therefore, came to the conclusion that what is needed is an institution which combines the local feel and familiarity with rural problems which the cooperative possess and the degree of business organisation, ability to mobilise deposits, access to the central money markets and modernised outlook which the commercial banks have.[14]

The Regional Rural Banks Act, 1976

3.3.3. Accordingly, the GOI, with certain modifications accepted the recommendations of the Group and the RRBs were set up under the Ordinance 1975 promulgated by the President of India on 26 September 1975 which was subsequently replaced by the RRBs Act, 1976 on 9 February 1976. The provision of this Act are broadly in conformity with the recommendations made by the Working Group. Initially 5 RRBs were set up on 2 October 1975 at Moradabad and Gorakhpur of Uttar Pradesh, Bhiwani in Haryana, Jaipur in Rajasthan and Malda in West Bengal. The principal features of the RRBs in the light of the important provisions enshrined in the RRBs Act 1976 and RRBs (Amendment) Act, 1987 have been highlighted in the next section.

Regional Rural Banks (Amendment) Act, 1987

3.3.4. The Regional Rural Banks Act, 1976 was amended in 1987 and the Regional Rural Banks (Amendment) Act, 1987 came into force on 28 September 1988. These amendments were done in pursuance to the recommendations of the Kelkar Working Group (1986). Some of the important amendments were: (a) Enhancement of the authorised capital of RRBs from Rs. 1 crore to Rs. 5 crore and paid-up share capital from Rs. 25 lakhs to Rs. 1 crore; (b) Provision for amalgamation of RRBs in consultation with all the concerned parties; and (c) Empowering the sponsor banks to monitor the progress of RRBs and also to arrange for their inspection, internal audit,etc.

Regional Rural Banks : Special Features

3.4.1. RRBs represent an innovation in Indian banking. The innovation is not only institutional but relates to objectives, functions, area of operation and its clientele. For this reason, RRBs be regarded as specialised institutions, i.e., distinct from commercial banks as well as cooperative credit agencies. It is, therefore, necessary to refer to the essential features of the RRBs.

Objectives

3.4.2. The objectives of the RRBs is to bring about progress with social justice to the rural poor, in conformity with the national objective of development with stability and social justice. RRBs are an institution meant exclusively for those sections of the rural society which did not benefit from the percolation of the fruits of development - i.e., a situation which could not be remedied by the cooperatives dominated by big farmers and other vested interests nor by the commercial banks with urban bias and with high operational costs. RRBs are, in other words, an institutional device for taking banking services to the doorsteps of the rural poor and making available to them institutional credit.

Sponsorship

3.4.3. Each RRB was to be sponsored by a scheduled commercial bank (mainly by a public sector bank). It will be set up at the initiative taken by the sponsor bank in consultation with the concerned State Government and the GOI and under license from the RBI. The Sponsor Bank will provide assistance to the RRBs in several ways. These include subscription of its share capital, provision of managerial and other staff assistance, training of RRBs' staff etc. to be mutually agreed upon within the period of first five years of its existence. The RRBs would be scheduled banks eligible for refinance facilities from the RBI (now from NABARD) and sponsor banks.

Management and Capital Structure

3.4.4. The management of the affairs and business of a RRB shall rest in a Board of Directors (BOD). The Chairman of the RRB is appointed by the GOI on the recommendation of the sponsor bank which pays the full salary of the Chairman and also of its other staff on deputation with the RRB. The authorised capital of each RRB was placed at Rs. 1 crore and the issued capital at Rs. 25 lakh. The issued capital would be subscribed by the GOI, sponsor bank and the concerned State Government in the ratio of 50 per cent, 35 per cent and 15 per cent respectively.

Location Policy

3.4.5. As a matter of policy RRBs are to be set up mainly in underbanked[15] and unbanked areas of the country. This means that RRBs are to function in remote rural areas which lack basic amenities like education, medical help, transport and communications. An important aspect of this policy is that RRBs would cover a compact area of not more than two or three districts where the weaker sections of the population are predominant and there is sufficient potential for agricultural development.

Low Cost Institution and Sectoral Approach to Rural Credit

3.4.6. RRBs would function as low cost institutions with staff drawn from the districts or the State in which the banks are located. The RRB staff would be paid salaries comparable to those of the respective State government functionaries. The very approach of RRBs to rural credit is sectoral. That they are to operate in a compact area of not more than two or three districts, gives them no scope for neutralising losses sustained in one area by the profits earned in another area. Similarly, since their development approach is sectoral (i.e., lending to specified categories of rural poor) and not spatial, they can not spread their overheads and operational costs over a wider clientele.

Operations

3.4.7. RRBs provide credit both directly and indirectly. RRBs grant direct loans and advances only to small and marginal farmers, rural artisans and agricultural labourers and others of small means for productive purposes. Indirect loans are given through cooperative societies operating within RRB's area. Like CBs, they are empowered to mobilise rural savings through deposits. Like Cooperatives they provide credit at cheaper rate of interest. The lending rates of RRBs should not be higher than the prevailing lending rates of cooperative societies in any particular State. RRBs enjoy some concessions with regard to requirement of cash reserves, liquidity, interest rates on deposits. The RRBs are allowed to offer half per cent additional rate of interest on its deposits over the rates offered by scheduled CBs. Thus, the sponsoring banks and the RBI provide many subsidies and concessions to RRBs to enable the latter to function effectively. The financial resources of the RRBs are utilised in the district where they operate. In other words, the resources of RRBs are not diverted to the outside of the area of operation. RRBs role is to supplement and not to supplant the other institutional agencies operating in the rural area.

3.4.8. These essential features built into the concept as well as the institutional structure of RRBs make it difficult for these banks to break-even right from the beginning. Recognising these limitations, Narasimham Committee, which had recommended the setting up of RRBs, had categorically stated that RRBs would be bound to make losses in initial years and that initial loss of these banks would be a price worth paying given the benefits sought to be achieved through these institutions.

A History of Committees on RRBs

3.5.1. The establishment of RRBs followed the acceptance by the GOI of the recommendations of the Working Group on Rural Banks appointed on 4th July 1975 under the Chairmanship of M.Narasimham. Since then the GOI, RBI and of late, NABARD have set up various expert committees and groups from time to time to probe into the various aspects of RRBs' performance over the years. Consequently, the role expectations of RRBs have undergone considerable changes with the passage of time. A Review Committee on RRBs, 1978, constituted on 23rd June 1977 by the RBI under the Chairmanship of M.L. Dantwala, was the first to evaluate the performance of RRBs. The Committee felt that the existing credit institutions even after necessary restructuring and modifications cannot be expected to meet the varied and growing needs for rural credit.[16] Hence, the Committee justified the establishment of RRBs with certain modifications. The Steering Committee constituted in December 1976 under the Chairmanship of the Deputy Governor, RBI gave the desired directions for the overall operations of RRBs to make them an effective link in the supply of rural credit. In the same year, the RBI appointed a Working Group under the Chairmanship of P.N.Khanna to suggest simplified operational and accounting procedures for RRBs. In February 1980, the RBI appointed a Committee on Control over Branches of RRBs with R.Sundaravaradam as Convenor to suggest appropriate guidelines for uniform system and procedures in order to ensure effective control over the branches of the RRBs. The Committee to Review Arrangements for Institutional Credit for Agriculture and Rural Development (CRAFICARD) appointed by the RBI under the Chairmanship of V. Sivaraman, examined the role of RRBs in the rural credit system. The Committee which submitted its report in 1981, recommended for the transfer of rural credit business of CBs to the RRBs, enhancement of the paid-up share capital of the RRBs and for continuance of various facilities provided by the RBI as well as sponsor banks to them. The Committee also suggested for the control, regulation and promotional responsibility of RRBs to be transferred to the newly proposed National Bank for Agriculture and Rural Development (NABARD). The GOI appointed a Working Group on RRBs under the Chairmanship of S.M. Kelkar, which made its report in 1986 after assessing the performance of RRBs over the decade 1975-84. It recommended *inter alia*, the provision of amalgamation of RRBs in consultation with NABARD, state government concerned and sponsor banks after taking into consideration public interest, development of the areas and interest of the RRBs concerned. This provision was incorporated into the RRB Act, 1976 by the Regional Rural Bank (Amendment) Act, 1987. The Committee, however, suggested that RRBs should continue along the lines originally envisaged, re-emphasising the need to maintain the image of the RRB as a 'poor man's bank'. Thus, the Dantwala Committee (1978), CRAFICARD (1981) and the Kelkar Working Group (1986) were of the view that in spite of serious organisational deficiencies and loss of viability, RRBs should continue their existence as the third arm of multi-agency approach and cater exclusively to weaker sections.

3.5.2. The Agricultural Credit Review Committee under the chairmanship of A.M. Khusro in its report published in 1989 has made a detailed review (Chapter IV) of the operations and performance of RRBs during 1975-1986. The Committee came to the conclusion that RRBs as a system had no justifiable cause for continuance and recommends their merger with sponsor banks. The Committee on the Financial System under the Chairmanship of M. Narasimham while making recommendations of financial sector reforms in 1992, had some changed perceptions on the role of RRBs in the future. It proposed for allowing RRBs to engage in all types of business in line with the CBs so as to improve their viability.[17] The Committee left the option open to the RRBs and the sponsor banks to decide whether the RRBs should retain their identity or go for the merger. At the instance of the GOI, the RBI constituted on 8th April 1994 a three-member Committee headed by M.C. Bhandari to spearhead the process of restructuring and to lay down the norms for identification of RRBs to be taken up in the first phase of restructuring. Another Committee headed by K. Basu and constituted in 1995-96, observed that mere recapitalising the RRBs will achieve nothing and strong supportive action must be taken to ensure the viability of these institutions. In July 1995, the RBI has set up an Expert Group on Policy Issues of RRBs under the Chairmanship of N.K. Thingalaya to advise RBI periodically on the issues on the policies on RRBs and to monitor the progress in this regard on an ongoing basis. The GOI, RBI and the NABARD have involved themselves in working out policies on the basis of the recommendations of these Committees and Working Groups to enable the RRBs to become financially viable on the one hand and to meet the rural credit needs on the other, in the changing economic scenario.

Liberalised Policy Measures for RRBs Under the New Economic Policy

3.6.1. The impact of the economic liberalisation initiated by the GOI in 1991 has been far-reaching, so far as the banking sector is concerned. The financial sector reforms (FSRs) have laid emphasis on the banks improving the quality of their customer service and the range of services offered by them. So far as RRBs are concerned, till recently, i.e., 1992, they were subjected to certain restrictions in their business operations and management which became critical to their viability. Some of these deficiencies were: directed credit to target group of beneficiaries having zero risk bearing capacity, centrally administered interest rate structure, limited and remote area of operation, poor recovery position, high cost of recovery, etc. Besides, from 1987 on account of the implementation of National Industrial Tribunal (NIT) Award providing remuneration package to staff of RRBs at par with the staff of PSBs, their financial burden increased substantially. The net impact of this has been that most of the RRBs accumulated heavy losses leading to rapid deterioration in their financial health and viability. Therefore, the Narasimham Committee (1991) while framing recommendations for FSRs, proposed that RRBs should be allowed to engage in all types of banking business in line with the CBs. In this context, the GOI, RBI and NABARD have announced certain liberalised policy measures exclusively for RRBs in view of their highly sustainable position. The aim is to give them greater flexibility in their operations so as to enable them to improve efficiency and attain viability. The policy measures implemented for the development of RRBs on viable lines are discussed in this section.

3.6.2. There has been complete deregulation of the interest rates allowing the RRBs to fix their own interest rates on advances and deposits made by them. The proportion of Non-Target Group (NTG) lending has been enhanced from 40 per cent to 60 per cent of the RRBs' fresh lending w.e.f. 1 January 1994. The RRBs were allowed to conduct non-fund business, i.e., to purchase/discount and issue demand drafts/ cheques, to provide locker facilities, to issue guarantee on behalf of their customers, to provide remittance facilities on agency basis under arrangement with their sponsor banks. The RRBs were brought at par with the CBs with regard to priority sector discipline w.e.f. 1 April 1997.

3.6.3. Investment portfolios of the RRBs have been broadened to improve their profitability. They can now invest their Non-SLR surplus resources in UTI listed schemes, fixed deposits of profit making term-lending institutions, bonds of nationalised banks and profit-making public sector institutions with top category rating by credit rating agencies, non-convertible debentures (NCD) of reputed blue-chip companies, etc. However, the RBI has stipulated that the investment of Non-SLR surpluses should not exceed 50 per cent of the refinance availed by the RRBs from the NABARD and sponsor banks. As a prudential measure aimed at better risk management and avoidance of concentration of credit risks, limits have been fixed on RRBs' exposure to different categories of borrowers. The GOI has advocated a more active role for the sponsor banks in the investment activities of their sponsored RRBs at least till such time as the RRBs develop the requisite technical expertise in investment management.

3.6.4. The issued capital of all the 196 RRBs stands enhanced to Rs. 1 crore from Rs. 25 lakh by the GOI since 1995-96. The GOI, with a view to facilitating revitalisation and strengthening of RRBs, initiated the recapitalisation programme in the year 1994-95. The additional share capital for cleansing of the balance sheets of the RRBs selected for restructuring is shared by the shareholders, i.e., GOI, Sponsor Banks and the State Governments in the proportion of 50:35:15 respectively and is held by the Sponsor Banks/RRBs under a special head "Share Capital Deposit Account" until eventual release of the entire amount by all the three shareholders. This amount is to be released to RRBs for deployment in their business only.

3.6.5. RRBs are allowed to open new branches besides relocation of loss-making branches with some conditions within their service area. NABARD initiated a comprehensive package of measures for revamping the operations of RRBs through the concept of Development Action Plan (DAP) for business improvement and viability attainment coupled with Memorandum of Understanding (MoU) between RRBs and sponsor banks to guide, control and facilitate DAP implementation. The DAPs were basically aimed at achieving Break-Even Level (BEL) to attain current viability in the short-run and sustainable viability in long-term by wiping out accumulated losses and making adequate provisions against bad debts. The annual MoU is a fresh commitment from RRBs every year and is envisaged as an instrument for implementation of the DAP towards realisation of the set objectives and targeted business levels.

3.6.6. The RBI has introduced income recognition and asset classification norms from the year 1995-96 and provisioning norms from the year 1996-97. Accordingly, the RRBs were required to recognise income in respect of their Non-Performing Assets (NPAs) only on cash basis and not on accrual basis and they have to classify their assets into four categories, viz.- standard, sub-standard, doubtful and loss assets based on the performance of assets. RRBs were advised to make provision as per the asset classification. The objective is to bring transparency in the operations of RRBs by identifying their strengths and weaknesses and also to provide durability to the reform process.

3.6.7. The areas of control over RRBs have been defined; while the entire managerial and operational responsibility has been entrusted to Sponsor Banks, the supervisory and regulatory matters of RRBs will continue to rest with RB1/NABARD.

3.6.8. The reform measures discussed in the foregoing sections have brought about far-reaching changes, both quantitative and qualitative in the working of RRBs in the country. This constitutes the theme of the discussion in the following section.

Growth and Performance of RRBs at All India Level

3.7.1. The present section deals with the analysis of the progress and performance of RRBs at the All-India level. An attempt has been made to concentrate mainly on the essential features of the performance of RRBs like branch expansion, resource mobilisation, credit dispensation, recovery performance and the working results. The progress and performance of the RRBs at the All-India level has been studied in two parts. The first part deals with the Structural Growth of the RRBs in terms of their geographical reach and coverage ever since their inception in 1975. This part also seeks to make an analysis of the average annual growth and the decadal growth of RRBs in India. The second part of the study deals with the operational analysis of RRBs at all-India level during the period from 1994-95 to 1999-2000, the latest period for which data were available.

Growth of the Structure[18]

3.7.2. The six RRBs established in 1975 on an experimental basis, have eventually grown to 196 by April 1987. No RRB was established thereafter. However, the overall coverage of RRBs has increased on account of bifurcation of districts and opening of new branches. As of March 2000, all the 196 RRBs sponsored by 25 public and 2 private sector CBs and 1 State Cooperative Bank, covering 492 districts, had 14,517 branch offices functioning in 23 States. The branches are comprised of 6 metropolitan branches, 326 urban branches, 1837 semi-urban branches and 12,330 rural branches. The rural branch network of the RRBs constituted 37.5 per cent of the total rural credit outlets of all the Scheduled Commercial Banks (including RRBs). The share of RRBs in mobilising rural deposits stood at 18.25 per cent whereas it was 21.25 per cent with regard to the dispensation of credit. An important and noteworthy feature is that as many as 94 out of 115 (82 per cent) districts identified by the Planning Commission under Tribal Sub-Plan Area are covered by the RRBs.[19]

Geographical Coverage

3.7.3. The RRBs had by March 2000, opened 14,517* branches in 23 States in India. Amongst the States, Uttar Pradesh had the largest number of branches (3008) with largest number of RRBs (40), followed by Bihar with 1,886 branches (of 22 RRBs), Madhya Pradesh with 1,568 branches (of 24 RRBs), Andhra Pradesh with 1,137 branches (of 16 RRBs), Karnataka with 1,090 branches (of 13 RRBs) and Rajasthan with 1,067 branches (of 14 RRBs). All the North-Eastern States have one RRB each except Assam which has 5 RRBs. The State of Nagaland has only one RRB with lowest number of (8) branches. The above mentioned six states accounted for more than two-thirds (68 per cent) of the total number of branches.

Progress at a Glance

3.7.4. Table 3.2 shows the progress of RRBs at a glance. In terms of growth rates, the RRBs have achieved phenomenal progress between 1975, the year of setting up of these banks and 2000, the latest year for which data are available. Over a 25-year period of existence, the number of RRBs increased from 6 to 196, the branches from 17 to 14,517 and the districts covered from 12 to 492. Similarly, the amount of deposits increased from Rs. 0.20 crore to Rs. 32,008.48 crore and outstanding advances from Rs. 0.10 crore to Rs. 13,102.47 crore during the same period. Thus, these statistics reflects the sizeable geographical reach and significant functional growth of the RRBs in the sphere of savings mobilisation and dispensation of rural credit.

Table 3.2
Progress of RRBs at a Glance
(From 1975 to 2000)

Sl. No.	*Indicators*	*1975*	*As on March 2000*
1.	No. of RRBs	6	196
2.	No. of Districts Covered	12	492
3.	No. of Branches	17	14,517
4.	Deposits (Rs. in Crore)	0.20	32,008.48
5.	Outstanding Advances (Rs. in Crore)	0.10	13,102.47
6.	Credit-Deposit Ratio (in per cent)	50	41

Source : *Statistics on RRBs,* NABARD Publications, Mumbai;
RBI, *Banking Statistics, Quarterly Handout*, March 2000, p. 37.

Annual and Decadal Growth Analysis

3.7.5. The average annual increase or decrease in the various operational parameters of RRBs in India are shown in Table 3.3. It is evident from this table that the structural growth and coverage achieved by RRBs during the 25-year period was most occurred during the five years from 1981 to 1985. During these five-year period the average number of RRBs established, the number of districts covered per year, the number of branches opened per year were highest. In the subsequent three five-year periods, i.e., 1986-90, 1991-95 and 1996-2000, though the structural growth in terms of the number of RRBs established, districts covered and the number of branches opened, slowed down compared to the preceding five-year period (1981-85), the functional growth in terms of deposits and advances was considerably high. The decadal analysis of the growth of RRBs presented in Table 3.4 reveals that in the seventies (1975 to 1980) the expansion of such banks was slow because of some sort of reservations and reconsideration about the speed with which new RRBs should be opened. The structural growth of RRBs in all respects namely in terms of number of RRBs, districts covered, expansion of branches was substantial in the eighties. However, the consolidation of the existing set up of the RRB structure and giving more emphasis on the functional growth became the guiding principle in the nineties.

Table 3.3

Average Annual Increases/Decreases in Operational Parameters of RRBs in India (From 1975 to 2000)

Sl. No.	*Indicators*	*1976-1980*	*1981-1985*	*1986-1990*	*1991-1995*	*1996-2000*
1.	No. of RRBs	14	21	-	-	-
2.	No. of Districts Covered	24	38	8	11	13
3.	No. of Branches of RRBs	547	1866	367	20	2
4.	Deposits (Rs. in Crore)	33	217	573	1400	4172
5.	Outstanding Advances (Rs. in Crore)	41	233	429	779	1344
6.	Credit Deposit Ratio (Increase/ Decrease)	91-122 6.8%	121-109 (-) 1.98%	104-86 (-)13.46%	72-56 (-) 4.44 %	53-41 (-) 4.53%

Source : Statistics on RRBs, NABARD Publications, Mumbai.

Table 3.4

Decadal Growth of RRBs in India (1975-2000)

Sl. No.	*Indicators*	*1975-80*	*1981-90*	*1991-000*	*Total*
1.	No. of RRBs	85	111	Nil	196
2.	No. of Districts Covered	144	228	120	492
3.	No. of Branches of RRBs	3279	11164	74	14517
4.	Deposits (Rs. in Crore)	200	3951	27858	32009
5.	Outstanding Advances (Rs. in Crore)	243	3311	9459	13013
6.	Credit Deposit Ratio (Increase/Decrease)	50 to 122 144%	121 to 86 (-) 29%	72 to 41 (-) 43%	

Source : Statistics on RRBs, NABARD Publications, Mumbai.

Resource Base

3.7.6. The total resources of the RRBs are comprised of owned funds, deposits and borrowings. Table 3.5 presents the resource position of RRBs in India as a whole for the period from 1994-95 to 1999-2000. The owned funds of RRBs consisting of share capital, share capital deposit account balance and reserves and surplus have registered increase both in absolute terms from Rs. 253.07 crore in 1994-95 to Rs. 3047.45 crore in 1999-2000 and in terms of percentage share to the total resources of RRBs from 1.85 per cent to 7.81 per cent during the said period. Throughout the period of study deposits account for nearly 82 per cent of the total resources and constitute the major resource component of RRBs. The borrowings of RRBs from NABARD, sponsor banks, SIDBI and others increased from Rs.2274.01 crore in 1994-95 to Rs. 3756.75 crore in 1999-2000. However, in terms of percentage share, it steadily declined from 16.64 per cent to 9.63 per cent during the said period. Thus, the total resources of RRBs have grown from Rs. 13667.74 crore in 1994-95 to Rs. 39008.54 crore in 1999-2000 at an average annual rate of about 23 per cent.

Deposit Mobilisation

3.7.7. Data on deposits mobilisation of RRBs in India have been shown in Table 3.6. Aggregate deposits mobilised during the period of study (March 1995 to March 2000) increased from Rs. 11150.01 crore to Rs. 32204.34 crore recording an average annual growth rate of 24.11 per cent. The average deposits per RRB and per branch increased from Rs. 56.89 crore and Rs. 0.77 crore as on March 1995 to Rs. 164.31 crore and Rs. 2.22 crore as on March 2000 respectively. Similarly, the Deposits per Account increased from Rs. 2978 to Rs.6239 during the period from 1995 to 2000. These data indicate that the RRBs have shown significant achievement in mobilisation of savings in rural areas both in quantitative and qualitative terms.

Classification of Deposits by Type

3.7.8. Table 3.7 presents the classification of deposits by type from March 1995 to March 2000. The term deposits which constituted 48.1 per cent as on March 1995 increased to 55.02 per cent as on March 2000. Savings deposits which formed 46.5 per cent of the total deposits have reduced to 40.34 per cent during the same period. The proportion

Table 3.5
Resources of RRBs in India (1994-95 to 1999-2000)

(Rs. in Crore)

Sl. No.	*Particulars*	*1994-95*	*1995096*	*1996-97*	*1997-98*	*1998-99*	*1999-00*
	Share Capital	151 61	155.64	190.12	195.20	195.57	195.66
	Share Capital Deposits	NA	NA	NA	1100.92	1615.72	1984.62
	Reserves and Surplus	101.46	364.30	902.93	311.57	539.26	867.17
1.	Owned Funds	253.07 (1.85)	519.94 (3.01)	1093.05 (4.96)	1607.69 (5.94)	2350.55 (7.11)	3047.45 (7.81)
2.	Deposits	11140.66 (81.51)	14170.96 (82.01)	17976.20 (81.61)	22189.23 (82.07)	27065.74 (81.88)	32204.34 (82.56)
3.	Borrowings	2274.01 (16.64)	2588.84 (14.98)	2958.10 (13.43)	3240.55 (11.99)	3639.54 (11.01)	3756.75 (9.63)
4.	Total	13667.74 (100)	17279.74 (100)	22027.35 (100)	27037.69 (100)	33055.83 (100)	39008.54 (100)
5.	Growth Rate (%)	-	26.43	27.47	22.75	22.26	18.01

***Note*:** Figures in brackets indicate the percentage to total resources.
Source: Statistics on RRBs, NABARD Publications, Mumbai.

of current deposits to total deposits remain almost constant at around 5 per cent during this period. The steady increase in the share of term deposits from 48 per cent to 55 per cent of total deposits has correspondingly increased the servicing cost of deposits which is bound to affect the profitability of the RRBs.

Credit Deployment

3.7.9. Table 3.8 shows the outstanding advances of RRBs, which increased from Rs. 6290.97 crore in March 1995 to Rs. 13184.40 crore in March 2000 at an average rate of above 16 per cent per annum. The trend shows that the outstanding advances of RRBs have increased in absolute terms but at a declining growth rate initially for the period from 1995 to 1998. However, the growth rate in advances improved from 13.1 per cent in 1998 to 16.10 per cent in the year 2000. The advances outstanding per account increased from Rs. 4993 to Rs. 10362 during

Table 3.6
Deposit Mobilisation by RRBs in India (1994-95 to 1999-2000)

(Rs. in Crore)

Sl. No.	*Year*	*Aggregate Deposits Amount*	*Growth (%)*	*Number of Accounts*	*Deposit per Account (in Rs))*	*Average Deposit per RRB*	*Average Deposit per branch*
1.	March 1995	11150.01	26.32	37437869	2978	56.89	0.77
2.	March 1996	14187.91	27.25	38857716	3651	72.39	0.98
3.	March 1997	17970.18	26.66	40491372	4437	92.00	1.25
4.	March 1998	22189.23	23.48	43013088	5158	113.21	1.54
5.	March 1999	27065.74	21.98	47701797	5674	138.09	1.87
6.	March 2000	32204.34	18.99	51620424	6239	164.31	2.22
Average			**24.11**				

Source: (i) *Statistics on RRBs,* NABARD Publications, Mumbai.
(ii) *Financial Statements of RRBs* (As on 31 March 2000), NABARD Publications, Mumbai, p. 1.

the study period. Average advances per RRB and per branch increased from Rs. 32.10 crore and Rs. 0.43 crore as in March 1995 to Rs. 67.27 crore and Rs.0.91 crore as on March 2000 respectively.

Purpose-wise Break-up of Outstanding Advances

3.7.10. Purpose-wise break-up of outstanding advances of RRBs is given in Table 3.9. The table reveals that outstanding advances to the agricultural sector increased from Rs. 3008.93 crore in March 1995 to Rs. 5402.79 crore as in March 1999 registering an annual growth rate of 15.75 per cent. Among the advances to the non-farm sector, advances for the retail trade, small business and self-employment purposes increased from Rs. 1555.21 crore to Rs. 2493.14 crore at an annual growth rate of Rs. 12.91 per cent. Advances for rural artisans, village and cottage industries increased from Rs. 523.29 crore to Rs.

Table 3.7
Classification of Deposits by Type of RRBs in India (1994-95 to 1999-2000)

(Rs. in Crore)

Sl. No.	*Type of Deposits*	*1994-95*	*1995-96*	*1996-97*	*1997-98*	*1998-99*	*1999-00*
1.	Current	599.93 (5.4)	739.91 (5.2)	984.10 (5.4)	1081.60 (4.9)	1375.84 (5.1)	1494.31 (4.64)
2.	Savings	5186.86 (46.5)	6179.25 (43.6)	7306.38 (40.5)	9329.48 (42.1)	11088.41 (41.0)	12992.61 (40.34)
3.	Term	5363.22 (48.1)	7268.75 (51.2)	9741.53 (54.1)	11778.15 (53.0)	14601.49 (53.9)	17717.42 (55.02)
4.	Total	11150.01 (100)	14187.90 (100)	17970.18 (100)	22189.23 (100)	27065.74 (100)	32204.34 (100)

Note: Figures in brackets indicate the percentage share of total deposits.

Source: *Statistics on RRBs*, NABARD Publications, Mumbai.

Table 3.8
Outstanding Advance of RRBs in India (1994-95 to 1999-2000)

(Rs. in Crore)

Sl. No.	*Year*	*Outstanding Advances (Amount)*	*Growth (%)*	*Number of Accounts*	*Advances per Account (in Rs.)*	*Average Advances per RRB*	*Average Advances per branch*
1.	March 1995	6290.97	19.8	12597890	4993	32.10	0.43
2.	March 1996	7505.03	19.3	12659365	5928	38.29	0.52
3.	March 1997	8718.08	16.2	12038607	7241	44.48	0.60
4.	March 1998	9860 81	13.1	12181141	8095	50.31	0.68
5.	March 1999	11355.84	15.2	11611288	9780	57.94	0.78
6.	March 2000	13184.40	16.10	12724378	10362	67.27	0.91
Average			16.62				

Source : (i) *Statistics on RRBs*, NABARD Publications, Mumbai.
(ii) Financial Statements of RRBs (As on 31 March 2000), NABARD Publications, Mumbai, p. 1.

741.39 crore as on March 1998. It declined to Rs. 721.35 crore in 1999. This sector witnessed an average growth rate of 8.55 per cent per annum. The proportion of outstanding advances to agriculture was the highest forming about 47 per cent of the total outstanding advances of RRBs. In the non-farm category, the share of advances for retail-trade, small business purpose constitutes the largest at about 23 per cent, followed by the advances for miscellaneous purposes (21 per cent) and that for rural artisans, village and cottage industries etc. accounting for about 7.6 per cent of the total outstanding advances of RRBs during the period of study.

Investments

3.7.11. Data on investments of RRBs in terms of growth percentage and Investment to Deposit Ratio (I-D Ratio) are given in Table 3.10. Investments which also includes cash and bank balances with RBI and other banks, increased from Rs. 6127.83 crore as on March 1995 to Rs. 23925.64 crore in March 2000 registering an average annual growth rate of 30.90 per cent. Investment to Deposit Ratio (I-D Ratio) of RRBs has registered an increase from 54.96 per cent to 74.29 per cent in the same period. With the deposit growth rate of about 19 per cent to 27 per cent during the last six years and 13 per cent to 19 per cent growth rate in advances, parking of their surplus funds in investments was an easier option for the RRBs.

Credit-Deposit Ratio

3.7.12. Table 3.11 shows that the deposits of RRBs have been higher than their advances not only in absolute terms but also in terms of growth rates in all the years. It further shows the steady decline in the C-D Ratios of RRBs from 56 per cent in 1994-95 to 41 per cent in 1999-2000.

Recovery Performance

3.7.13. Recovery of amo unts lent in case of RRBs which is a good indicator of the success of any lending institution, has been around 64.09 per cent on an average as on June 2000, as can be found in the Table 3.12. As at the end of June 1994, the loans recovered as a proportion of the loans due for repayment amounted to only 46.23 per cent. During the last seven years period from 1994 to 2000, the

Table 3.9

Purpose-wise Break-up of Outstanding Advances of RRBs in India (1994-95 to 1999-2000)

(Rs. in Crore)

Sl. No.	Year As at the end of March	Agriculture		Non-Agricultural Purposes						Total Outstanding advances #
		Amount	Growth (%)	Rural Artisans etc.		Retail Trade etc.		Other purposes		
				Amount	Growth (%)	Amount	Growth (%)	Amount	Growth (%)	
1.	1995	3008.93 (47.83)	-	523.29 (8.32)	-	1555.21 (24.72)	-	1170.74 (18.61)	-	6290.97 (100)
2.	1996	3466.51 (46.20)	15.22	586.40 (7.81)	12.04	1836.40 (24.46)	18.07	1581.18 (21.07)	35.01	7505.03 (100)
3.	1997	4044.27 (46.42)	16.64	672.18 (7.72)	14.68	1972.30 (22.64)	7.41	1980.18 (22.73)	25.24	8711.82 (100)
4.	1998	4683.01 (47.49)	15.80	741.39 (7.51)	10.27	1992.02 (20.20)	1.01	1943.9 (19.71)	(-)1.85	9860.81 (100)
5.	1999	5402.79 (47.58)	15.37	721.35 (6.35)	(-)2.77	2493.14 (21.95)	25.15	2286.26 (20.13)	17.59	11355.84 (100)
6.	2000	NA		NA		NA		NA		13184.40
	Average	(47)	15.75	(7.6)	8.55	(23)	12.91	(21)	18.99	

Note: (i) Figures in brackets indicate percentage to the total outstanding advances.
(ii) # Total outstanding advances include indirect advances.

Source: *Statistics on RRBs*, NABARD Publications, Mumbai.

Table 3.10

Investments of RRBs at all-India Level (1994-95 to 1999-2000)

(Rs. in Crore)

Sl. No.	*Year (As on)*	*Aggregate Investments*	*Growth (In per cent)*	*Investment-Deposit Ratio (In per cent)*
1.	March 1995	6127.83	28.40	54.96
2.	March 1996	8342.86	36.15	58.80
3.	March 1997	1150.40	37.88	64.01
4.	March 1998	14903.66	29.56	67.17
5.	March 1999	18956.89	27.20	70.04
6.	March 2000	23925.64	26.21	74.29
	Average		30.90	

Source : *Statistics on RRBs*, NABARD Publications, Mumbai.

Table 3.11

C-D Ratios of RRBs of all-India Level (1994-95 to 1999-2000)

(Rs. in Crore)

Sl. No.	*Year*	*Deposits*		*Advances*		*C-D Ratio (%)*
		Amount	*Growth Rate (%)*	*Amount*	*Growth Rate (%)*	
1.	1994-95	11150.01	26.32	6290.97	19.8	56
2.	1995-96	14187.91	27.25	7505.03	19.3	53
3.	1996-97	17970.18	26.66	8718.08	16.2	48
4.	1997-98	22189.23	23.48	9860.81	13.1	44
5.	1998-99	27065.74	21.98	11355.84	15.2	42
6.	1999-2000	32204.34	18.99	13184.40	16.10	41
7.	Average		24.11		16.62	

Source : Statistics on RRBs, NABARD Publications, Mumbai.

Table 3.12
Recovery Performance of RRBs in India: Demand, Collection, Balance Position (June 1994 to June 2000)

(Rs. in Crore)

Sl. No.	*As at the end of*	*Demand*	*Collection*	*Balance*	*% of Recovery to Demand*
1.	June 1994	3159.95	1460.85	1699.10	46.23
2.	June 1995	3669.07	1870.36	1798.71	50.98
3.	June 1996	4426.88	2439.18	1987.70	55.10
4.	June 1997	5521.73	3144.91	2376.82	56.96
5.	June 1998	5884.99	3556.95	2328.04	60.44
6.	June 1999	NA	NA	NA	60.43
7.	June 2000	NA	NA	NA	64.09

Note: Position is from July to June every year.

Source: Statistics on RRBs, NABARD Publications, Mumbai.

percentage of recovery has been increasing steadily. The maximum recovery recorded was in the year 2000, i.e., 64.09 per cent. State-wise analysis of data on the recovery performance of the RRBs was presented in Table 3.13 which shows that as many as 12 out of States have recorded more than 60 per cent recovery rate as on 30 June 2000; Kerala has shown the highest percentage of recovery at 89.98 per cent followed by Punjab and Tamil Nadu (above 80 per cent) and Gujarat, Haryana, Karnataka and Himachal Pradesh (above 74 per cent). Recovery performance was very unsatisfactory in respect of RRBs in three North-Eastern States viz.- Assam (34.56 per cent), Manipur (33.69 per cent) and Tripura (15.78 per cent). The recovery performance of RRBs in the remaining eight states have been in the range of 40 per cent to 60 per cent.

Asset Classification and Non-Performing Assets (NPAs)

3.7.14. RBI has introduced asset classification norms from the fiscal year 1995-96 for the RRBs. Since the application of these norms, the asset quality of these banks has shown significant improvement as is evidenced by the data given in the Table 3.14. The share of Standard Assets in the total loans of RRBs steadily increased from 56.93 per cent in 1995-96 to 76.93 per cent in 1999-2000. Similarly, the

Table 3.13

Recovery Performance : Percentage of Recovery to Demand (State-wise Data on all RRBs) as on 30 June 2000

Sl. No.	60% and above		40% to 60%		20% to 40%	
	State	*%of Recovery*	*State*	*%of Recovery*	*State*	*% of Recovery*
1.	Kerala	89.98	Madhya Pradesh	58.77	Assam	34.56
2.	Punjab	81.40	Uttar Pradesh	56.21	Manipur	33.69
3.	Tamil Nadu	80.63	Arunachal Pradesh	54.00	Tripura	15.78
4.	Haryana	76.32	Nagaland	48.84		
5.	Gujarat	74.93	West Bengal	43.98		
6.	Himachal Pradesh	74.28	Jammu and Kashmir	41.99		
7.	Karnataka	74.11	Bihar	41.80		
8.	Rajasthan	66.56	Meghalaya	41.74		
9.	Maharashtra	64.18				
10.	Orissa	63.85				
11	Mizoram	63.39				
12.	Andhra Pradesh	63.04				

Source : Statistics on RRBs, NABARD Publications, Mumbai.

NPAs have declined from 43.07 per cent to 23.07 per cent during the said period. However, the level of NPAs at Rs. 3041.64 crore constituting nearly 23 per cent of the total loans outstanding as on 31 March 2000 was still very high and was a cause of concern for the RRBs.

Working Results

3.7.15. Table 3.15 presents the working results of RRBs from March 1994-95 to March 1999-2000. The amount of annual profit earned increased from Rs. 28.96 crore (by 32 RRBs) in March 1995 to Rs. 543.52 crore (by 162 RRBs) in March 2000. The amount of loss incurred (by 164 RRBs) decreased from Rs. 423.21 crore to Rs. 113.55 crore (by 34 RRBs) in the corresponding period. Thus, the overall working results

Table 3.14

Assets Classification and Non-Performing Assets (NPAs) of RRBs in India (1995-96 to 1999-2000)

(Rs. in Crore)

Sl. No.	*Assets Classification*	*1995-96*	*1996-97*	*1997-98*	*1998-99*	*1999-00*
1.	Standard Assets	4272.71	5507.65	6622.83	8194.49	10142.76
		(56.93)	(63.21)	(67.16)	(72.16)	(76.93)
	Growth (%)	—	28.90	20.25	23.73	23.78
2.	NPAs	3232.32	3210.44	3237.99	3161.35	3041.64
		(43.07)	(36.83)	(32.84)	(27.84)	(23.07)
	Growth (%)	—	(-) 0.68	0.86	(-) 2.35	(-) 3.79
3.	Total Assets	7505.03	8718.08	9860.82	11355.84	13184.40

Notes: Figures in brackets indicate the percentage of Assets to total loans and advances outstanding.

Source: *Statistics on RRBs,* NABARD Publications, Mumbai.

of RRBs have shown that there was operating loss of Rs.394.26 crore in 1994-95 and operating profit of Rs. 429.97 crore in 1999-2000. It may be observed that, the loss went on increasing to reach the highest level of Rs. 811.39 crore (even after taking into account the amount of profit of Rs. 69.68 crore earned by 44 RRBs) in 1996-97. The RRBs, taken as a whole, started reporting operating profits of Rs.73.66 crore for the first time in 1997-98 and have been improving since then to reach a level of Rs. 429.97 in 1999-2000.

Loss Incurring RRBs—The Magnitude and Concentration

3.7.16. Out of 196 RRBs, 162 RRBs earned a total profit of Rs. 543.52 crore during 1999-2000 whereas 34 RRBs incurred an aggregate loss of Rs. 113.55 crore. Of the 23 States in which the RRBs are operating, as many as 12 States had no loss-incurring RRBs. Of the 34 loss-incurring RRBs as many as 26 RRBs constituting 77 per cent were concentrated in 5 States, namely, Bihar (29 per cent), Madhya Pradesh (18 per cent), Orissa (12 per cent), Rajasthan (9 per cent) and West Bengal (9 per cent). The remaining six States have only one to two loss-incurring RRBs each as on 31 March 2000.

Table 3.15

Working Results of RRBs at all-India Level (1994-95 to 1999-2000)

(Rs. in Crore)

Sl. No.	*Working Results*	*1994-95*		*1995-06*		*1996-97*		*1997-98*		*1998-99*		*1999-2000*	
		No. of RRBs	*Amount*	*No. of RRBs*	*Amount*	*No. of RRBs*	*Amount*	*No. of RRBs*	*Amount*	*No. of RRBs*	*Amount*	*No. of RRBs*	*Amount*
1.	Profit Making RRBs	32	28.96	45	42.44	44	69.68	126	304.22	147	425.83	162	543.52
2.	Loss Incurring RRBs	164	423.21	151	465.37	152	881.07	70	230.57	49	178.10	34	113.55
3.	Working Results	196	394.26 (Loss)	196	422.93 (Loss)	196	811.39 (Loss)	196	73.66 (Profit)	196	247.73 (Profit)	196	429.97 (Profit)

Source : *Statistics on RRBs*, NABARD Publications, Mumbai.

Table 3.16
Accumulated Losses of RRBs in India (1995-96 to 1999-2000)

Sl. No.	*Year*	*No. of RRBs*	*Amount*	*Growth Rate*
1.	March 1995	175	1691.72	-
2.	March 1996	173	2176.09	28.60
3.	March 1997	174	3052.67	40.50
4.	March 1998	168	3116.19	2.06
5.	March 1999	153	3100.85	-0.48
6.	March 2000	121	2978.90	-3.93

Source : Financial Statements of RRBs, NABARD Publications, Mumbai.

Accumulated Losses

3.7.17. Huge amount of accumulated losses of RRBs have become a prime cause of concern for the RRBs. Accumulated losses have increased from Rs. 1691.72 crore as on March 1995 to Rs. 3116.19 crore as on March 1998 as can be observed from the Table 3.16. The table reveals that the accumulated losses of RRBs decreased only marginally from Rs. 3116.19 crore in 1997-98 to Rs. 3100.84 crore in 1998-99 and to Rs. 2978.90 crore in 1999-2000. It may also be noticed that the number of RRBs with accumulated losses have decreased from 175 to 140 during this period. The growth rate of accumulated losses was the highest (40.30 per cent) in 1996-97.

Viability Structure

3.7.18. Another evidence of the qualitative improvement in the performance of RRBs has been the gradual but steady increase in the number of RRBs attaining sustainable viability. The viability status of the RRBs presented in the Table 3.17 reveals that the number of RRBs in India which have attained sustainable viability, i.e., made profit and wiped out accumulated losses from their balance sheets, has gone up from 22 in 1995-96 to 56 in 1999-2000. Similarly, the number of RRBs with current viability, i.e., have earned operating profit but still have accumulated losses, has increased from 23 to 106 and that of loss incurring RRBs has decreased from 151 to 34 during the same period.

Table 3.17
Classification of RRBs According to Viability at all-India Level

Sl. No.	*Classification of RRBs*	*Number of RRBs*				
		1995-96	*1996-97*	*1997-98*	*1998-99*	*1999-2000*
1.	Attained Sustainable Viability	22	21	28	43	56
2.	Attained Current Viability	23	23	98	104	106
3.	Incurring Losses	151	152	70	49	34
	(i) Incurred lesser losses than previous year and having accumulated losses	67	33	62	31	22
	(ii) Incurred Higher losses than previous year and having accumulated losses	78	107	8	15	10
	(iii) Shifted from profit to losses	6	12	0	3	2
4.	Total	196	196	196	196	196

Source : *Financial Statements RRBs*, NABARD Publications, Mumbai.

3.7.19. In Banking sector, RRBs have occupied a significant place among the financing institutions for strengthening rural financial network. As a new group of State-sponsored, regionally based, rural-oriented and low-cost banks RRBs were set up in 1975 to project the ethos of business attitude of commercial banks through providing credit in rural areas, especially to the weaker sections of the society and for mobilising rural savings through neighbouring banking. The RRBs have come a long way since their inception in realising their avowed objectives.

Summary

3.8.1. The institutional agencies catering to the rural credit prior to the establishment of RRBs in 1975 were the cooperatives and the commercial banks. In commercial banks with all their new found enthusiasm, were still new to rural lending. The staff of the bank with their urban orientation had problems of adjustment in a rural setting. As against these, they had, on the positive side, vast resources at their command and professional ability to deploy them. The cooperatives, on the other hand, were very much rooted in rural ethos and enjoyed decades of experience in agricultural finance. But as a financial agency, they were quite weak due to various problems such as low level of efficiency, delays, politicisation, overdues etc. Besides, the volume of credit required, spatial diversities and social complexities of rural life called for a third financial agency in rural areas. Given the rising demand for rural credit and the need to replace moneylenders with institutional agencies, there existed scope for another agency. This agency would combine the feel of the cooperatives and the business acumen of the CBs leaving out the disadvantages of the both. This was then the background in which the Working Group on Rural Banks headed by Narasimham recommended the setting up of RRBs in 1975. The RRBs, by mandate were, therefore, required to take banking services to the doorsteps of rural masses, particularly to hitherto unbanked far-flung rural areas and make available institutional credit especially to the weaker sections of the society. The operations of the RRBs were governed as per the provisions of the RRBs Act, 1976 which was amended in 1987 and the RRBs (Amendment) Act, 1987 came into force on 28 September 1988.

3.8.2. In order to ensure easy access to credit for the rural poor the RRBs until 1992 were subjected to certain restrictions in their business operations and management which became critical to their viability. Therefore, a number of Committees (2 Working Groups and 4 Committees) were established to look into the various problems of RRBs. A package of reform measures were announced by the GOI to make them financially sound and viable. NABARD also initiated revamping measures and asked the RRBs to prepare bank-specific Development Action Plans (DAPs) and to enter into MoU with their sponsor-banks for business improvement in the short-run and viability attainment in the long-run. As a result of these reform measures; the RRBs have shown both quantitative and qualitative improvement in their performance over the last few years.

3.8.3. The annual and decadal growth analysis of RRBs confirms the fact that there has been substantial development in the overall performance of RRBs. The structural growth and development of RRBs were concentrated mainly during early eighties and their functional growth gained momentum in the nineties and is still continuing. These findings on structural and financial growth of RRBs reflects the impact of branch incensing policy for 1985-90 followed in the line of the recommendations of the Kelkar Committee laying emphasis on the consolidation of the banking system and also the need to go slow on setting up of RRBs in the context of rise in the number of loss-incurring RRBs.

3.8.4. The resource base of the RRBs have been strengthened during the period of study from March 1995 to March 2000. Deposit, the major resource component of RRBs as a proportion of total resources has remained constant at around 82 per cent over these years. Borrowing as proportion to the total resources of RRBs has decreased from 16.64 per cent to 9.63 per cent. The most remarkable aspect has been the steady improvement in the owned funds position of the RRBs in absolute terms and in terms of percentage share to the total resources of the RRBs during this period. This may be attributed to the recapitalisation measures initiated since 1995-96 by the GOI as a policy to strengthen the financial position of RRBs. Consequently, these banks have been provided with additional share capital by the GOI, sponsor banks and the State Governments. This reflects a welcome trend for the RRBs to involve more of their own resources and deposits in their business and to depend less on the external resources especially borrowings.

3.8.5. The performance of RRBs with regard to deposit mobilisation and credit deployment has been overwhelming as revealed through different indicators, i.e., in absolute terms, in terms of growth rate, number of deposits or advances accounts, deposits or advances per RRB, per branch and per account. The composition of deposit structure shows that the share of savings deposits has varied between 40 per cent to 44 per cent whereas that of the current account deposits remained constant at around 5 per cent during the period of study. The steady increase in the share of term deposits from 48 per cent to 55 per cent during the study period may result in high servicing cost of deposits ultimately affecting the profitability of the RRBs. On the other hand, in the break-up of outstanding advances of RRBs, the farm-sector advances have shown a lower proportion of 47 per cent than nearly 52 per cent of advances to the non-farm sector. In the non-farm sector, retail-trade category has recorded the highest percentage share of 23 per cent followed by the share of 21 per cent and 7.6 per cent of other purposes and rural artisans categories respectively during the period under review.

3.8.6. The investments and I-D Ratios of the RRBs have shown noticeable improvement. The performance of the RRBs in the recovery front has been consistently improving from 46.23 per cent in June 1994 to 64.09 per cent in June 2000. The recovery performance of the RRBs in the three North-Eastern States namely Tripura, Manipur and Assam has been the lowest. The RRBs in Kerala recorded the highest recovery percentage of 89.98 per cent in 1999-2000. There has been steady improvement in the amount of profit and the number of profit-making RRBs. Out of 23 States where RRBs have been operating, 12 States have no loss-incurring RRBs at all and 6 States have only 1 or 2 loss-incurring RRBs. The loss-incurring RRBs were concentrated mainly in 5 States, viz. Bihar, Madhya Pradesh, Orissa, Rajasthan and West Bengal. The number of RRBs attaining sustainable viability and current viability were 56 and 106 respectively and those of loss-incurring RRBs were 34 in India as on 31 March 2000.

3.8.7. Thus, while majority of the RRBs have made good progress, a few others continued to be plagued by certain problems. The continuously declining C-D Ratios especially in the nineties, mounting overdues, high percentage of NPAs, huge amount of operating and accumulated losses are a few crucial problems that have been unearthed in course of analysis of their operations during the study period from 1994-95 to 1999-2000.

References

1. GOI, *Report of the Committee (Working Group) on Rural Banks,* New Delhi, 1975; Quoted in Wadhva, C.D., *Rural Banks for Rural Development*, Macmillan, Madras (1988), p. 6.
2. RBI, *Statistical Statements Relating to Cooperative Movement in India, 1975-76*, Part-I, Bombay, Credit Societies, 1977.
3. These findings are based on the data published in the various issues of *RBI Bulletin*, Bombay.
4. (i) *All India Debts and Investment Survey, 1980-81*, p. 40;

   (ii) All India Rural Credit Survey – *The Survey Report*, Vol. I, Part II, p. 3 (Credit Agencies).
5. Ghosh, B.K., and Patel, K.V., "Role of Banks in the Promotion of Agriculture and Rural development, Indian Experience", National Institute of Bank Management (NIBM), (1995), Pune.
6. *Ibid.*
7. Patel, K.V., "Rural Development; Strategies and Experience", *Pigmy Economic Review*, Diamond Jubilee Year, November, 1984.
8. Shete, N.B. and Karkal, G.L., "Regional Rural Banks: Problems and Perspectives of Rural Credit", *Prajnan*, 18(2), April-June 1989, p. 133.
9. GOI, *Report of the Banking Commission*, New Delhi, 1972, pp. 164-166.
10. *Banking Commission Report, op. cit.*, pp. 164-174.
11. RBI, *Report of the Review Committee on Rural Banks* (1978), p. 4.
12. 'RRBs : Problems and Perspectives of Rural Credit", Shate, N.B. and Karkal, G.L., *Prajnan*, 18(2), April-June, 1989, p. 134.
13. GOI (1975), *Report of the Working Group on Rural Banks*, Government of India, New Delhi, pp. 2-3.
14. *Ibid.*, p. 5.
15. Underbanked District : A district having a minimum population of 75,000 per branch office of the Commercial Bank. A district having a population below 75,000 as considered as well-banked. This was the norm adopted by the Steering Committee, 1976 appointed by the GOI to workout the operational details of the RRB Scheme.
16. *Report of the Review Committee on RRBs* (1978), RBI, Bombay, p. 4.

17. *Report of the Committee on the Financial System* (1991), RBI, Bombay,
18. Data were collected from:
    (a) RBI, *Banking Statistics Quarterly Handout,* March, 2000.
    (b) *Statistics on RRBs*, NABARD Publications.
    (c) *Review of the Performance of RRBs as on 31.3.1999,* NABARD Publications, Mumbai.
19. *Working of RRBs—Review for the year ended 31 March 1996*, NABARD Publications, Mumbai, p. 2.

4

Socio-Economic Background of and Imperatives for RRBs in Orissa

Introduction

4.1.1. This chapter entitled "The socio-economic background of and the imperatives for Regional Rural Banks in Orissa" is comprised of five sections including the introductory one. Section - 2, throws light on the economic profile of Orissa. It covers the geographical and demographic features of the State, the State's income, per capita consumer expenditure, the standard of living of the people, the availability of different resources and the extent of their utilisation etc. Subject to the availability of data and the necessity of the study, the economic features of Orissa have been discussed in comparison to those of India. Section - 3 highlights the different environmental and economic reasons that led to the establishment of RRBs in Orissa. Section - 4 contains an empirical analysis of the role of RRBs in the economic development of Orissa. Section - 5, the concluding section, summarises the findings of this chapter.

Economic Profile of Orissa

Physical Features

4.2.1. The economic profile of Orissa throws light on the status of the State's Economy, its strengths and weaknesses. "The State of Orissa has a geographical area of 1.56 lakh square kilometres which accounts for about 4.74 per cent of India's landmass of the country. It lies between 17.31 degree and 22.27 degree North Latitude and 81.27 degree and 87.30 degree East Latitude".[1] For administrative convenience, it is divided into 30 Districts, 314 Blocks and 51,536 villages. The State is surrounded by West Bengal, Bihar and Jharkhand in the North, Chattisgarh in the West, Andhra Pradesh in the South and the Bay of Bengal in the East. The length of its coast line is nearly 480 km.

Agro-Climatic Conditions[2]

4.2.2. The State can be divided into ten agro-climatic zones with varied characteristics. Its land can be classified into three categories, low (25.6 per cent), medium (33.6 per cent) and up-lands (40.8 per cent). The land comprises of various types of soil like red, yellow, red-loamy, alluvial, coastal alluvial, laterite and black soil etc. with low and medium texture. The characteristics of different agro-climatic zones and the physical features of Orissa determine the nature and extent of her agricultural obtaining. The main controlling physical features of Orissa are the Bay of Bengal in the East, the alluvial plains, the plateau of the North and Western part of the State and the mountains of the Southern Orissa which forms the part of the long chain hills known as "Eastern Ghats". All these have their determining influence on the agricultural pattern of Orissa. The alluvial plains are highly fertile and suitable for digging irrigation canals and providing water at shallow depths for lift irrigation. But, these regions are prone to frequent flood and cyclone. The North, South and West parts of Orissa comprising plateau areas, hilly areas and river valley are helpful for agriculture. In addition, these parts are rich in mineral and forest wealth. The average rainfall in Orissa is 1532 mm. of which 77 per cent is contributed by the South-west Monsoon. It breaks in Orissa usually towards mid-June and prevails up to mid-September. The Northern Plateau gets about 1584 mm. rainfall per annum. The Eastern Ghat receives an annual rainfall of nearly 1547 mm. The rainfall of the Coastal Plateau is about 1449 mm. per year as against that of the Central Table land which is 1421 mm. Thus, the distribution of rainfall in Orissa is not even which makes the State liable to suffer from drought and floods.

Demographic Profile[3]

4.2.3. The demographic profile of Orissa in comparison to that of India and the decadal growth of population in Orissa shows that, the population of the State according to 2001 Census was 367.92 lakh which is 3.60 per cent to that of India. Nearly 87 per cent of the total population of the State live in rural areas and the remaining 13 per cent constitutes the urban population of the State as compared to 74 per cent and 26 per cent respectively at All India level. The decennial growth rate of population of 15.94 per cent in the State during the decade 1991-2000 was lower than the growth rate of 20.06 per cent during the previous decade. The density of population which was 203 per sq. km. in 1991 increased to 236 per sq. km. in 2001, compared to the all India averages of 257 and 324 per sq. km. during the corresponding periods respectively. The sex-ratio in the State, i.e., number of females per 1000 males increased from 971 in 1991 to 972 in 2001 as compared to the all India average which increased from 927 in 1991 to 972 in 2001 during the corresponding period. On the literacy front, the achievement has been noticeable as the literacy rate increased from 49.1 per cent in 1991 to 63.61 per cent in 2001 as against the increase from 52.1 per cent to 65.38 per cent at the national level during the same period. "Every fourth person in the State is a Scheduled Tribe (ST) and every seventh person is a Scheduled Caste (SC). Both the ST and SC population constitute 38.41 per cent of the State's population while the national average is 24.34 per cent".[4]

Employment Situation

4.2.4. With the increase in the population of the State and the consequent addition to the labour force, the supply of labour continues to outstrip demand resulting in accentuation of the problem of unemployment and under-employment. "The levels of unemployment at the end of 1999-2000 was estimated to be around 8 lakhs".[5]

Incidence of Poverty

4.2.5. The economy of Orissa is characterised by high incidence of poverty. According to the Planning Commission's latest estimates of poverty (using the methodology contained in the Report of the Expert Group on Estimation of Proportion and Number of Poor headed by Lakdawala) covering the period July 1999 to June 2000, the number of persons living below poverty line was 143.69 lakhs in rural areas and 25.40 lakhs in urban areas of Orissa with a combined figure 169.09 lakhs. Proportion of people living below poverty line was 47.15 per cent with a break up of 48.01 in rural areas and 42.83 per cent in urban areas. Incidentally, this figure was the highest in the country and is much higher than the national average of 26 per cent. Thus, Orissa is now the poorest State in the country and the magnitude of poverty is more prevalent in rural areas of the State. Worse still is the fact that "the State has fallen into a debt trap with an outstanding loan burden pegged at more than Rs. 21,000 crore as at the end of March 2001. This is about 51 per cent of the estimated Gross State Domestic Product (GSDP)".[6]

State Income

4.2.6. The size of the State Income depends on the share and growth of the four major sectors namely primary, secondary, tertiary and service sectors. The sectoral contribution of each of these sectors to the State Income was 40 per cent, 18.7 per cent 20.1 per cent and 21.2 per cent respectively in 1997-98 at 1980-81 prices.[7] Thus, the primary sector which includes agriculture plays a key role in the State's economy. "The per capita income of the State at 1980-81 prices was Rs. 1688 compared to the national average of Rs. 2814 and was one of the lowest in the country. The gap in the per capita income of the State and the national average in 1980-81 was Rs. 316 and this gap has increased nearly four-fold to Rs. 1126 in 1997-98".[8]

Consumer Expenditure

4.2.7. The expenditure incurred by a household on domestic consumption is the household's consumer expenditure. The level of consumer expenditure is a measure of the economic well-being of the household. The data on private consumption are also useful for observing changes in the quality of life over a period of time. The data given here are based on the findings of the 55th Round of National Sample Survey Organisation (NSSO) covering the period from July 1999 to June 2000. The Monthly Per Capita Expenditure (MPCE) in rural areas of Orissa, as per this Survey, was Rs. 323.92 as against the all-India average of Rs. 327.56 and was also lower than that of many other States in the country like Assam, Bihar, Himachal Pradesh, Kerala, Punjab, Rajasthan, U.P., West Bengal, etc. MPCE for urban area in Orissa was Rs. 473.12 which is considerably higher than the MPCE for rural area as stated above. It can be inferred that the average living standard of rural area of Orissa is not only worse than that of the urban area but also is lower than that of many other States and India as a whole.

Agriculture

4.2.8. Agriculture is the dominant sector of the State's economy. Nearly 65.75 per cent of the total workforce of the State depend on agriculture for their livelihood. The primary sector which includes agriculture contributed nearly 40.41 per cent of the NSDP and the contribution of agriculture alone was about 30 per cent of the State Income (NSDP) in 1997-98.

(a) **Operational Holdings in the State :** Table 4.1 presents the number and area of operational holdings in the State. It shows that there were 39.48 lakh operational holdings in Orissa of which small and marginal holdings account for 79.88 per cent while the remaining 20.12 per cent came under the category of semi-medium, medium and large holdings. As much as 46.66 per cent of the total operated area was owned by small and marginal farmers (SF/MF) whose number is nearly 31.54 lakhs and the remaining 53.34 per cent by the semi-medium and large farmers. The average size of the holding is 1.34 hectare.

(b) **Cropping Pattern :** Cropping pattern is one of the thrust areas for the economic use of the scarce natural resources like land. More than 70 per cent of the cultivated area in the State is covered under paddy crop. "During 1998-99 paddy was the major cereal crop in the State with coverage about 74.4 per cent of the total gross cropped area under principal crops followed by pulses (11.8 per cent) and oil seeds (6.4 per cent). The area under fibre crops accounted for only 1.2 per cent and other cash crops which include sugarcane, potato, ginger, onion and tobacco etc. constituted only 3.0 per cent of the total gross cropped area under principal crops".[10]

(c) **Irrigation**[11]**:** According to the estimate of the Central Ground Water Board, only 10.12 per cent of ground water resources had been harnessed till 1992. In spite of plenty of water resources in the State, nearly 63 per cent of the

Table 4.1
Number and Area of Operational Holdings in Orissa (According to Agricultural Census 1990-91)

Sl. No.	*Holding Size*	*No. of Operational Holdings (thousand)*	*Area of Operation (thousand hectare)*
1.	Marginal (below 1.0 hect.)	2118 (53.65)	1045 (19.73)
2.	Small (1.0 hect. to 2.0 hect.)	1035 (26.22)	1426 (26.93)
3.	Semi-Medium (2.0 hect. to 4.0 hect.)	594 (15.04)	1561 (29.47)
4.	Medium (4.0 hect. to 10.0 hect.)	186 (4.71)	1012 (19.11)
5.	Large (10.0 hect. and above)	15 (0.38)	252 (4.76)
6.	Total	3948 (100.0)	5296 (100.0)

N.B. : Figures in brackets indicate percentage to total.
Source : Board of Revenue, Agricultural Census Division, Government of Orissa, Cuttack.

cultivable land is rainfed and exposed to the vagaries of monsoon. "Out of the total cultivable land of 65.59 lakh hectare total land which can be brought under assured irrigation is 59 lakh hectare. Irrigation facilities provided (up to 1998-99) to 24.69 lakh hectare of land was only 41.85 per cent of the total irrigable land. Further, the proportion of net area irrigated to net area sown in the State was 32.8 per cent during 1992-93 as against 35.2 per cent at the all-India level and was much below the corresponding proportion in agriculturally advanced States like Punjab (93.3 per cent), Haryana (75.6 per cent), Uttar Pradesh (65.6 per cent), Bihar (46.7 per cent), Tamil Nadu (46.4 per cent)". Thus, the irrigation facilities in the State is inadequate and there is over-dependence of agriculture on monsoon.

Table 4.2
Performance of Industrial Sector in Orissa up to the end of 1998-99

Sl. No.	*Type of Industries*	*Number*	*Investment in Rs. Crore*	*Employment Generation*
1.	Large and Medium Scale	334	1841.99	81,188
2.	Small Scale	59,079	1233.08	3,99,000
3.	Cottage	50,607	58.69	92,822

Source : 1 Directorate of Industries, Cuttack.
2. Directorate of Handicrafts and Cottage Industries, Bhubaneswar.

Industry

4.2.9. The performance of industrial sector in the State by the end of 1998-99 has been given in the Table 4.2. The table indicates that by the end of 1998-99, Orissa had 334 large and medium industries with an investment of Rs. 1841.99 crore generating employment opportunities for 81,188 persons. Similarly, as on the said period 59,079 small-scale industries with an investment of Rs. 1233.08 crore were operating in the State providing employment to 3.99 lakh persons. Besides, 50,607 cottage industries had been set up in the State with an investment of Rs. 58.69 crore and provision of employment to 92,822 persons.

Minerals and Forest Resources[12]

4.2.10. As per the All India Mineral Resources Estimates made for 1998-99, the reserve of coal was the highest at 49,406 million tonne followed by iron ore (3567 million tonnes), bauxite (1733 million tonne) and lime stone (1032 million tonnes) in Orissa. The mineral deposits of Orissa in respect of chromite, bauxite, iron ore were about 98.4 per cent, 69.7 per cent, 26.0 per cent and 23.8 per cent respectively of the total deposits of India. Though Orissa is rich in mineral resources, the rate of exploitation of minerals in the State is less than 1 per cent in all cases except graphite (4.5 per cent), lead ore (3.4 per cent) and manganese (1.1 per cent). The forest area in the State was 59,963 sq. km. which constituted 38.44 per cent of the total geographical area of the State in 1981, and has reduced to 58,135 sq. km. constituting 37.3 per cent in 1991. The main thrust in the forestry sector is on afforestation of waste lands and restoration of degraded forests.

Infrastructure Facilities

4.2.11. The infrastructure facilities available in the State shows the extent of socio-economic development of the State. These facilities include the transport, communication, health, medical services, family welfare, education, supply of electricity, banking and insurance facilities. Table 4.3 presents the level of infrastructural development in the State in comparison to that of India in terms of various socio-economic indicators. It may be observed that the basic infrastructure in the State is lagging far behind in comparison to that of India in terms of many indicators such as percentage of villages electrified, per capita government expenditure on education, health and family welfare, per capita milk production in the State. As far as banking facilities are concerned, there is one bank office for every 17 thousand of population as against the figure of 15 thousand of people per bank at the all-India level. The availability and deployment of bank credit is also lesser in Orissa (39.75 per cent) in comparison to the national level (57.05 per cent) as indicated by the Credit-Deposit Ratio (C-D Ratio). Thus, the analysis of the above data leads to the conclusion that there has been inadequate development of socio-economic infrastructure in the State and it shows all the characteristics of backwardness.

Imperatives for Regional Rural Banks in Orissa

4.3.1. Paradoxically, there is widespread poverty in Orissa in the midst of plenty of resources. The prime task of economic development is therefore to remove poverty from the State. In order to achieve this goal, heavy investment of capital in the economy is necessary. The State Government is unable to meet all the required investment on account of limited budgetary resources. The central assistance to the State is inadequate. The private sector is also unable to undertake large scale investment in the State on account of paucity of resources. Accordingly, more reliance is placed upon the institutional agencies assisting the investment efforts of the private sector in the economy. It is worthwhile to mention that as per 1971, 1981, 1991 and the just recently concluded 2001 Census, in no other States of India, the concentration of population in the rural areas was as high as that in Orissa. This, therefore, draws the need for paying greater attention for the development of the rural sector in the State. The Regional Rural

Table 4.3
Infrastructure Facilities in Orissa Compared to that of India

Sl. No.	*Facilities*	*Orissa*	*India*
1.	Length of Roads per 1000 sq. km. area (1996-97)	1687 km.	750 km.
2.	Registered Motor Vehicles per 1000 persons (1996-97)	21	40
3.	Percentage of villages connected with all weather roads (1995-96)	40	48
4.	Railway Route Length per 1000 sq. km. of area (1997-98)	14.04 km.	19.01 km.
5.	Railway Route Length per one lakh of population (1997-98)	6.21 km.	6.56 km.
6	No. of Post Offices per 100 sq. km. (1997-98)	5.2(5)	4.7(5)
7.	Average No. of Post Offices per One lakh population (1997-98)	23	16
8.	No. of Telephone connections per 1000 persons (1998-99)	4	9
9.	Percentage of Villages covered under Telephone Services (1998-99)	44	NA
10.	Percentage of Villages Electrified up to March 1999	73.43	86.4
11.	**Banking** : Population in '000 covered per Bank Office as on March 2000	17	15
12.	**Banking** : Credit-Deposit Ratio as on March 2000	39.75	57.05
13.	**Education** : Per capita Government expenditure on Education, Art and Culture in Rs. (1998-99)	Rs. 354.40	Rs. 456.10
14.	**Health & Family Welfare** : Per capita Government Expenditure on Medical, Public Health and Family Welfare (1998-99)	Rs. 76.20	Rs. 110.80
15.	**Milk Production** : Per capital Milk production in kg. (1994-95)	17.5 kg.	70 kg.

Source : *Economic Survey, 1999-2000,* Bureau of Economics and Statistics, Orissa, Bhubaneswar.

Banks were set up in Orissa with the objective of supplementing the existing sources of institutional credit for the rural sector and thus harnessing the socio-economic development of the State. Against this backdrop, the imperatives for the RRBs in Orissa should be considered.

Rural Character of the State's Economy

4.3.2. The economy of Orissa is rural-oriented in nature in view of several reasons. Nearly 86.62 per cent of the State's population live in the rural areas comprising of 51,536 villages. 89 per cent of the State's total workforce belong to the rural areas. It has the highest density of rural population in India. The State is characterised by the highest incidence of poverty in the country and the magnitude of poverty is more in rural areas than in urban areas of the State. Therefore, the economic development of Orissa, in real sense would mean the development of the rural areas of the State.

Incidence of Poverty and Natural Calamities

4.3.3. Orissa is a poor State as evidenced by the largest percentage of people living below poverty line, low per capita income and low MPCE. These data have also shown that the magnitude of poverty has been more in rural areas of the State than in urban areas. There has been wide difference between the per capita income at the State and national level. The devastation caused by the Super Cyclone in 1999, the severe drought situation especially in the Western parts of the State in 2000, followed by an unprecedented flood in 2001 would make it difficult to bridge this gap in near future. Thus, the frequent occurrence of flood, cyclones and drought has become the main barrier in the socio-economic development of the State.

Dominance of the Agricultural Sector in the State's Economy

4.3.4. (a) Agriculture is the dominant sector of the State's economy contributing nearly 40 per cent of the NSDP. Further, 65.75 per cent of the total workforce depends directly or indirectly on agriculture for their livelihood. The State has around 31.54 lakh small and marginal farmers and they account for 79.88 per cent of the total occupational holdings. After the introduction of new technology, agriculture has became a costly proposition. It is beyond the means of these small and marginal farmers to make appropriate investment due to poverty. In addition to this, it has been found that "the yield rate of food-grains for Orissa is 9 qtl./hect. for the year 1996-97 which was the lowest in India and was much below the figure of 16 qtl./hect. for the country as a whole. During the same year contribution of Orissa to the food grains basket of the country was only 2.4 per cent. Consumption of fertilisers was 30.52 kg./hect. which was much below the national average of 77.5 kg./hect. The proportion of net area irrigated to the net area sown in the State was only 32.8 per cent as against 35.2 per cent at the national level".[13] By the end of 1998-99, nearly 63 per cent of the cultivable land was rainfed and was exposed to the vagaries of monsoon. By the end of 1999-2000, the proportion of net irrigated area to the irrigable land was only 41.85 per cent. Thus, on the one hand, there is over-dependence on agriculture, on the other hand, agriculture in Orissa is characterised by low productivity, inadequate irrigation facilities and low investment. In view of favourable ground water potential and existence of a number of rivers and rivulets, there is ample scope for enhancing the area under irrigation in the State. These measures will also be useful for drought proofing.

(b) The varied agro-climatic condition of the State provide good scope for horticulture, cultivation of vegetables, plantation crops, species, flowers and medicinal herbs. Suitable cropping patterns need to be designed keeping in view the agro-climatic conditions of different zones in the State, both for horticultural and agricultural crops. Agro-based industries have to be set up to absorb the unutilised man power from the agricultural sector, generate income through value addition and solve the problem of unemployment and under employment in rural areas.

(c) All these enterprises to be implemented require huge amount of investment in agriculture. "But the investment in agriculture is only Rs. 773.51 crore which accounts for only 15.28 per cent of the total bank credit of Rs. 5062.15 crore in Orissa as in the year ending March 2000. Further, the investment in agriculture in Orissa is only 2.4 per cent of the total in the country and is lower than that of many other States of India".[14] Therefore, agriculture being the staple occupation of the ruralites in Orissa, an increased quota of bank credit is needed with a view to imparting greater impetus to this sector.

Scope for Promotion of Village and Cottage Industries

4.3.5. The performance of the industrial sector indicates that small-scale, village and cottage industries need lesser investment but have larger employment generating potential than the large-scale and medium industries. Promotion of these type of industries in rural area will not only help in diverting surplus labour from agriculture but also in income generation, creation of assets and employment opportunities leading to the better standard of living of the rural masses. This calls for the need to provide institutional and financial support in addition to various incentives and concessions, for promotion of this sector in rural areas.

Scope for Exploitation of Natural Resources

4.3.6. Orissa is rich in mineral resources, but the rate of exploitation, when compared to the reserves is quite low for most minerals. "The mineral sector contributed substantial income, i.e., Rs. 316 crore to the State exchequer during 1998-99, which is about 49 per cent of the State's own non-tax revenue".[15] Mineral exploitation also generates large employment. Therefore, there is need to attract greater investment in this sector so as to increase the rate of exploitation and generate further employment. Orissa shows all the characteristics of backwardness partly due to the lack of efficient exploitation and optimum utilisation of natural resources like mineral, forest, water and marine resources but mainly to lack of adequate infrastructural facilities.

Need for Enhancing Banking Facilities in the State

4.3.7. Bank credit in general as a means for sustaining the livelihood of the poor in a State like Orissa hardly needs any emphasis. The overall performance of the banking sector in Orissa shows that "the Credit-Deposit Ratio (C-D Ratio) of all scheduled commercial banks (Sch. CBs) in Orissa was 39.75 per cent against the all-India average of 57.05 per cent as on 31st March 2000. This ratio has sharply fallen from 80.59 per cent in 1990-91 to 39.75 per cent in 1999-2000 and was low when compared to States like Andhra Pradesh (63.60 per cent), Karnataka (61.01 per cent), Kerala (42.29 per cent), Tamil Nadu (88 per cent), Maharashtra (83.79 per cent), Gujarat (49.85 per cent), West Bengal (45.17 per cent), Rajasthan (46.69 per cent) and Haryana (41.41

per cent) as on 31 March 2000. Further, the population covered per bank in the State was 17 thousand as compared to 15 thousand at the all-India level".[16] Hence, the banking facilities in the State need to be enhanced by stimulating domestic savings and improving the volume of advances by all the scheduled commercial banks in the State.

4.3.8. The above mentioned socio-economic reasons justify the fact that the key to the economic development of the State lies in the development of the rural areas. Rural Development is a comprehensive programme of activities which encompasses agricultural growth, development of economic and social infrastructure, provision of gainful employment to the rural poor and the removal of poverty. Therefore, there is invariably the need for launching initiatives for stimulating the all round growth of the State's economy. Establishment of the Regional Rural Banks (RRBs) in Orissa in 1976 was an effort in this direction. These banks which have been working in Orissa since then were promoted as ideal low-cost banks primarily meant for economic upliftment of the weaker sections through credit dispersion in rural area.

Role of RRBs in the Economic Development of Orissa

4.4.1. The economy of Orissa has been characterised by high incidence of poverty, greater magnitude of poverty in rural area, highest density of population in rural area, dominance of agriculture etc. This calls for giving more emphasis on the development of rural areas of the State. Bank credit has been recognised as an important tool to improve the lot of the rural masses. In an economically backward State like Orissa, mere credit extension by CBs may not meet the emerging credit requirements of the rural areas. The RRBs were established in 1976 in the State with the aim of increasing banking facilities and serving more people specifically the weaker sections of the rural areas. Therefore, these banks were expected to operate mainly in rural areas and to cater to the needs of small and marginal farmers, agricultural labourers, rural artisans and other small borrowers. Against this background, an attempt has been made in this section to assess the role of RRBs in the economic development of Orissa through coverage of rural areas and extension of credit facilities in the State. The role of the RRBs in the economic development of Orissa can be gauged from three main indicators:

(i) RRBs' place in the banking scenario of Orissa,

(ii) Coverage of rural areas by RRBs in terms of rural branch network, deposit mobilisation and credit dispensation in rural areas, and

(iii) Assets creation and employment generation in rural areas through financing of agriculture, village and cottage industries, various government sponsored anti-poverty programmes including Integrated Rural Development Programme (IRDP).

RRBs' place in the Banking Scenario of Orissa

4.4.2. Table 4.4 gives an overall idea about the place the RRBs occupy in the banking scenario of Orissa. RRBs' share in the aggregate bank deposits and gross bank credit in the State have been consistently increasing from 9.43 per cent to 11.72 per cent and from 11.17 per cent to 14.88 per cent respectively during the period from 1994-95 to 1999-2000. This becomes more evident in Figure-4.1 which exhibits the trend of the RRBs' overall performance in three basic areas viz. branch expansion, deposit mobilisation, credit deployment in terms of percentage shares to the total of all scheduled CBs in the State. The overall share of RRBs in the total offices of all scheduled CBs in the State was constant at around 38 per cent in all these years. It becomes evident from this that the achievement by the banking system of population-branch ratio of 17000:1 (As against 15000:1 at the All India level) in the State could not have been possible but for the RRBs. It is further observed that the RRBs in the State stay considerably ahead of those at the all-India level in terms of their share in the total branch-network, deposit mobilisation and credit dispensation of all scheduled CBs.

Coverage of Rural Areas by RRBs in Orissa

4.4.3. The RRBs are supposed to be a nucleus of rural development in view of their low-cost structure, local ethos and professional management. They are rural oriented banks to supplement the existing institutional credit agencies.

(a) Coverage of Rural areas by RRBs in Orissa

Table 4.5 contains the data about the coverage of rural areas by the RRBs in Orissa and India as on 31 March 2000. It shows that out

Table 4.4

RRBs' Place in the Banking Scenario of Orissa

[Rs. in Crore]

Sl. No.	Year	Bank Offices		Aggregate Deposits		Gross Credit	
		All Sch. CBs	RRBs	All Sch. CBs	RRBs	All Sch. CBs	RRBs
1.	1994-95	2150	819 (38.09)	5077.04	478.87 (9.43)	2822.17	315.19 (11.17)
2.	1995-96	2154	819 (38.02)	6005.96	611.32 (10.18)	3291.82	379.65 (11.53)
3.	1996-97	2160	816 (37.78)	7152.72	767.65 (10.73)	3504.49	437.83 (12.49)
4.	1997-98	2170	817 (37.65)	8817.54	950.04 (10.77)	3984.40	531.13 (13.33)
5.	1998-99	2209	842 (38.12)	10239.54	1193.77 (11.66)	4352.59	624.00 (14.34)
6.	1999-2000	2219	843 (37.99)	12733.96	1492.10 (11.72)	5062.15	753.14 (14.88)
7.	Average		(37.94)		(10.75)		(12.96)
8.	All India (as on 31 Mar. 2000)	65521	14517 (22.16)	822132.77	32197.68 (3.92)	469031.71	13178.58 (2.81)

Population covered per Branch by All Sch. CBs : India : 15000 per branch Orissa : 17000 per branch

Note: Figures in brackets indicate percentage to the total of all Sch. CBs.

Sources : (a) *Economic Survey,* Govt. of Orissa, 1999-2000, p. 13/1.

(b) *Review of the Performance of RRBs in Orissa, As on 31 March 2000,* NABARD Publications, Bhubaneswar, p. 14.

(c) *RBI Banking Statistics, Quarterly Handout,* March 2000, pp. 14 & 18.

Fig. 4.1

Trend of RRBs' Overall Performance in Orissa
(in terms of percentage share to the total of all Scheduled CBs)

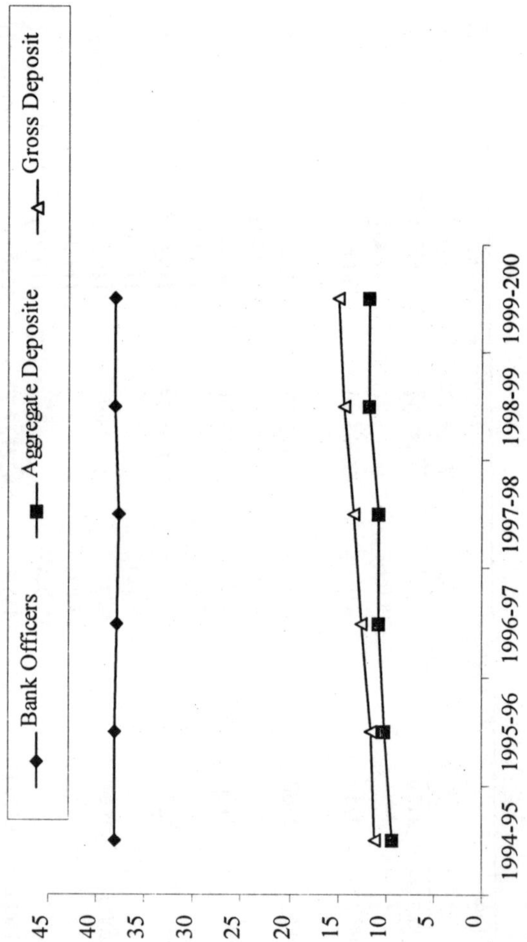

Table. 4.5
Coverage of Rural Areas by RRBs in Orissa and at All-India Level
(As on 31 March 2000)

Sl. No.	*Indicators*	*RRB's Coverage in Orissa*		*RRBs' Coverage in India*	
		Rural area	*Total*	***Rural area***	*Total*
1.	Offices	**764** (**90.63**)	843 (100)	**12178** (**83.89**)	14517 (100)
2.	Deposits (Rs. in Crore)	**1138.39** (**76.30**)	1492.09 (100)	**22404.99** (**69.59**)	32197.68 (100)
3.	Credit (Rs. in Crore)	**625.41** (**82.11**)	761.71 (100)	**9592.91** (**72.79**)	13178.58 (100)
4.	Business (Rs. in Crore)	**1763.80** (78.56)	2245.23 (100)	**31997.90** (**70.52**)	45376.26 (100)

Note : Figures in brackets indicate percentage to the total.
Sources: (a) *Statistics on RRBs,* NABARD Publications, Regional Office, Bhubaneswar. .
(b) RBI, *Banking Statistics, Quarterly Handout,* March 2000.

of the total 843 branches of the RRBs in Orissa, 764 were operating in rural areas which was 90.63 per cent of their total branch network in the State and rest are in urban areas. Deposits mobilised by the RRBs only in rural areas were Rs. 1138.39 crore which constitutes 76.30 per cent of the total deposits mobilised by them in the State. Similarly, rural credit deployment was to the tune of Rs. 625.41 crore which accounted for 82.11 per cent of their gross outstanding advances of Rs. 761.71 crore as on the said date. The coverage of rural areas by RRBs in Orissa was better than that at the all-India level as is evidenced by the lower percentage of rural branch network, rural deposit mobilisation and rural credit deployment of RRBs at the national level. This has also been highlighted in Fig. 4.2 in the form of graph.

(b) RRB's Share in Coverage of Rural Areas by all Scheduled CBs in Orissa and India

Comparative analysis of the coverage of rural areas by RRBs in the State and at all-India level presented in Table 4.6 shows that, as on

Fig. 4.2
Coverage of Rural Area by RRBs in Orissa and All India Level on March 2000

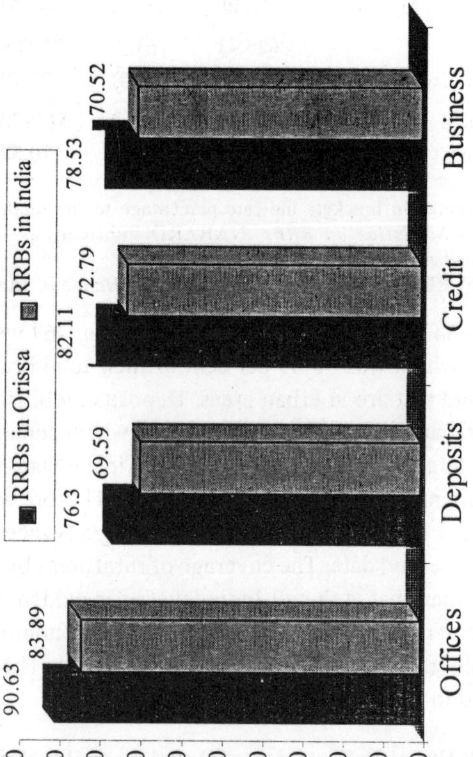

Table 4.6
RRB's Shares in the Coverage of Rural Areas by all Sch. CBs in Orissa and at All-India Level (As on 31 March 2000)

Sl. No.	*Indicators*	*Orissa*		*India*	
		All Sch CBs	*RRBs*	*All Sch. CBs*	*RRBs*
1.	Rural Branches	1614 (100)	764 (47.34)	32719 (100)	12178 (37.22)
2.	Rural Deposits (Rs. in Crore)	4174.29 (100)	1138.39 (27.27)	120446.75 (100)	22404.99 (18.60)
3.	Rural Advances (Rs. in Crore)	1837.20 (100)	625.41 (34.04)	47396.02 (100)	9592.91 (20.24)

Note : Figures in brackets indicate percentage to the total of all Sch. CBs.
Source : Banking Statistics, Quarterly Handout, March 2000, RBI, Mumbai.

31 March 2000, the RRBs' rural branch network constituted 47.34 per cent to the total rural branch network of all Scheduled CBs (including RRBs) in the State against 3.79 per cent at all-India level. The share of RRBs in mobilising rural deposits stood at 27.27 per cent in the State against 18.60 per cent at the all-India level. With regard to credit dispensation the percentages were 34.04 per cent and 20.24 per cent of the total outstanding advances at the State and national level respectively as on the said date. Thus, the RRBs in Orissa stay ahead of those at the all-India level with regard to coverage of rural areas. This has been displayed in the form of graph in Fig. 4.3.

(c) Relative Performance of Difference Banks in Rural Areas of Orissa

Table 4.7 and Fig. 4.4 reveal the relative coverage of rural areas by RRBs, Nationalised Banks and State Bank of India (SBI) and its associates in terms of percentage share to the total of all Scheduled CBs. It is observed that RRBs have the largest branch network which constitutes 47.34 per cent of the total branches of all the Scheduled CBs in the State against 33.33 per cent and 19.33 per cent of Nationalised Banks and SBI and its associates respectively. Similarly, RRBs have largest C-D Ratio of nearly 55 per cent against 38 per cent,

Fig. 4.3

RRBs Shares in the Coverage of Rural Areas by All Scheduled CBs in Orissa and at All-India Level as on 31 March 2000

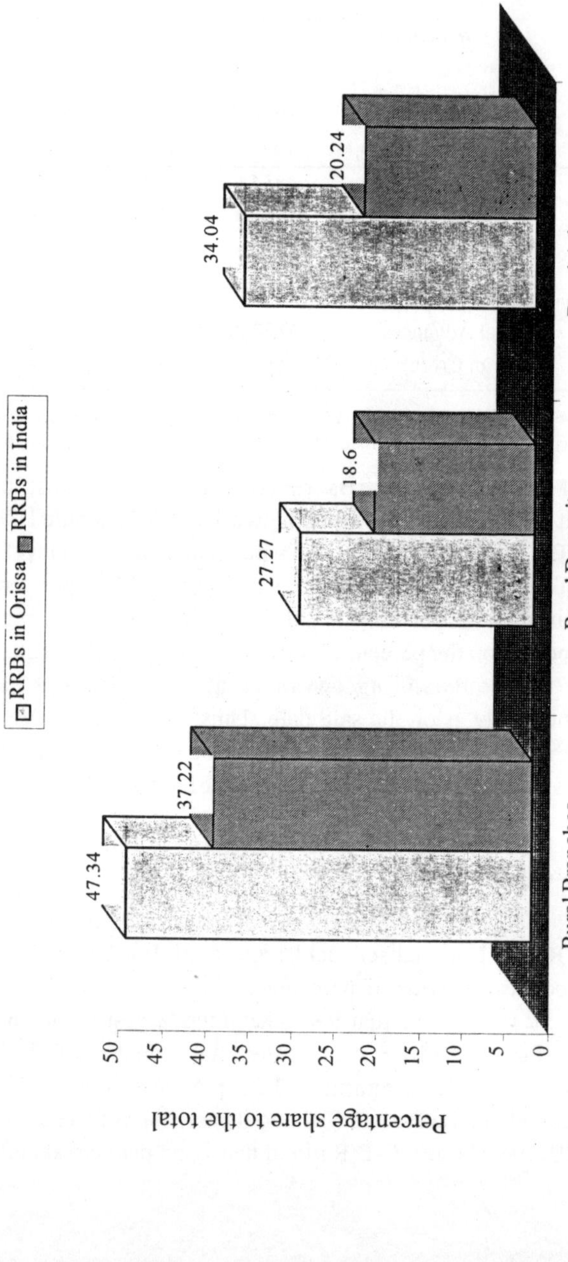

Table 4.7
Relative Performance of Different Banks in Rural Areas in Orissa (As on 31 March 2000)

(Rs. in Crore)

Sl. No.	*Indicators*	*RRBs*	*Nationalised Banks*	*SBI and Associates*	*All Scheduled CBs*
1.	Rural Offices	764 (47.34)	538 (33.33)	312 (19.33)	1614 (100)
2.	Rural Deposits	1138.39 (27.27)	1785.67 (42.78)	1250.23 (29.95)	4174.29 (100)
3.	Rural Credits	625.41 (34.04)	677.91 (36.90)	533.88 (29.06)	1837.20 (100)
4.	C-D Ratios (%)	54.94	37.96	42.70	44.01
5.	Business per branch (Rs. in Crore)	2.31	4.58	5.72	3.73

Note : Figures in brackets indicate percentage share to the total of all the Sch. CBs.

Source : RBI, Banking Statistics, Quarterly Handout, March, 2000.

43 per cent and 44 per cent of the Nationalised Banks, SBI and its associates and all Scheduled CBs respectively. But, RRBs lagged behind all other banks in terms of rural deposit mobilisation and business per branch in rural area in the State as on the said date.

Sectoral Disbursements of Advances by RRBs in Orissa

4.4.4. Table 4.8 presents the sector-wise classification of outstanding advances of RRBs in Orissa as on 3 1 March 2000. The share of credit assistance to different sectors were: crop loan 16.10 per cent, agricultural investment 19.99 per cent, village and cottage industries, rural artisans etc. 5.69 per cent, retail trade, small business and self-employed persons 24.51 per cent. The advances for miscellaneous purposes which included advances to small-scale industries, small road transport operators, professionals, Self-Help Groups (SHGs), Non-Governmental Organisations (NGOs), housing loans, staff loans, consumer advances etc. constituted 33.71 per cent of the total advances. The farm and non-farm sector advances accounted for 36.09 per cent and 63.91 per cent of the total outstanding

Fig. 4.4
Comparative Performance of Different Banks in Rural Areas of Orissa as on 31 March 2000

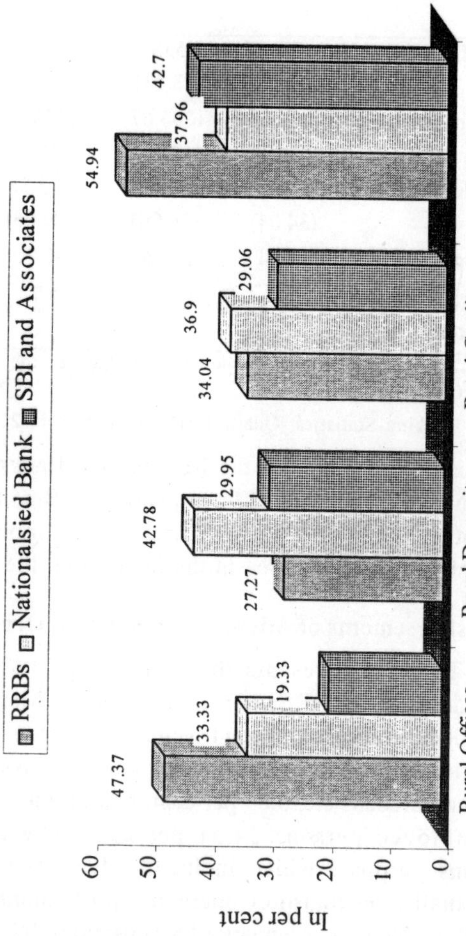

Table. 4.8
Sector-wise Classification of Outstanding Advances of RRBs in Orissa (As on 31 March 2000)

Sl. No.	*Sectoral Advances*	*No. of Accounts*	*Amount (Rs. in Crore)*
1.	Short-Term Crop Loan	207144 (22.10)	122.65 (16.10)
2.	Agricultural Investments & Allied Activities (Medium and Long-term)	221892 (23.66)	152.26 (19.99)
3.	Agricultural Advances	429036 (45.76)	274.91 (36.09)
4.	Rural Artisans, Village & Cottage Industries	21165 (2.26)	43.38 (5.69)
5.	Retail Trade, Small Business and Self-employed Persons etc.	214188 (22.86)	186.70 (24.51)
6.	Advances for Miscellaneous purposes	273001 (29.12)	256.72 (33.71)
7.	Non-Agricultural Advances	508354 (54.24)	486.80 (63.91)
8.	Total Outstanding Advances	937390 (100)	761.71 (100)
9.	Primary Sector Advances	785321 (83.78)	576.07 (75.63)
	Non-Priority Sector Advances	152069 (16.22)	185.64 (24.37)
10.	Total Outstanding advances	937390 (100)	761.71 (100)

Note : Figures in brackets indicate percentage share to the accounts and total outstanding advances.

Source : Working of the RRBs in Orissa for the year ending on 31 March 2000, NABARD Publications, Regional Office, Bhubaneswar.

advances covering more than 4 lakhs and 5 lakhs beneficiaries respectively. Similarly, the priority sector advances constituted 75.63 per cent of the total advances and 83.78 per cent of the total number of borrowal accounts covering nearly 8 lakh beneficiaries in the State up to the end of March 2000. The sectoral distribution of credits of RRBs have been presented in pictorial form in Fig. 4.5.

Fig. 4.5
Sector-wise Classification of Outstanding Advances of RRBs in Orissa (As on 31 March 2000)

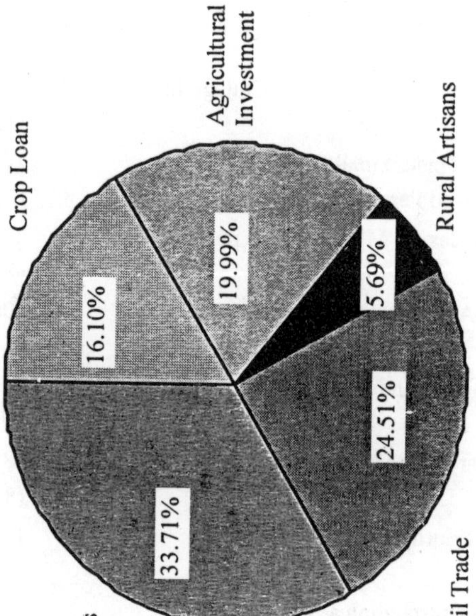

Table 4.9
Classification of Outstanding Advances of RRBs under Government Sponsored Programmes (As on 31 March 2000)

(Rs. in Crore)

Sl. No.	*Category of Borrowers*	*Number of Accounts*	*Amount*
1.	SC/ST	363922	143.43 (18.74)
2.	Minorities	18311	11.05 (1.44)
3.	Small and Marginal Farmers, Agricultural Labourers	560732	362.74 (47.41)
4.	1RDP	373190	192.15 (25.11)
5.	Other Government sponsored Programmes	109070	55.87 (7.30)
6.	Total	1425225	765.24 (J00)

Note : Figures in brackets indicate percentage share to the total outstanding advances under government sponsored programmes.

Source : *Performance of the RRBs in Orissa as on 31 March 2001,* NABARD Publications, Bhubaneswar, p. 46.

Financing of Government Sponsored Anti-Poverty Programmes; Programme-wise Classification

4.4.5. By mandate, the RRBs were required to take banking services to the doorsteps of the rural poor. Therefore, the clientele of RRBs belonged to only one category, i.e., weaker sections of the rural area and included poor people belonging to SC, ST and minority group, small and marginal farmers, landless agricultural labourers and other small borrowers. Financial assistance under several government sponsored anti-poverty programmes including Integrated Rural Development Programme (IRDP) is provided to the weaker sections of the rural area for their economic upliftment. Classification of outstanding advances of RRBs under government sponsored programmes as on 31 March 2000 displayed in the Table 4.9 shows that the largest chunk, i.e., 47.41 per cent of this advances has been

Table 4.10
Financing of Government Sponsored Anti-Poverty Programmes (1994-95 to 1999-2000)

(Rs. in Crore)

Sl. No.	Year	No. of Accounts	Amount	Growth (%)	Loan per Account (in Rs.)	Total Bank Loans under this programme No. of Accounts	Total Bank Loans under this programme Amount
1.	1994-95	46273 (30.05)	21.31 (30.82)	62.75	4605	139837 (100)	64.14 (100)
2.	1995-96	54233 (44.94)	29.51 (31.68)	38.50	5442	120669 (100)	93.15 (100)
3.	1996-97	31274 (33.05)	39.22 (32.39)	32.89	12540	94636 (100)	121.09 (100)
4.	1997-98	21774 (25.51)	36.98 (29.70)	-5.71	16982	85344 (100)	124.52 (100)
5.	1998-99	28984 (30.62)	49.59 (30.65)	34.10	17109	94671 (100)	161.75 (100)
6.	1999-2000(P)	17689 (9.06)	29.75 (12.63)	-40.01	16818	195311 (100)	235.59 (100)
7.	Average	35940 (28.88)	37.61 (27.98)	20.42	12250	124446	134.42

Note : (P) - Provisional
Figures in brackets indicate percentage share of RRBs to total of all Scheduled CBs' loan under this category.

Sources: (i) *Statistics on RRBs*, NABARD Publications, Mumbai and Bhubaneswar.
(ii) *Economic Survey*, 1999-2000, Government of Orissa, p. 13/4.

provided to the small and marginal farmers followed by advances under IRDP with 25.11 per cent. The advances to poor people belonging to SC/ST and minorities group constituted 18.74 per cent and 1.44 per cent of the total advances under this category respectively. Thus, in aggregate RRBs have made provisions for means of livelihood through credit assistance to the tune of Rs. 765.24 crore to more than 14 lakh hands belonging to the weaker sections of the rural area in the State.

Financing of Government Sponsored Anti-Proverty Programmes: Annual Disbursements

4.4.6. The annual disbursement of bank loans under various government sponsored anti-poverty programmes from 1994-95 to 1999-2000 in Orissa have been presented in Table 4.10. It reveals that RRBs' loan assistance in the State under these programmes were averaged at Rs. 37.61 crore with an average annual growth rate of 20.42 per cent and accounted for 27.98 per cent of the total bank loans under this category. These banks have served about 36000 beneficiaries per annum which was nearly 28.88 per cent of the total beneficiaries covered by all the banks in the State. The average loan per account though worked out at Rs. 12250, has remained constant at around Rs. 17000 since last three years. This analysis precisely speaks of the role played by the RRBs in the economic development of the rural poor by participating in various government sponsored anti-poverty programmes including IRDP, the largest ever rural development programme in India.

Financing of Agriculture

4.4.7. Table 4.11 presents the agricultural financing of RRBs in Orissa. The annual disbursement of loan by RRBs has displayed a continuously upward trend in absolute terms and in terms of number of beneficiaries covered (i.e., loan accounts). The loan per account has been more than Rs. 10,000/- since last 4 years. But, the share of RRBs' agricultural loan to total bank loan for the agricultural sector in Orissa has declined from 17.31 per cent in 1996-97 to 14.06 per cent in 1999-2000.

Financing of Village and Cottage Industries

4.4.8. Table 4.12 presents the data on RRBs' role in the financing of the village and cottage industries in Orissa during the period from 1994-95 to 1999-2000. RRBs' share in the total investment in this sector in the State varied between 12 per cent and 43 per cent. The amount of RRBs' investment in this sector was Rs. 1685.84 lakhs constituting 42.94 per cent of the total investment in the year 1996-97, the highest during the period under review both in absolute terms and also in terms of percentage share. On the other hand, the share of RRBs in the total

Table 4.11
Financing of Agriculture by RRBs in Orissa
(1994-95 to 1999-2000)

(Rs. in Crore)

Sl. No.	*Year*	*RRBs Loan to Agriculture*	*Growth*	*No. of Accounts*	*Loan per Account (in Rs.)*	*Total Bank loan for agriculture*
1.	1994-95	42.47 (12.10)	—	67673	6300	351.06 (100)
2.	1995-96	49.47 (13.11)	16.48	68745	7200	377.35 (100)
3.	1996-97	76.28 (17.31)	54.19	71348	10700	440.56 (100)
4.	1997-98	79.18 (16.92)	3.80	76477	10400	467.95 (100)
5.	1998-99	101.90 (16.33)	28.69	82957	12300	624.05 (100)
6.	1999-2000(P)	108.73 (14.06)	6.70	89161	12200	773.51 (100)
7.	Average	(15.55)	22.01	76058	9900	—

Note : (P) - Provisional
Figures in brackets indicate percentage share of RRBs to total of all Scheduled CBs' loan under this category.

Sources: (i) *Statistics on RRBs*, NABARD Publications, Mumbai and Bhubaneswar.
(ii) *Economic Survey*, 1999-2000, Government of Orissa, p. 4/14.

employment generation in this sector in the State remained in the range of 6.99 per cent to 14.37 per cent. On an average, RRBs' investment has been Rs. 1078 lakh per annum constituting nearly 23 per cent of the total investment in the village and cottage industries sector in the State. Similarly, these banks have provided employment opportunities to about 9500 people per annum constituting 10.32 per cent of the total employment created in this sector in the State during the period covered under the analysis. Thus, RRBs have been playing a vital role in providing means of livelihood to the rural artisans belonging to weavers, cobblers, potters, blacksmith and other communities, augmenting their financial resources and promoting their age-old ancestral occupation.

Table 4.12
Financing of Village and Cottage Industries by RRBs in Orissa (1994-95 to 1999-2000)

(Rs. in Crore)

Sl. No.	*Year (April to March)*	*Investment**		*Employment Generation #*	
		Total Investment in the State	*RRBs' Share*	*Total in the State (No. of persons)*	*RRBs' Share (No. of Accounts)*
1.	1994-95	2853.66	501.87 (17.59)	104185	8883 (8.53)
2.	1995-96	3616.86	672.26 (24.26)	91484	13147 (14.37)
3.	1996-97	3925.68	1685.84 (42.94)	76516	10049 (13.13)
4.	1997-98	4886.16	1196.45 (24.49)	82941	9753 (11.76)
5.	1998-99	5869.00	752.08 (12.81)	92822	6492 (6.99)
6.	1999-2000	6860.72	1128.98 (16.46)	101634	7276 (7.16)
7.	Average	4668.68	1078.00 (23.09)	91597	9453 (10.32)

Note : Figures in brackets indicate percentage share to the total.
* Investment in Village and Cottage Industries.
\# Employment generation in village and cottage industries. Number of Accounts through which loans under this category have been issued were taken as number of persons employed.

Source : (i) *Economic Survey,* 1999-2000, Government of Orissa, p. 9/14.
(ii) *Statistics on RRBs,* NABARD Publications, Mumbai and Bhubaneswar.

Summary

4.5.1. The economic profile of Orissa reveals that despite the existence of vast natural human resources in the State, the economy of the State is characterised by poverty, unemployment, low per capita income and low productivity in agriculture which is the main occupation of the people in the State. This dismal state of affairs may be due to over dependence on agriculture, inadequate development of socio-economic infrastructure and inadequate exploitation of vast natural resources in the State. The frequent occurrence of natural calamities has made it worse. This is why Orissa continues to be a less developed State in the country.

4.5.2. In view of the rural character of the State's economy and the incidence of poverty being more in rural areas, the development of the rural sector will lead to the overall development of the State. Rural development covers development of agriculture, trade, industry in the rural area. It will strengthen the rural economy by diverting sizeable proportion of surplus workers dependent on agriculture to some non-farm occupations, village and cottage industries which can be started in rural areas. It would reduce the pressure on agriculture, create employment opportunities and productive assets and generate income in rural areas. Therefore, substantial amount of financial resources are essential for implementation of all these enterprises. Availability of bank credit would supplement these resources to a considerable extent. Viewing in this context, the establishment of RRBs in Orissa seems to have been justified in the sense that these banks would be assigned with the specific task of catering to the credit requirements of the rural poor. They would supplement the existing institutional sources of rural credit and would play a crucial role in the process of rural development of a poor and economically backward State like Orissa.

4.5.3. RRBs have been playing a key role in the socio-economic development of Orissa through extensive coverage of rural area and making credit available under different categories for poverty alleviation and development of agriculture and village and cottage industries in the State.

4.5.4. RRBs' share in the total bank offices of all the scheduled commercial banks in Orissa was around 38 per cent. Their shares in aggregate bank deposits and gross bank credit, averaged at 11 per cent and 13 per cent respectively, have been consistently increasing over the last six years in the State.

4.5.5. True to the spirit of their setting up, RRBs in Orissa have accorded priority to their operation in rural area as is evidenced by the fact that 91 per cent of their branches are located in rural areas of the State against 84 per cent at the national level as on 31 March 2000. Secondly, they have mobilised 76 per cent of their deposits from the rural areas compared to 70 per cent at the all-India level. Thirdly, their credit deployment in rural area was 82 per cent and 73 per cent at the State and national level respectively. The overall business transacted by the RRBs in rural areas was 79 per cent in Orissa compared to 71 per cent at the all-India level. These findings show that RRBs' operate primarily in rural areas and their coverage of rural area in Orissa is fairly better than at the all-India level.

4.5.6. RRBs' shares in the total rural branch network, total rural deposits and total rural credits of all Scheduled CBs in Orissa as on 31 March 2000 were 47.34 per cent, 27.27 per cent and 34.04 per cent compared to 37.22 per cent, 18.60 per cent and 20.24 per cent respectively at the all-India level. In this case also, the RRBs in Orissa are performing better than those at the all-India level.

4.5.7. The analysis of the relative performance of different banks in rural areas of the State as on 31 March 2000, reveals that, though the RRBs have mobilised lower volume of rural deposits but have deployed higher volume of credit in rural areas than the Nationalised Banks and SBI and its associates. This becomes evident from the higher C-D ratios of 54.94 per cent of RRBs than 37.96 per cent of Nationalised Banks and 42.70 per cent of SBI and associates respectively. The RRBs volume of business per branch in rural areas, however, was lower than those of other banks as mentioned above in the State.

4.5.8. The classification of the total outstanding advances of RRBs in Orissa shows that almost 66 per cent of the total advances was absorbed by four types : crop loans, term loans for agriculture and allied activities, retail trade, small business and self-employed persons etc., and rural artisans, village and cottage industries which have generated employment for nearly 7 lakh persons. In aggregate, RRBs have provided gainful means of employment to more than 9 lakh hands in various capacities through credit assistance of Rs. 761.71 crore up to 31 March 2000. The classification also reveals that the farm-sector advances of RRBs in the State was lower than the advances to the non-farm sector in absolute terms as well as in terms of number of borrowal accounts and percentage share to the total advances. The priority and non-priority sector advances constituted around 2/3rd and l/3rd of the total outstanding advances of RRBs in the State respectively as on the said date.

4.5.9. Under the government sponsored anti-poverty programmes, cumulative credit assistance to the tune of Rs. 765.24 crore has been extended to more than 14 lakh beneficiaries belonging to SC/ST, small and marginal fanners, agricultural labourers, minorities group and other weaker sections of the rural population in the State as at the end of the said period. RRBs played a key role in the economic development of the rural poor by providing 28 per cent of the total bank loans under the said anti-poverty programmes in the State including IRDP. The average loan per account under this category has remained constant around Rs. 17000 per annum since last three years. The above analysis leads to the conclusion that there has been a great deal of diversification in the advances sanctioned by RRBs. Further, by sanctioning term loans for acquisition of productive assets, these banks have been contributing directly to asset creation in underdeveloped region.

4.5.10. Agricultural loan disbursement by RRBs have increased in absolute terms as well as in terms of number of borrowal accounts and loan per account. RRBs' share in the total bank loan to the farm sector in Orissa has declined from 17.31 per cent in 1996-97 to 14.06 per cent in 1999-2000.

4.5.11. The RRBs in Orissa have, on an average, shared nearly 23 per cent of the total funds invested and 10 per cent of the employment opportunities created in the village and cottage industries sector per annum during the period covered under the analysis. In this way, the RRBs have not only augmented the financial resources of rural artisans, but also have assisted in promotion of their age-old ancestral occupation in the State.

References

1. *Economic Servey, 1999-2000*, Bureau of Economics and Statistics, Government of Orissa, Bhubaneswar, p. 1/1.
2. *Ibid.*
3. *The Sambad,* 3 April 2001, p. 3.
4. Pattnaik, Nageswar, "Navin Demands Special Category Status for Orissa", *The Economic Times,* 7 June 2001, p. 6.
5. *Economic Servey of Orissa,* 1999-2000, *op.cit.*, p. 1/3.
6. *The Economic Times,* op. cit., 7 June 2001, p. 6.
7. *Economic Servey of Orissa,* 1999-2000, *op.cit.*, Annex.-6.

8. *Ibid.*
9. "Poverty Estimates for 1999-2000", *Kurukshetra*, Vol. 49, No. 7, April 2001, IInd cover page.
10. *Economic Servey*, 1999-2000, *op.cit.*, p. 4/15.
11. *Economic Servey*, 1999-2000, *op.cit.*, p. 4/15.
12. *Ibid.*
13. *Ibid.* Annexures–74 and 75.
14. *Ibid.*, p. 4/14.
15. *Ibid.*, Chapter 21, para 21-22, page 21/4.
16. (i) C-D Ratio computed from the data collected from *Statistical Abstracts of Orissa, 1996,* Bureau of Economics and Statistics. Government of Orissia, Bhubaneswar, p. 182.

    (ii) RBI, *Banking Statistics,Quarterly Handout*, March 2000, pp.17-18.

5

Analysis of the Progress and Performance of RRBs in Orissa (Total Sample)

Introduction

5.1.1. The fulfilment of the objective of rural development is very much connected to the availability of bank credit to the weaker sections in rural areas. The institutional credit was given an impetus with the establishment of RRBs in the year 1975. It was made a statutory obligation for the RRBs to take banking services to the doorsteps of rural masses, particularly to unbanked far-flung rural areas and to make available institutional credit especially to the weaker sections of the society. Ever since their inception, RRBs have made considerable achievements in rural development in terms of branch expansion, deposit mobilisation and credit deployment at all-India level. Therefore, the setting-up of RRBs was a development of great significance in the recent past in the field of rural finance. In this chapter, an attempt has been made to make a macro-analysis of the operations of RRBs in Orissa.

Growth and Progress of RRBs in Orissa The Structural Aspects

Establishment of RRBs in Orissa

5.2.1. The era of Regional Rural Banking in Orissa began with the establishment of the Puri Gramya Bank on 25 February 1976.

Table 5.1
Establishment of RRBs in Orissa

Sl. No.	*Name of the RRB*	*Date of Establishment*
1.	Puri Gramya Bank	25.02.1976
2.	Bolangir Anchalika Gramya Bank	14.04.1976
3.	Cuttack Gramya Bank	11.10.1976
4.	Koraput Panchabati Gramya Bank	13.11.1976
5.	Kalahandi Anchalika Gramya Bank	26.05.1980
6.	Baitarani Gramya Bank	23.06.1980
7.	Balasore Gramya Bank	06.08.1980
8.	Rushikulya Gramya Bank	14.02.1981
9.	Dhenkanal Gramya Bank	12.08.1981

Source : Statistics on RRBs, NABARD Publications, Mumbai.

Though, at the all-India level, the RRBs were established in the year 1975, but the RRBs came into existence in the State in 1976 only after the promulgation of the RRB Ordinance on 26 September 1975. The establishment of RRBs in chronological order is given in Table 5.1.

The table shows that the establishment of RRBs in Orissa took place in three phases in 1976, 1980 and 1981. In the first phase, 4 RRBs, viz., Puri GB*, Bolangir Anchalika GB, Cuttack GB and Koraput Panchabati GB were established in 1976. In the second phase 3 RRBs viz., Kalahandi Anchalika GB, Baitarani GB and Balasore GB were established in 1980. The third phase witnesses the establishment of the other two RRBs, i.e., Rushikulya GB and Dhenkanal GB in 1981. Thus, by 1981, all the nine RRBs in Orissa came into existence.

Geographical Coverage

5.2.2. Table 5.2 presents the RRBs' coverage of districts in Orissa in terms of number of branches opened in each district. The RRBs in Orissa were established keeping in view the banking requirements of all the 13 undivided districts of Orissa. These 13 districts have been bifurcated and reorganised into 30 districts for administrative convenience since April 1993. Therefore, all the 30 districts of the State are covered by the 9 RRBs in Orissa. Thus, the geographical coverage in terms of the percentage of total districts covered in the State is 100 per cent as on 31 March 2000. Orissa has only 4.50 per cent of the

Table 5.2
District-wise and RRB-wise Distribution of Branches of RRBs in Orissa (As on 31 March 2000)

Sl. No.	*RRB*	*No. of Branches*	*No. of Districts*	*Districts covered*	*No. of Branch Offices*
1.	Puri GB	112	1.	Puri	43
			2.	Nayagarh	26
			3.	Khurda	43
2.	Bolangir Anchalika GB	156	1.	Bolangir	47
			2.	Bargarh	32
			3.	Sonepur	19
			4.	Deogarh	07
			5.	Sambalpur	25
			6.	Jharsuguda	10
			7.	Sundargarh	16
3.	Cuttack GB	121	1.	Cuttack	45
			2.	Kendrapara	24
			3.	Jagatsinghpur	22
			4.	Jajpur	30
4.	Koraput Panchabati GB	90	1.	Koraput	33
			2.	Malkangiri	14
			3.	Nowrangpur	23
			4.	Rayagada	20
5.	Kalahandi Anchalika GB	77	1.	Kalahandi	44
			2.	Boudh	07
			3.	Kandhamal	08
			4.	Nawapara	18
6.	Baitarani GB	91	1.	Keojhar	36
			2.	Mayurbhanj	55
7.	Balasore GB	63	1.	Balasore	46
			2.	Bhadrak	17
8.	Rushikulya GB	81	1.	Ganjam	65
			2.	Gajapati	16
9.	Dhenkanal GB	52	1.	Dhenkanal	26
			2.	Angul	26
10.	Total	843	30	All districts	843

Source. Reserve Bank of India (RBI), *Banking Statistics, Quarterly Handout,* March 2000, Mumbai.

total RRBs in the country. On the basis of the geographical area covered by each RRB, it appears that largest number of districts for a RRB is seven (by BAGB - Bolangir Anchalika GB) and minimum is two (by Baitarani GB, Balasore GB and Dhenkanal GB each covering 2 districts) in Orissa. Two or three districts per RRB appears to be the preferred area of operation for one RRB. On an average, the number of districts covered by an RRB is 3 in Orissa which is same as the number of districts covered at the all-India level.[1]

The Distribution of Branch Network

5.2.3. The RRB-wise and district-wise distribution of branch network of RRBs are also given in Table 5.2. As on 31 March 2000, there were 843 branches of RRBs operating in Orissa. The Bolangir Anchalika GB has the largest branch network with 156 branches followed by Cuttack GB with 121 branches and Puri GB with 112 branches. Viewing from the bottom, the Dhenkanal GB has the smallest branch network with 52 branches. The table further indicates that among the 30 districts of Orissa, Ganjam district has the largest number of branches of RRBs with 65 branches followed by Mayurbhanj district with 55 branches and Bolangir district with 47 branches. On the other hand, Boudh and Deogarh districts have the least number of branches with 7 each. The undivided Kalahandi, Bolangir and Koraput districts (KBK Districts) accounted for nearly 38 per cent of the branches spread over 50 per cent of the total newly constituted districts in Orissa.

Sponsoring of RRBs in Orissa

5.2.4. The 9 RRBs in Orissa are sponsored by 5 public sector nationalised commercial banks. In Orissa, the oldest and the youngest RRBs, i.e., Puri GB and Dhenkanal GB are sponsored by the Indian Overseas Bank. The sponsor bank-wise distribution of RRBs and their branches are given in the Table 5.3. As regards the distribution of RRBs among the sponsoring banks, the State Bank of India (SBI) has sponsored 3, the Indian Overseas Bank (IOB) and the United Commercial Bank (U.Co. Bank) 2 each and the Allahabad Bank and Andhra Bank 1 each respectively. Branch-wise, the 5 sponsoring banks are looking after all the 843 branches of the RRBs in Orissa. The SBI covers about 38.32 per cent followed by the U.Co. Bank and the IOB covering 21.83 per cent and 19.45 per cent of the total number of

Table 5.3
Sponsor Bank-wise Distribution of RRBs in Orissa
(As on 31 March 2000)

Sl. No.	*Sponsoring Bank*	*No. of RRBs sponsored*	*RRBs sponsored*	*No. of RRB Branches*	*Total No. of Branches*
1.	State Bank of India	3	Bolangir Anchalika GB	156	323
			Koraput Panchabati GB	90	(38.32)
			Kalahandi Anchalika GB	77	
2.	United Commercial	2	Cuttack GB	121	184
	Bank		Balasore GB	63	(21.83)
3.	Indian Overseas Bank	2	Puri GB	112	164
			Dhenkanal GB	52	(19.45)
4.	Allahabad Bank	1	Baitarani GB	91	91
					(10.79)
5.	Andhra Bank	1	Rushikulya GB	81	81
					(9.61)
6.	Total	9	All	843	853
					(100)

Note : Figures in brackets indicate percentage to total branches of RRBs in Orissa.
Source : *Statistics on RRBs*, NABARD Publications, Mumbai.

branches of the RRBs in the State respectively. Thus, these public sector banks (PSBs) can be regarded as the leading banks in establishing and spreading the network of RRBs in Orissa.

Growth and Progress of RRBs in Orissa: The Functional Aspects

Trend of Overall Progress

5.3.1. Table 5.4 presents the data on growth and progress of RRBs in Orissa at 4 different points of time, i.e., 1976, the year of their inception in the State, 1986, 1996 and 2000. The first 4 RRBs in the State commenced their operations in 1976 and by December 1981, as many as 9 RRBs were organised covering 11 out of the 13 districts in the State. No new RRBs have been established so far. They had, by December 1984 covered all the undivided 13 districts in the State. As on 31 March 2000, RRBs in Orissa have a network of 843 branches comprising 764 rural branches, 59 branches in semi-urban and 20 branches in urban areas. The rural branches account for 90.63 per cent of the total branch network of RRBs in the State. Deposits and advances of RRBs amount to Rs. 1492.10 crore and Rs. 761.71 crore respectively at the end of March 2000. The total number of deposit accounts and loan accounts was 22 lakh and 9 lakh respectively. The average size of the deposits per account was Rs. 6782 and that of advances per account worked out to Rs. 8126. C-D Ratio of RRBs was nearly 51 per cent as on the said date.

Reach and Coverage

5.3.2. In terms of growth rate, RRBs made phenomenal progress between 1976, the year of setting up of these banks and March 2000, the latest year for which data were available. Over a period of two and half decade of operation, the number of RRBs rose from 4 to 9, the number of districts covered from 4 to 30, the number of branches increased from 43 to 843, i.e., an increase of more than 19 times. Deposits of RRBs increased from a mere Rs. 0.38 cr. to a high of Rs. 1492.10 crore and advances to Rs. 761.71 crore from a small figure of Rs. 0.45 crore during the same period. Besides, these quantitative achievement, the qualitative aspects of the growth and performance of

Table 5.4
Growth and Progress of RRBs in Orissa

Sl. No.	*Indicators*	*December 1976*	*December 1986*	*March 1996*	*March 2000*
1.	No. of RRBs	4	9	9	9
2.	No. of Districts covered	4	13	30	30
3.	No. of Branches	43	778	819	843
4.	Deposits (Rs. in Crore)	0.38	75.48	611.32	1492.10
5.	Advances (Rs. in Crore)	0.45	130.82	379.65	761.71
6.	Credit-Deposit (C-D) Ratios	119.53	173.31	62.10	50.48
7.	Deposits per Branch (Rs. in Lakhs)	0.88	9.70	94.07	179.35
8.	Advance per Branch (Rs. in Lakhs)	1.05	16.81	47.59	90.43
9.	Per Capita Deposits (in Rs.)	NA	811	2880	6782
10.	Per Capita Advance (in Rs.)	9.50	1767	3164	8126
11.	Rural Population Covered per Branch	467000	30000	33000	33000
12.	No. of village Covered per Branch	1138	64	62	61

Source : Statistics on RRBs, NABARD Publications, Mumbai.

RRBs are worth noting. Firstly, these banks have done well in meeting the credit needs of the target groups. The advances outstanding per branch which was just Rs. 1.05 lakh in December 1976, rose to Rs. 16.81 lakh by December 1986, to Rs. 47.59 lakh by March 1996 and to Rs. 90.43 lakh by the end of March 2000. Advances per account worked out to Rs. 9.50, Rs. 1767, Rs. 3164 and Rs. 8126 for the same years respectively. The total amount lent by the RRBs in Orissa by the end of March 2000 included advances of Rs. 351.48 crore (accounting for nearly 46 per cent of the total RRBs' advances) through nearly 6 lakh borrowal accounts exclusively for weaker sections.[2] Secondly, these banks mobilised deposits worth Rs. 1492.10 crore at the end of March 2000 from about 22 lakh persons. Deposits per branch rose from a mere Rs. 0.88 lakh in December 1976 to Rs. 94.07 lakh in March 1996. As at the end of March 2000, deposits per branch and per account were amounted to Rs. 179.35 lakh and Rs.6782 respectively. Another noteworthy achievement of RRBs is their contribution to the coverage of rural area. Not only about 90 per cent of their branches are operating in rural area but also, each branch served nearly 61 villages and covered 33,000 of the rural population in the State as at the end of March 2000.

Decadal Growth Analysis

5.3.3. Though, the number of RRBs established remained constant at 9 since 1981 in Orissa, the last two and half decade of their operation has witnessed significant progress in terms of branch expansion, coverage of districts and population and increase in the volume of business of RRBs which is becoming evident from the foregoing analysis. Table 5.5 presents the decadal growth in various operational magnitudes of RRBs in Orissa. The analysis has been made by dividing the entire period ever since their inception in 1976 up to 1999-2000 into three parts, viz. the period from 1976 to 1980 (seventies), from 1981 to 1990 (eighties) and from 1991 to 2000 (nineties). It is evident from the table that the period from 1976 to 1990 was marked for the structural growth of RRBs.

During this period all the 9 RRBs were set-up covering the 13 undivided districts of Orissa. However, the branch expansion programme of RRBs was concentrated in the eighties during which the number of branches established was 591, which was more than twice the number (228) during the preceding period, i.e., seventies. The decadal growth of the branch expansion programme and volume of business of RRBs are presented in graphical form in Fig. 5.1. It is observed from the table as well as from the figure that the structural growth in terms of number of branches opened by the RRBs was the highest during the eighties and has slowed down in the nineties. However, the volume of business in the form of deposits and credits was the highest during the nineties.

Table 5.5
Decadal Growth of RRBs in Orissa

Sl. No.	*Indicators*	*1976-1980*	*1981-1990*	*1991-2000*	*Total*
1.	Number of RRBs	7	2	—	9
2.	Number of Districts covered	9	4	17*	30
3.	Number of Branches	228 (27.05)	591 (70.11)	24 (2.84)	843 (100)
4.	Total Deposits (Rs. in Crore)	16.72 (1.12)	138.60 (9.29)	1336.78 (89.59)	1492.10 (100)
5.	Outstanding Advances (Rs in Crore)	28.84 (3.81)	194.06 (25.46)	538.81 (70.73)	761.71 (100)
6.	Total Business (Rs. in Crore)	45.56 (2.02)	332.66 (14.76)	1875.59 (83.22)	2253.81 (100)

Notes : I. *—The old 13 districts are reorganised into 30 districts since 1 April 1993.
2. Figures in brackets indicate percentage to the total.

Source: Statistics on RRBs, NABARD Publications, Mumbai and Bhubaneswar.

Comparative Analysis of the Operations of RRBs in Orissa between the Pre- and Post-Reform Period (Total Sample)

5.4.1. Since the inception of RRBs in Orissa in 1976, significant changes have taken place in the banking scenario of the State particularly in rural areas. The scale and scope of RRBs' operations have undergone substantial changes in sequence to the changes that have been taking place in the social, economic and political environments in rural areas. Along with the branch expansions, the RRBs have adopted new approaches in banking operations in rural areas in tune with the New Economic Policy (NEP) and banking sector reforms initiated in the early nineties. Against this background, an attempt has been made in this section to assess the quantitative and qualitative improvements that have taken place in the performance of

Fig. 5.1
Decadal Growth of RRBs in Orissa

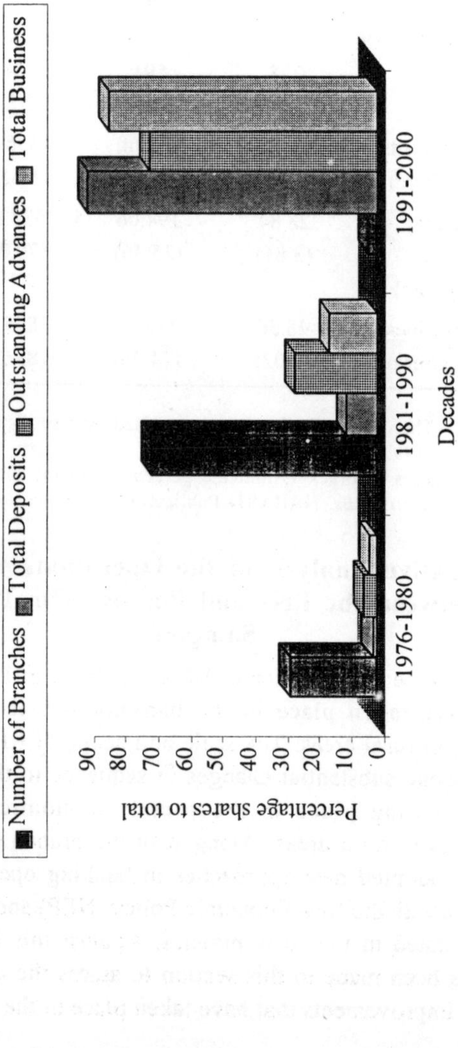

RRBs in Orissa through a comparative analysis of their basic operations between the pre- and post-reform periods. In this section, all the 9 RRBs have been taken as a whole, i.e., as a single unit for the purpose of analysis.

Quantitative Analysis

Resource Mobilisation

5.4.2. The financial resources of the RRBs are comprised of owned funds and procured funds. Procured funds consist of deposits and borrowings. The resource components of RRBs in Orissa, their growth rates and percentage shares to the total resources for the period from 1986 to 1999-2000 are presented in Table 5.6. The table reveals that the total resources of the RRBs in Orissa have increased from Rs. 170.39 crore in December 1986 to Rs. 1910.39 crore at an overall rate of 17.78 per cent per annum showing consistently an upward trend. The post-reform period has not only witnessed a higher average growth rate of 22.17 per cent than the pre-reform period average growth rate of 12.76 per cent, but also the growth rate of total resources at above 20 per cent from 1993-94 onwards. The increase in the total resources of RRBs is on account of steady increase in the amount of all individual resource components, especially, the deposits and owned funds in the form of recapitalisation support from GOI and other stakeholders.

Owned Funds

5.4.3. Owned funds have increased both in absolute terms and in terms of percentage shares especially from 1995-96 onwards. It was Rs. 7.72 crore in 1994-95 and increased to Rs. 170.54 crore in 1999-2000. Similarly, the percentage shares of owned funds to total resources went up from 1.12 per cent in 1994-95 to 8.93 per cent in 1999-2000 whereas it was around 2 per cent in all the preceding years. The increase in the owned funds was due to the recapitalisation measures adopted by the GOI with a view to strengthening the financial position of the RRBs since 1994-95. Till March 31, 2000 all the RRBs in Orissa except Balasore GB have been selected for restructuring and have been recapitalised. Besides this, the paid-up capital of all the RRB has been enhanced to Rs. I crore in March 1996 in terms of the RRBs (Amendment) Act, 1987. All the RRBs in the State have achieved this target. The average annual growth rates of owned funds in the pre-reform period and post-reform period are 10.53 per cent and 72.42 per cent respectively. The average share of owned funds in the total resources of the RRBs in the State in the post-reform period was 5.16 against 2.09 per cent in the pre-reform period.

Deposits

5.4.4. Table 5.6 reveals that deposits have shown consistently upward trend and have increased from Rs. 75.48 crore in December 1986 to Rs. 1492.10 crore in March 2000 at an average rate of nearly 24 per cent per annum. It records higher average annual growth rate of 26.98 per cent and percentage share of 73.80 per cent in the post-reform period than the respective figures of 21.58 per cent and 48.46 per cent in the pre-reform period.

Borrowings (Total)

5.4.5. It is found from the Table 5.6 that borrowings have also registered a continuous increase from Rs. 90.65 crore in December 1986 to Rs. 247.75 crore in March 2000 at an average growth rate of around 8 per cent per annum except in 1993 and 1994. The average annual growth rate of borrowings during the post-reform was 5.15 per cent which was about one-half of the growth rate of 10.90 per cent in the pre-reform period. Borrowings as percentage share to the total resources of the RRBs in Orissa constitute 49.46 per cent and 21.04 per cent in the pre-reform and post-reform period respectively. The percentage shares of different resource components to the total resources of the RRBs in Orissa has been presented graphically in Fig. 5.2. The figure shows that the percentage shares of deposits have shown steadily upward trend against the sharply downward trend of the borrowings during the study period. The owned funds' share remained constant around 2 per cent till 1993-94 and then started rising from 1994-95 onwards. This is due to the re-capitalisation measures initiated since 1994-95 by NABARD for these banks.

Composition of Deposits by Category

5.4.6. Composition of deposits by category in terms of their percentage share to total deposits and the average annual growth rates of each type of deposits of RRBs in Orissa for the study period have

Table 5.6
Resource Mobilization of RRBs in Orissa (From 1986 to 1999-2000)

(Rs. in Crore)

Sl. No.	*Resource Components*	*Pre-Reform Period*							
		1986	1987	1988	1988-89	1989-90	1990-91	1991-92	Avg.
1.	Owned Funds	426	4.54	4.78	5.01	5.79	6.69	7.72	-
		(2.50)	(2.17)	(2.20)	(1.98)	(1.82)	(1.94)	(1.99)	(2.09)
	Growth (%)	–	6.57	5.29	4.81	15.57	15.54	15.40	10.53
2.	Deposits	75.48	95.88	100.51	118.00	155.32	177.96	214.82	-
		(44.30)	(45.68)	(46.35)	(46.83)	(48.88)	(51.65)	(55.51)	(48.46)
	Growth (%)	–	26.32	5.2	16.83	31.36	14.84	20.79	21.58
3.	Borrowings	90.65	108.95	111.57	128.89	156.63	159.90	164.49	-
		(53.20)	(52.15)	(51.45)	(51.19)	(49.30)	(46.41)	(42.50)	(49.46)
	Growth (%)	–	20.19	2.40	15.52	21.52	2.90	2.87	10.90
4.	Total Resources	170.39	209.37	216.86	251.90	317.74	344.55	387.03	-
		(100)	(100)	(100)	(100)	(100)	(100)	(100)	(100)
	Growth (%)	–	22.88	3.58	16.16	25.90	8.44	12.33	12.76

(Cont. Table 5.6)

(Cont. Table 5.6)

Sl. No.	Resource Components	1992-93	1993-94	1994-95	Post-Reform Period 1995-96	1996-97	1997-98	1998-99	1999-2000	Avg.	Whole Period Avg.
1.	Owned Funds	9.04	7.99	7.22	32.43	76.20	80.17	134.14	170.54	-	-
		(2.07)	(1.52)	(1.12)	(4.01)	(7.50)	(6.52)	(8.58)	(8.93)	(5.16)	(2.81)
	Growth (%)	17.10	–11.62	–9.64	349.16	134.97	5.22	67.32	27.13	72.42	43.54
2.	Deposits	276.20	370.33	478.87	611.32	767.65	949.93	1200.17	1492.10	-	-
		(63.23)	(70.23)	(74.88)	(75.42)	(75.56)	(77.24)	(76.76)	(78.10)	(73.80)	(61.98)
	Growth (%)	28.37	29.84	29.31	27.66	25.57	24.86	25.21	24.32	26.98	24.46
3.	Borrowings	151.55	14.898	153.50	166.76	172.14	199.71	229.13	247.75	-	-
		(34.70)	(28.25)	(24.00)	(20.57)	(16.94)	(16.24)	(14.66)	(12.97)	(21.04)	(35.21)
	Growth (%)	–7.87	–1.70	3.03	8.64	3.23	16.02	14.73	8.13	5.15	7.83
4.	Total	436.79	527.30	639.59	810.51	1015.99	1225.97	1563.44	1910.39	-	-
	Resources	(100)	(100)	(100)	(100)	(100)	(100)	(100)	(100)	(100)	(100)
	Growth (%)	12.86	20.72	21.30	26.72	25.35	20.67	27.53	20.19	22.17	17.78

Notes : Figures in brackets indicate percentage of total resources of RRBs.
Source: Statistics on RRBs, NABARD, Mumbai.

Fig. 5.2

Trends of Percentage Shares of Owned Funds, Deposits and Borrowing to Total Resources of RRBs in Orissa

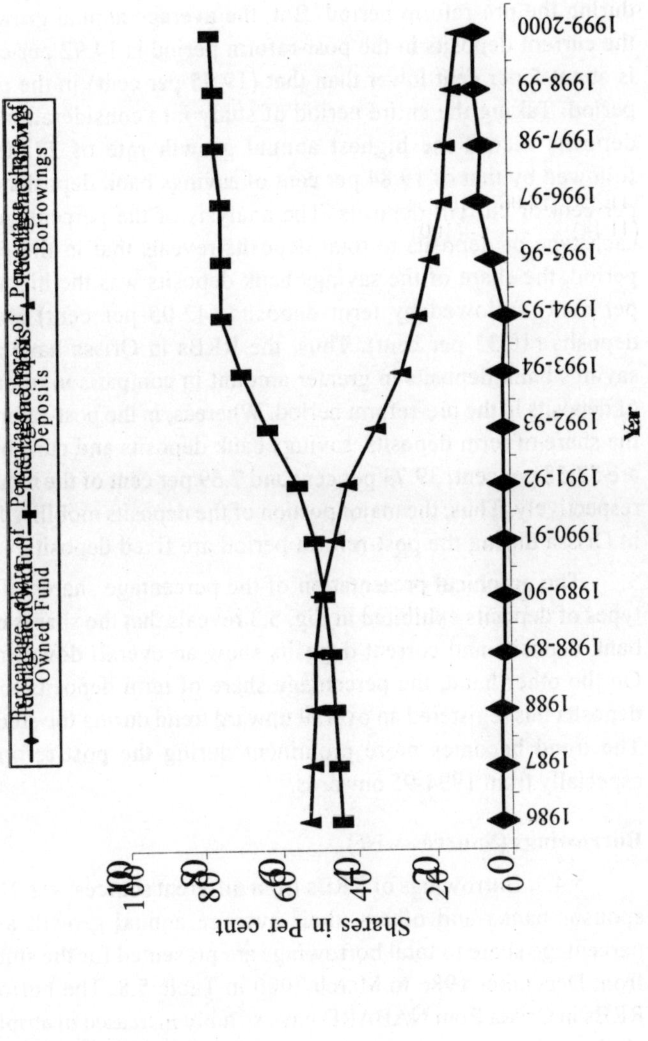

been displayed in Table 5.7. The table shows that the average annual growth rates of term deposits (30.37 per cent) and savings bank deposits (23.08 per cent) in the post-reform period are higher than their corresponding rates (24.23 per cent and 16.13 per cent respectively) during the pre-reform period. But, the average annual growth rate of the current deposits in the post-reform period is 14.92 per cent which is about 5 per cent lower than that (19.95 per cent) in the pre-reform period. Taking the entire period of study into consideration, the term deposits record the highest annual growth rate of 27.50 per cent followed by that of 19.84 per cent of savings bank deposits and 17.27 per cent of current deposits. The analysis of the percentage share of each type of deposits to total deposits reveals that in the pre-reform period, the share of the savings bank deposits was the highest (47.62 per cent) followed by term deposits (42.05 per cent) and current deposits (10.33 per cent). Thus, the RRBs in Orissa have mobilised savings bank deposits in greater amount in comparison to other types of deposits in the pre-reform period. Whereas, in the post-reform period, the share of term deposits, savings bank deposits and current deposits are 52.58 per cent, 39.73 per cent and 7.69 per cent of the total deposits respectively. Thus, the major portion of the deposits mobilised by RRBs in Orissa during the post-reform period are fixed deposits.

The graphical presentation of the percentage shares of different types of deposits exhibited in Fig. 5.3 reveals that the shares of savings bank deposits and current deposits show an overall downward trend. On the other hand, the percentage share of term deposits to the total deposits lias registered an overall upward trend during the study period. The trend becomes more prominent during the post-reform period especially from 1994-95 onwards.

Borrowings (Sources-wise)

5.4.7. Borrowings of RRBs from different sources, viz. NABARD, sponsor banks and others, their average annual growth as well as percentage share to total borrowings are presented for the study period from December 1986 to March 2000 in Table 5.8. The borrowings of RRBs in Orissa from NABARD have steadily increased in absolute terms all through the period of study except in the year 1992-93. The growth rate, however, does not follow any specific trend during the said period.

Table 5.7
Composition of Deposits by Category of RRBs in Orissa (From 1986 to 1999-00)

(Rs. in Crore)

	Sl. No.	*Study Period*	*Saving Bank Deposits Amount*	*Saving Bank Deposits Growth*	*Current Deposits Amount*	*Current Deposits Growth*	*Term Deposits Amount*	*Term Deposits Growth*	*Total Deposits Amount*
Pre-Reform Period	1.	1986	38.32		8.18		28.98		75.48
			(50.77)		(10.84)		(38.39)		(100)
	2.	1987	50.13	30.82	10.73	31.17	35.02	20.84	95.88
			(52.28)		(11.19)		(36.53)		(100)
	3.	1988	49.40	-1.46	9.76	-9.04	41.35	18.06	100.51
			(49.15)		(9.71)		(41.14)		(100)
	4.	1988-89	51.39	4.03	14.55	49.08	52.06	25.90	118.00
			(43.55)		(12.33)		(44.12)		(100)
	5.	1989-90	78.39	52.54	13.00	-10.65	63.93	22.80	155.32
			(50.47)		(8.37)		(41.16)		(100)
	6.	1990-91	82.88	5.73	17.27	32.85	77.81	21.71	177.96
			(46.57)		(9.70)		(43.72)		(100)
	7.	1991-92	87.12	5.12	21.81	26.29	105.89	36.09	214.82
			(40.56)		(10.15)		(49.29)		(100)
	8.	Average	-	16.13	-	19.95	-	24.23	-
			(47.62)		(10.33)		(42.05)		(100)
Post-Reform Period	9.	1992-93	109.06	25.18	31.79	45.76	135.35	27.82	276.20
			(39 49)		(11.51)		J49.00)		(100)
	10.	1993-94	152.62	39.94	37.66	18.46	180.04	33.02	370.33
			(41.21)		(10.17)		(48.62)		(100)
	11.	1994-95	208.71	36.75	49.67	31.89	220.49	22.47	478.87
			(43.58)		(10.37)		(46.05)		(100)
	12.	1995-96	258.66	23.93	48.85	-1.65	303.81	37.79	611.32
			(42.31)		(7.99)		(49.70)		(100)
	13.	1996-97	302.02	16.76	50.43	3.23	415.20	36.66	767.65
			(39.34)		(6.57)		(54.09)		(100)
	14.	1997-98	361.77	19.78	51.55	19.19	536.61	29.24	949.93
			(38.08)		(5.43)		(56.49)		(100)
	15.	1998-99	441.14	21.94	59.43	15.29	699.61	30.38	1200.17
			(36.76)		(4.95)		(58.29)		(100)
	16.	1999-00	558.57	26.62	54.92	-7.59	878.61	25.59	1492.10
			(37.44)				(58.88)		(100)
	17.	Average	–	23.08	–	15.57		30.37	-
			(39.73)		(7.69)		52.58		(100)
	Whole Period	Average	–	19.84	–	17.45	47.67	27.50	–
			(43.41)		(8.92)				(100)

Note: Figures in brackets indicate percentage of Total Deposits of RRBs.
Source: Statistics on RRBs, NABARD Publications, Mumbai and Bhubaneshwar.

Fig. 5.3

Trends of Percentage Shares of Different Types of Deposits of RRBs in Orissa

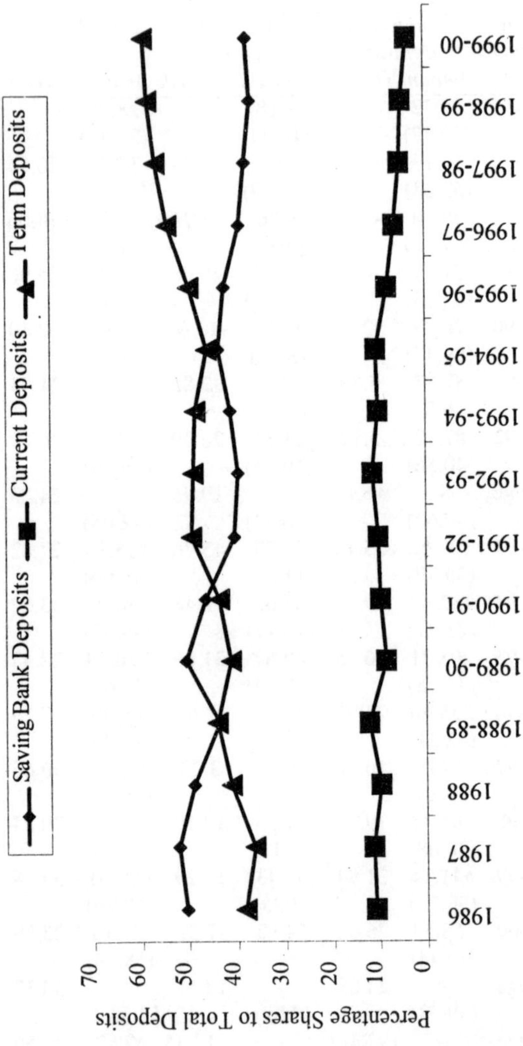

The table further shows that the borrowings of RRBs from NABARD have increased at a lower rate of 7.22 per cent in the post-reform period from that of 11.85 per cent in the pre-reform period. The overall annual growth rate of the borrowings from NABARD for the entire period of study was 9.36 per cent. The borrowings from sponsor banks have increased at an average rate of 2.94 per cent per annum in the pre-reform period and have steadily decreased in absolute terms during the post-reform an average annual rate of -4.04 per cent. The borrowings from sponsor bank is decreasing at an average rate of -0.82 per cent per annum during the entire period of study. The overall growth rate of the borrowings from all sources were 10.77 per cent and 5.15 per cent in the pre-reform and post-reform periods respectively implying that the borrowings of RRBs in the State have increased at a lower rate in the post-reform period. The table also reveals that the average percentage share of the borrowings of RRBs from NABARD to their total borrowings in the post-reform period was 82.60 per cent which was higher than the corresponding figure of 70.66 per cent in the pre-reform period. Whereas, the same from the sponsor bank in the post-reform period was 17.23 per cent of the total borrowings of RRBs which was lower than the average share of 25.82 per cent in the pre-reform period. It was further observed that borrowings from NABARD is steadily increasing in absolute terms from Rs. 117.67 crore in 1992-93 to Rs.220.88 crore in 1999-2000 and in terms of percentage from 77.64 per cent to 89.15 per cent during the same period. On the other hand, RRBs' borrowings from sponsor banks has decreased in absolute terms from Rs. 33.37 crore to Rs. 26.69 crore and in terms of percentage share from 22.82 per cent to 10.77 per cent during the same period. Taking the entire period of study into account, 76.63 per cent of the borrowings of RRBs come from NABARD followed by 21.53 per cent from the sponsor banks and 1.84 per cent from other sources.

Deployment of Credit

5.4.8. The outstanding advances of RRBs in Orissa, their purpose-wise classification and the amount of overdue from the year ending on December 1986 to the year ending on March 2000 have been presented in Table 5.9. The total advances increased steadily in absolute terms from Rs. 122.05 crore to Rs. 761.71 crore at an average annual growth rate of 14.21 per cent. The total outstanding advances

Table 5.8

Borrowings of RRBs in Orissa (From 1986 to 1999-2000)

(Rs. in Crore)

	Sl. No.	Study Period	NABARD		Sponsor Banks		Others		Total Borrowings	
			Amount	*Growth (%)*	*Amount*	*Growth (%)*	*Amount*	*Growth (%)*	*Amount*	*Growth (%)*
Pre-Reform Period	1.	1986	58.58 (64.62)		31.69 (34.96)		0.38 (0.42)		90.65 (100)	–
	2.	1987	77.99 (71.58)	32.20	30.63 (28.11)	–3.35	0.33 (0.31)		108.95 (100)	20.19
	3.	1988	72.34 (64.84)	–7.69	27.66 (24.79)	–9.68	11.57 (10.37)		111.57 (100)	2.40
	4.	1988-89	98.07 (76.09)	36.11	30.27 (23.49)	7.14	0.55 (0.42)		128.89 (100)	15.52
	5.	1989-90	90.46 (63.50)	–15.79	37.39 (23.87)	23.33	19.78 (12.63)		156.63 (100)	21.52
	6.	1990-91	122.94 (76.89)	23	36.42 (22.77)	–2.59	0.54 (0.34)		159.90 (100)	2.09
	7.	1991-92	126.78 (77.07)	3.25	37.43 (22.76)	2.77	0.28 (0.17)		164.49 (100)	2.87
	8.	**Average**	– **(70.66)**	**11.85**	– **(25.82)**	**2.94**	– **(3.52)**		– **(100)**	**10.77**

(Cont. Table 5.8)

(Cont. Table 5.8)

	Sl. No.	Study Period	NABARD		Sponsor Banks		Others		Total Borrowings	
			Amount	Growth (%)	Amount	Growth (%)	Amount	Growth (%)	Amount	Growth (%)
Post-Reform Period	9.	1992-93	1 17.67 (77.64)	–7.09	33.37 (22.02)	–10.85	0.51 (034)		151.55 (100)	–7.87
	10.	1993-94	117.71 (79.01)	0.03	30.94 (20.77)	–7.28	0.32 (0.22)		148.98 (100)	-1.70
	11.	1994-95	126.95 (82.70)	7.63	26.43 (17.22)	–14.29	0.12 (0.08)		153.50 (100)	3.03
	12.	1995-96	137.30 (82.03)	7.87	29.45 (17.96)	11.05	0.01 (0.01)		166.76 (100)	8.64
	13.	1996-97	143.19 (83.14)	4.38	28.95 (16.86)	–1.70	0		172.14 (100)	3.23
	14.	1997-98	170.85 (85.46)	20.28	27.78 (14.00)	–4.04	1.08 (0.54)		199.71 (100)	16.02
	15.	1998-99	201.67 (88.21)	17.44	27.46 (11.79)	–1.15			229.13 (100)	14.73
	16.	1999-00	220.88 (89.15)	9.53	26.69 (10.77)	–2.80	0.18 (0.07)		247.75 (100)	8.13
	17.	Average	– (82.60)	7.22	– (17.23)	–4.04	– (0.17)		– (100)	5.53
Whole Period		Average	– (76.63)	9.36	– (21.53)	–0.82	– (1.84)		– (100)	7.98

Notes : Figures in brackets indicate percentage of Total Borrowing of RRBs.
Source: Statistics on RRBs, NABARD Publications, Mumbai and Bhubaneswar.

have increased at a faster rate in the post-reform period. The slower growth-rate of the advances from 1996-97 onwards may be attributed to the cautious approach in dispensation of credit consequent to the introduction of income recognition and asset classification norms from 1995-96 and the provisioning norms in 1996-97. The growth rate analysis shows that agricultural and non-agricultural advances have shown higher average annual growth rates of 13.24 per cent and 19.67 per cent in the post-reform period against the growth rates of 6.01 per cent and 16.45 per cent respectively in the pre-reform period. Thus, in terms of growth rate, both the types of advances have shown upward trend throughout the period of study. But, the non-agricultural advances are increasing at a faster rate of 17.34 per cent than 10.14 per cent of the agricultural advances over the whole period of study.

The analysis of the percentage shares of advances further reveals that the pre-reform period average share of agricultural advances to total advances of RRBs in Orissa was 52.05 per cent against that of 42.44 per cent in the post-reform period. A steep decline in the share of agricultural advances from 46.02 per cent in 1992-93 to 36.09 per cent in 1999-2000 was observed during the post-reform period.

On the other hand, the average share of non-agricultural advances was 47.95 per cent in the pre-reform period which was considerably smaller than the post-reform period average share of 57.56 per cent. Taking the entire period of study into consideration, the average shares of agricultural and non-agricultural advances were 47.70 per cent and 52.30 per cent of the total advances respectively. Thus, the agricultural advances of RRBs were lower than their non-agricultural advances not only in absolute terms, but also in terms of growth rates and percentage shares during the period of study in Orissa especially in the post-reform period. The graphical presentation of the share of RRBs' advances to the farm and non-farm sector in the State displayed in Fig. 5.4 reveals that the trend of higher share of advances to the non-farm sector began since the year 1991-92 and is still continuing. This finding confirms the apprehensions of P.R. Dubhashi. He observes "With the advent of economic liberalisation, rural and agricultural economy seems suffering from neglect".[3]

Table 5.9

Purpose-wise Classification of Outstanding Advances of RRBs in Orissa (From Dec. 1986 to Mar. 2000)

(Rs. in Crore)

Sl. No.	Particulars	Pre-Reform Period							
		Dec 1986	Dec 1987	Dec 1988	1988-89	1989-90	1990-91	1991-92	Avg.
1.	Agricultural Advances	7185.57 (58.57)	8358.22 (54.15)	9705.38 (55.71)	10352.57 (52.75)	11536.46 (51.07)	10262 (46.74)	9917.40 (45.04)	(52.05)
	Growth (%)	–	16.32	16.12	8.52	9.53	–11.04	–3.07	6.01
2.	Non-Agricultrual Advances	5016.82 (41.13)	7076.08 (45.75)	7717.39 (44.29)	9433.60 (47.25)	11054.47 (48.93)	11692.46 (53.26)	12102.48 (54.96)	(47.95)
	Growth (%)	–	40.96	9.06	22.24	17.18	5.77	3.51	16.45
(a)	Rural Artisans. Village & Cottage Industries	730.61 (6.48)	1109.75 (7.19)	1483.62 (8.56)	1540.04 (7.71)	1989.61 (8.81)	1674.30 (7.63)	1806.94 (8.21)	(7.80)
	Growth (%)	–	51.90	33.69	3.80	32.28	–15.85	7.92	18.96
(b)	Retail Trade, Small Business, Self-emp	3564.14 (29.20)	4531.89 (29.36)	4713.82 (37.06)	6064.98 (30.38)	6943.32 (30.73)	7411.44 (33.76)	7615.35 (34.58)	(32.33)
	Growth (%)	–	27.15	4.02	28.66	14.48	6.74	2.75	13.97
(c)	Misc Purposes	725.07 (5.94)	1088.04 (7.05)	1175.48 (6.75)	1436.94 (7.20)	1720.16 (7.61)	2294.10 (10.45)	2561.95 (11.63)	(8.09)
	Growth (%)	–	50.06	8.04	22.24	19.71	33.37	11.68	24.18
4.	Overdue Advances	2785.69 (22.82)	3734.33 (24.84)	4830.55 (27.73)	5071.53 (25.40)	5234.33 (23.17)	6638.77 (30.24)	7493.81 (34.03)	(26.89)
	Growth (%)	–	37.62	26.00	4.99	3.19	26.74	12.88	18.59
5.	Total Advances	12205.39 (100)	15434.30 (100)	17422.77 (100)	19966.17 (100)	22590.93 (100)	21955.21 (100)	22019.88 (100)	(100)
	Growth (%)	–	24.45	12.88	14.60	13.15	–2.81	0.29	10.76

(Cont. Table 5.9)

(Cont. Table 5.9)

Sl. No.	Particulars	Post Reform Period 1992-93	1993-94	1994-95	1995-96	1996-97	1997-98	1998-99	1999-2000	Avg.	Whole Period Avg.
1.	Agricultural Advances	11247.70	12120.46	14920.56	16692.67	18756.91	22561.53	24114.74	27490.57		
		(46.02)	(45.23)	(46.72)	(42.79)	(41.55)	(42.46)	(38.65)	(36.09)	(42.44)	(47.70)
	Growth (%)	13.79	7.41	23.10	11.18	12.35	20.30	6.89	14.00	13.24	10.14
2.	Non-Agricultrual Advances	16235.35	14677.91	17018.31	22315.82	26379.10	30551.86	38285.78	48680.41		
		(53.98)	(54.77)	(53.28)	(57.21)	(58.45)	(57.52)	(61.35)	(63.91)	(57.56)	(52.30)
	Growth (%)	9.36	10.90	15.95	31.13	18.21	15.82	25.31	24.15	19.67	17.34
(a)	Rural Artisans. Village & Cottage Industries	1945.85	2197.14	2418.04	2944.00	3753.31	3733.38	4202.73	4337.61		
		(7.94)	(8.20)	(7.57)	(7.55)	(8.32)	(7.03)	(6.75)	(5.69)	(7.62)	(7.71)
	Growth (%)	7.69	1291	10.05	21.75	27.49	–0.53	12.57	3.21	13.13	15.82
(b)	Retail Trade, Small Business, Self-emp	7951.21	8554.15	10028.42	12520.55	13990.29	13647.92	16576.13	18670.42		
		(32.43)	(31.92)	(31.40)	(32.10)	(31.00)	(25.70)	(26.56)	(24.81)	(29.45)	(30.80)
	Growth (%)	4.41	7.58	17.23	24.86	11.73	–2.44	21.46	12.63	12.12	12.97
(c)	Misc Purposes	3219.17	3808.64	4444.48	6801.81	8315.96	10096.86	13582.62	25672.37		
		(13.13)	(14.21)	(13.92)	(17.45)	(18.43)	(19.01)	(21.29)	(33.70)	(18.49)	(13.85)
	Growth (%)	25.65	18.31	16.80	53..04	22.26	21.42	34.52	89.01	34.13	30.02
4.	Overdue Advances	6670.96	6201.24	7608.17	7809.40	9341.12	11130.72	12188.10	12510.96		
		(27.21)	(23.14)	(23.82)	(20.02)	(20.69)	(20.96)	(19.53)	(16.72)	(21.47)	(24.00)
	Growth (%)	–10.98	–7.04	22.69	2.64	19.62	19.16	9.50	2.65	7.28	12.56
5.	Total Advances	24520.05	26798.37	31938.87	39008.49	45133.01	53113.39	62400.52	76170.98		
		(100)	(100)	(100)	(100)	(100)	(100)	(100)	(100)	(100)	
	Growth (%)	11.35	9.26	19.18	22.13	15.70	17.68	17.49	22.07	16.87	14.21

Notes : Figures in brackets indicate percentage of total resources of RRBs.
Source: *Statistics on RRBs*, NABARD Publications, Mumbai and Bhubaneswar.

Fig. 5.4

Trends of Shares of RRBs' Advances to the Farm and Non-Farm Sector in Orissa

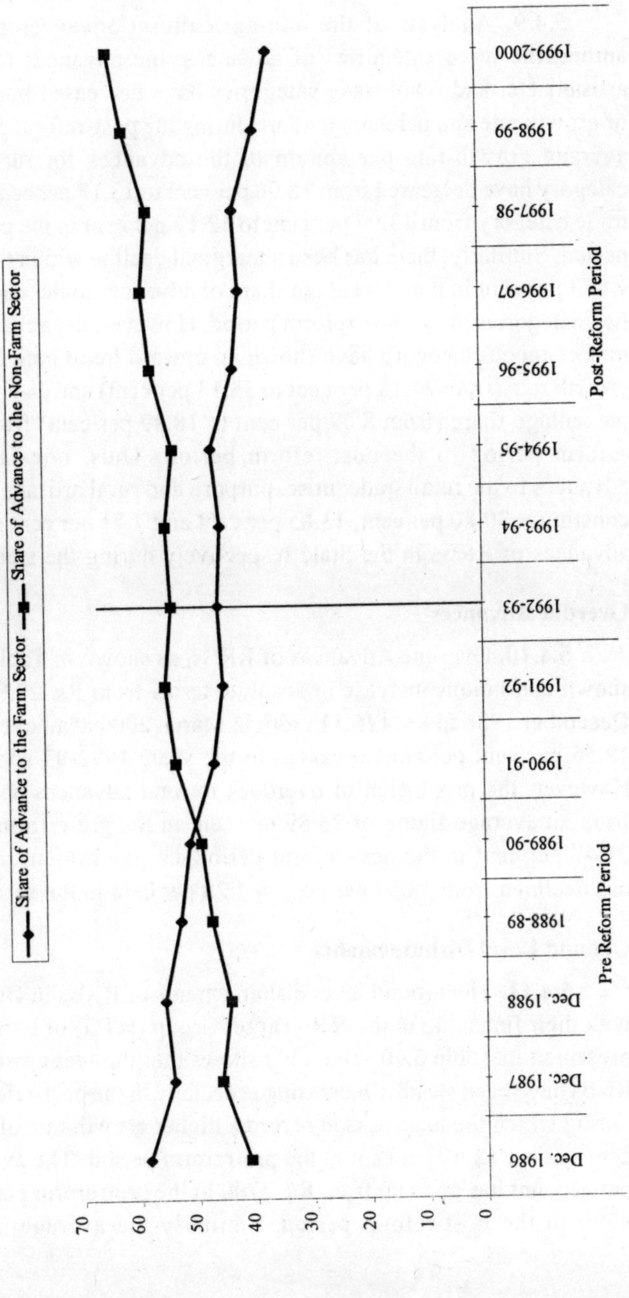

Non-agricultural Advances

5.4.9. Analysis of the non-agricultural advances shows that among the three categories of advances, the advances to the rural artisans etc. and retail trade categories have decreased both in terms of growth rate and percentage share during the post-reform period. The average growth-rate per annum of the advances for rural artisans category have decreased from 18.96 per cent to 13.13 per cent and retail trade category from 13.97 per cent to 12.12 per cent in the post-reform period. Similarly, there has been a marginal decline within the range of 1 to 3 per cent in the percentage share of advances under each of these two categories in the post-reform period. However, the advances under miscellaneous category have shown an upward trend both in terms of growth rate (from 24.18 per cent to 35.13 per cent) and also in terms of percentage share (from 8.09 per cent to 18.89 per cent) from the pre-reform period to the post-reform period. Thus, non-farm sector advances to the retail trade, misc. purpose and rural artisans categories constitutes 30.80 per cent, 13.85 per cent and 7.71 per cent of the total advances of RRBs in the State respectively during the study period.

Overdue Advances

5.4.10. Overdue Advances of RRBs, as shown in Table 5.9 have shown continuous increase in absolute terms from Rs. 27.86 crore in December 1986 to Rs. 125.11 crore in March 2000 at an overall rate of 12.56 per cent per annum except in the years 1992-93 and 1993-94. However, the proportion of overdues to total advances has declined from an average figure of 26.89 per cent in the pre-reform period to 21.47 per cent in the post-reform period and the growth rate thereof has declined from 18.59 per cent to 7.28 per cent in the same periods.

Ground Level Disbursements

5.4.11. The ground level disbursements of RRBs in Orissa along with their financing to the Non-Target Group (NTG) of borrowers are presented in Table 5.10. The table shows that the loans issued by the RRBs have been steadily increasing especially in the post-reform period during which the loans issued record a higher growth rate of 29.98 per cent against 12.65 per cent in the pre-reform period. The average loan per account has gone up from Rs. 2700 in the pre-reform period to Rs. 8200 in the post-reform period. Similarly the average number of

Table 5.10

Loans Issued-Ground Level Disbursement by RRBs in Orissa (From Dec. 1986 to Mar. 2000)

(Rs. in Crore)

Sl. No.	*Particulars*	*Pre-Reform Period*						
		1986	*1987*	*1988-89*	*1989-90*	*1990-91*	*1991-92*	*Avg.*
1.	Amount Disbursed in Rs. Cr.	28.53	40.25	30.05	44.18	27.02	47.31	–
	Growth (%)	–	41.08	-48.41	47.02	–38.82	75.03	12.65
2.	No. of Accounts	165423	180388	135457	168219	73557	129089	142022
3.	Average Loan per Account (in Rs.)	1725	2232	2218	2626	3675	3665	2700
4.	NTG Loan (Rs. in Lakhs)							
	Growth (%)							
	NTG Loan as % to Total Loan							

(Cont. Table 5.10)

(Cont. Table 5.10)

Sl. No	Particulars	Post-Reform Period									Whole period Avg.
		1992-93	1993-94	1994-95	1995-96	1996-97	1997-98	1998-99	1999-2000	Avg.	
1.	Amount Disbursed in Rs. Cr.	53.22	68.06	107.28	152.93	200.39	243.51	300.43	370.68	-	-
	Growth (%)	12.49	27.90	57.62	42.55	31.03	21.52	23.37	23.39	29.98	21.31
2.	No. of Accounts	109848	141668	176391	217867	218014	256604	257561	291289	196850	169436
3.	Average Loan per Account (in Rs.)	4845	4805	6082	7020	9191	9490	11664	12322	8200	5900
4.	NTG Loan (Rs. in Lakhs)	1057.52	1741.78	4034.67	7076.77	11025.98	14323.25	17066.20	18786.30		
	Growth (%)	-	64.70	131.64	75.40	55.81	29.90	19.15	39.69	59.47	59.47
	NTG Loan as % to Total Loan	19.87	25.59	37.61	46.27	55.02	58.82	56.81	50.68	43.83	43.83

Source: *Statistics on RRBs*, NABARD Publications, Mumbai and Bhubaneswar.

beneficiaries covered has also increased from 142022 to 196850 during the said periods respectively. The RRBs were allowed to finance NTG borrowers up to a limit of 40 per cent of their fresh loans since September 1992. This ceiling was further raised to 60 per cent with effect from January 1994. In pursuance to this policy, the RRBs have started providing NTG loans since 1992-93 onwards and their performance in this regard has been very impressive as can be found from the Table 5.10. The disbursement of NTG loans has increased continuously from Rs. 1057.52 lakh in 1992-93 to Rs. 18786.30 lakh in 1999-2000 at an average annual growth rate of 59.47 per cent. The NTG loans disbursed by the RRBs in the year 1994-95 recorded the highest growth rate of 131.64 per cent. The percentage of NTG loans to the total loans also has continuously risen from 19.87 per cent in 1992-93 to 58.82 per cent in 1997-98 and was averaged at nearly 44 per cent per annum over the last 8 years.

Investments

5.4.12. Table 5.11 contains the details of investments of RRBs in Orissa from the year 1987 to 2000. The table shows that the average annual growth rate of the total investment of RRBs in Orissa during the post-reform period is almost one and half times more than that during the pre-reform period. The growth rates of both SLR and non-SLR investments of RRBs have been higher in the post-reform period. It is further found from the said table that the growth of the non-SLR investments has been tremendous from 1994-95 onwards. This may be due to the announcement of the liberalised policy of investment by the RBI for the RRBs since 1994-95 with a view to improving their profitability. As a result, the RRBs were allowed to deploy a part of their surplus non-SLR funds in credit portfolios of their sponsor banks, in fixed deposits of profit making term-lending institutions, bonds of public sector institutions etc. in shares and debentures of corporations and units of mutual funds subject to certain conditions. They are also permitted to invest surplus non-SLR funds in risk sharing Participation Certificates (PCs) of their sponsor banks. On account of low yield on loans and advances due to low recovery and high transaction cost, the RRBs went for investment in a big way particularly for non-SLR avenues of investment.

Table 5.11

Investments of RRBs in Orissa (From Dec. 1986 to Mar. 2000)

(Rs. in Crore)

Sl. No.	*Particulars*	*Pre-Reform Period*					
		1987	1988-89	1989-90	1990-91	1991-92	Avg.
1.	SLR-Investments Amounts	44.07	46.76	63.16	77.32	97.26	–
	Growth (%)		6.10	35.07	22.42	25.79	17.88
2	Non-SLR Investments Amounts	1.90	1.90	2.10	7.45	6.10	-
	Growth (%)	–	-	10.53	254.76	–18.12	49.43
3.	Total Investments Amount	45.97	48.66	65.26	84.77	103.36	-
	Growth (%)	-	5.86	34.11	29.89	21.93	18.36

(Cont. Table 5.11)

(*Cont. Table 5.11*)

Sl. No.	*Particulars*	*Post-Reform Period*									*Whole Period*
		1992-93	*1993-94*	*1994-95*	*1995-96*	*1996-97*	*1997-98*	*1998-99*	*1999-2000*	*Avg.*	*Overall Avg.*
1.	SLR-Investments Amounts	136.22	186.90	124.84	148.27	242.70	255.73	336.13	431.37	-	-
	Growth (%)	40.06	37.20	-33.20	18.77	63.69	5.37	31.44	28.33	23.96	21.62
2	Non-SLR Investments Amounts	5.45	6.10	78.43	130.81	188.78	223.98	294.95	386.73	-	-
	Growth (%)	-10.66	11.93	1185.74	66.79	44.32	18.64	31.69	31.12	172.45	125.13
3.	Total Investments Amount	141.67	193.00	203.27	279.08	431.48	479.71	631.08	818.10	-	-
	Growth (%)	37.07	36.23	5.38	37.23	54.61	11.18	31.56	29.63	30.36	25.75

Note: Data for 1986 were not available.

Source: *Statistics on RRBs*, NABARD Publications, Mumbai and Bhubaneswar.

Working Results

5.4.13. The working results of RRBs in Orissa in terms of income, expenditure, operating losses and accumulated losses for the periods from 1986 to 2000 have been presented in the Table 5.12. All through the period of study, the expenditure of RRBs have been more than their income. Consequently, the RRBs have been making losses. This is also reflected in terms of their higher overall average growth rate of 21.92 per cent of expenditure against 20.56 per cent growth of income during the study period. The table though exhibits a continuous rise in the income of RRBs in absolute terms from Rs. 15.62 crore in 1986 to Rs. 172.10 crore in 2000, but the growth rate thereof is very uneven, varying between -2.14 per cent in 1989-90 and 46.42 per cent in 1996-97. The operating losses and accumulated losses of RRBs have witnessed an overall average annual growth rate of 33.48 per cent and 35.79 per cent respectively during the period of study.

The annual losses of RRBs increased sharply by 71.33 per cent from Rs. 4796.45 lakhs in 1995-96 to Rs. 8217.88 lakhs in 1996-97. This was due to provisioning by the RRBs to the tune of Rs. 4376.09 lakhs and payment of NIT Arrears to the employees. However, the annual losses of RRBs came down from Rs. 8217.88 lakhs in 1996-97 to Rs. 2150.33 lakhs in 1999-2000 in absolute terms and from 71.33 per cent to -28.63 per cent in terms of growth rate during the same period. Accumulated losses though recorded an increase in absolute terms from Rs. 758.54 lakhs in 1986 to Rs. 38430.22 lakhs in 1999-2000, the decline in their growth rate from 59.45 per cent to a small 5.94 per cent during the same period is remarkable. The steady decline in the growth rate of accumulated losses consistently from 1994-95 onwards is indeed a positive feature of their working result position.

Qualitative Analysis

5.4.14. This section seeks to analyse the qualitative aspects of the operations of the RRBs in Orissa in terms of 10 indicators of performance. The first eight parameters seek to analyse the operational efficiency of RRBs in Orissa whereas the last two aim at analysing their productivity. The chosen indicators are defined as follows:

Table. 5.12
Working Results of RRBs in Orissa
(From year ended in Dec. 1986 to the year ended in Mar. 2000)

(Rs. in Crore)

Sl. No.	*Particulars*	*Pre-Reform Period*						
		1986	*1987*	*1988-89*	*1989-90*	*1990-91*	*1991-92*	*Avg.*
1.	Income	1561.80	1835.84	2616.13	2559.68	3158.37	3204.81	–
	Growth (%)	18.24	17.54	42.48	-2.14	23.36	1.49	16.83
2.	Expenditure	1832.07	2111.97	3497.89	3343.84	3890.67	5180.79	–
	Growth (%)	20.05	1528	65.63	-4 40	16.36	33.15	24.35
3.	Operating Profit/Loss	-270.27	-276.13	-881.76	-784.16	-732.30	-1975.98	–
	Growth (%)	31.71	2.22	219.57	-11.11	-6.63	169.95	57.96
4.	Accumulated Losses	-758.54	-1054.46	-1957.54	-2784.59	-3602.59	-5605.88	–
	Growth (%)	59.45	38.87	85.64	42.25	29.38	55.61	44.46

(Cont. Table 5.12)

(Cont. Table 5.12)

Sl. No.	Particulars	Post-Reform Period									Overall Avg.
		1992-93	1993-94	1994-95	1995-96	1996-97	1997-98	1998-99	1999-2000	Avg.	
1.	Income	3715.06	4276.12	4885.86	5529.46	8096.50	10307.66	13452.00	17209.51	-	-
	Growth (%)	15.91	15.10	14.27	13.16	46.42	27.31	30.50	27.93	23.83	20.56
2.	Expenditure	6404.65	7169 65	10337.99	10325.91	16314.38	14141.37	16464.96	19359.85	-	-
	Growth (%)	23.62	11.94	44 19	-0.12	57.99	-13.32	16.43	17.58	19.79	21.92
3.	Operating Profit/Loss	–2689.59	-2663.65	-5489.36	-4796.43	-8217.88	-3834.01	-3012.96	-2150.33	-	-
	Growth (%)	36.11	-0.96	106.08	-12.62	71.33	-53.35	-21.41	-28.63	12.07	33.48
4.	Accumulated Losses	-8435.85	-10959 16	–16448.52	-21244.95	-29462.82	-33296.83	-36309.79	-38430.22	-	-
	Growth (%)	50.48	29.91	50.09	29.16	38.68	13.01	9.05	5.94	28.20	35.79

Note: For 1986, the growth rate has been calculated over the previous year's figure.
Source: *Statistics on RRBs*, NABARD Publications, Mumbai and Bhubaneswar.

A. Perameters of Operational Efficiency

1. C-D Ration (in per cent) = $\frac{\text{Total Outstanding Advances}}{\text{Aggregate Deposit}} \times 100$

2. Recovery Performance (in per cent) = $\frac{\text{Total Collection}}{\text{Total Demand}} \times 100$

3. NPA (in per cent) = $\frac{\text{Gross Non-Perfoming Assets (NPAs)}}{\text{Gross Loans and Advances}} \times 100$

4. I-D Ratio (in per cent) = $\frac{\text{Investment} - \text{Share Capital Deposit}}{\text{Deposits}} \times 100$

5. Accumulated Losses to

   Total Assets (in per cent) = $\frac{\text{Accumulated Losses}}{\text{Total Assets}} \times 100$

6. Assets per staff

   (Rs. in Lakhs) = $\frac{\text{Total Assets} - \text{Accumulated Losses}}{\text{Total Staff}} \times 100$

7. Interest paid to interest recevied

   (in per cent) = $\frac{\text{Total Interest paid}}{\text{Interest received on Loans and Advances}} \times 100$

8. Salary to Income (in per cent) = $\frac{\text{Wage Bill}}{\text{Total Income}} \times 100$

B. Parameters of Productivity

9. Branch Productivity

   (Rs. in Lakhs)= $\frac{\text{Total Deposits} + \text{Gross Advances}}{\text{No. of Branches}} \times 100$

10. Employee Productivity

    (Rs. in Lakhs) = $\frac{\text{Total Deposits} + \text{Gross Advances}}{\text{No. of Employees}} \times 100$

Explanations

(i) The number of branches indicated against the RRBs and used in calculation of the branch productivity, incl udes the Satellite Offices and Extension Counters.

Table 5.13

Deposits, Advances and Credit-Deposit Ratio of RRBs in Orissa (From 1986 to 1999-2000)

(Rs. in Crore)

Sl. No.	*Indicators*	*Pre-Reform Period*							
		1986	*1987*	*1988*	*1988-89*	*1989-90*	*1990-91*	*1991-92*	*Avg.*
1.	Deposits	75.48	95.88	100.51	118.00	155.32	177.96	214.82	–
	Growth Rate (%)	–	26.32	5.2	16.83	31.36	14.84	20.79	21.58
2.	Advance	122.05	154.34	174.23	199.66	225.91	219.55	220.20	–
	Growth Rate (%)		26.45	12.88	14.60	13.15	–2.81	0.29	10.76
3.	C-D Ratio (%)	161.70	160.97	173.35	169.20	145.49	123.37	102.50	–
	Growth Rate (%)		–0.45	7.69	–2.39	–14.01	–15.20	–16.92	–6.88
4.	All India C-D Ratio	106	101	98	93	85	72	69	–

(Cont. Table 5.13)

(Cont. Table 5.13)

Sl. No.	Indicators	Post-Reform Period								
		1992-93	1993-94	1994-95	1995-96	1996-97	1997-98	1998-99	1999-2000	Avg.
1.	Deposits	276.20	370.33	478.87	611.32	767.65	949.93	1200.17	1492.10	–
	Growth Rate (%)	28 37	29.84	29.31	27 66	25.57	24.86	25.21	24.32	26.98
2.	Advance	245.20	267.98	319.39	390.09	451.62	531.13	624.00	761.71	–
	Growth Rate (%)	11.35	9.29	19.18	22.13	15.70	17.68	17.49	22.07	16.87
3.	C-D Ratio (%)	88.78	72.36	66.70	63.81	58.83	55.91	51.99	51.05	–
	Growth Rate (%)	-13.39	-18.50	-7.82	-4.33	-7.80	-4.96	-7.01	-3.02	-8.35
4.	All India C-D Ratio	66	59	56	52	48	44	42	41	–

Source: *Statistics on RRBs*, NABARD Publications, Mumbai and Bhubaneswar.

Fig. 5.5

C-D Ratios of RRBs in Orissa and at All-India Level

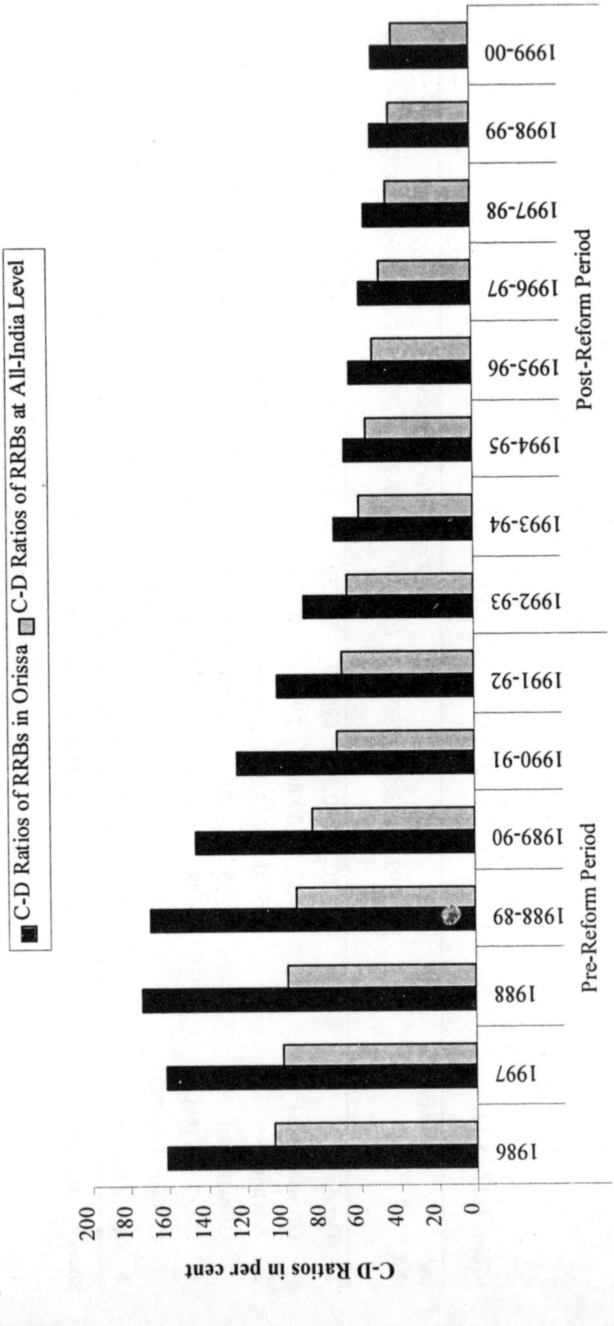

(ii) The staff position indicated and used for calculating Per Employee Productivity and Assets per Staff Ratios, excludes Sponsor Bank Staff.

A. Analysis of Operational Efficiency

C-D Ratios

5.4.15. Deposits, Outstanding Advances and C-D Ratios of RRBs in Orissa along with their growth rates are presented in Table 5.13. The deposits and advances are increasing in absolute terms at fairly good rate during the period of study from 1986 to 2000. But, it is observed from the table that the growth rates of advances have been lower than the growth rates of deposits all through the period of study except in the two initial years. The reasons for the slower growth rates of advances, while cannot be explained during the pre-reform period, can be attributed to the cautious approach in dispensation of credit consequent to the introduction of income recognition and asset classification norms from 1995-96 and the provisioning norms in 1996-97. The slow growth rate in the loan portfolio was reflected in terms of the progressive fall in the C-D Ratios of RRBs from 173 per cent in December 1988 to a mere 51 per cent in the year ending on 31 March 2000. It may be observed that the C-D Ratios decline at a faster average rate of -8.35 per cent in the post-reform period than that of -8.16 per cent in the pre-reform period. However, one noteworthy feature is that C-D Ratios of RRBs in Orissa have been higher than their corresponding figures at the all-India level in all the years during the period of study. This has been exhibited in graphical form in Fig. 5.5.

Recovery Performance

5.4.16. Table 5.14 shows the recovery performance of RRBs in the State in terms of percentage of recovery to demand during the study period from 1986 to 1999-2000. It is observed that the RRBs have shown an uneven recovery performance during the pre-reform period. On the other hand, the post-reform period has witnessed a steady improvement in their performance in the recovery front. This is reflected in terms of the higher average of recovery percentage and growth rate of 57.34 per cent and 4.68 per cent in the post-reform period against those of 39.61 per cent and 4.13 per cent respectively in the pre-reform period.

Table. 5.14

Recovery Performance of RRBs in Orissa (As on June 30 every year) (From 1986 to 2000)

(Figures in Per cent)

Sl. No.	Indicators	Pre-Reform Period							
		1986	*1987*	*1988*	*1989*	*1990*	*1991*	*1992*	*Avg.*
1.	Orissa % of Recovery to Demand	39.55	41.32	38.29	34.23	30.17	48 08	4561	39.61
	Growth (%)	-	4.48	-7.33	-10.60	-11.86	59.36	-5 14	4.13
2.	India % of Recovery to Demand	NA	NA	NA	NA	33.5	45.2	40.89	

Sl. No.	Particulars	Post-Reform Period									Overall Avg.
		1993	*1994*	*1995*	*1996*	*1997*	*1998*	*1999*	*2000*	*Avg.*	
1.	Orissa % of Recovery to Demand	47.72	48.80	53.39	57.57	60.07	61.62	63.85	65.64	57.34	49.07
	Growth (%)	4.63	2.26	9.41	7.83	4.34	2.58	3.62	2.80	4.68	4.43
2.	India % of Recovery to Demand	41.20	46.23	50.98	55.10	56.96	60.54	60.43	64.09	54.34	

Fig. 5.6

Recovery Performance of RRBs in Orissas and at All-India Level

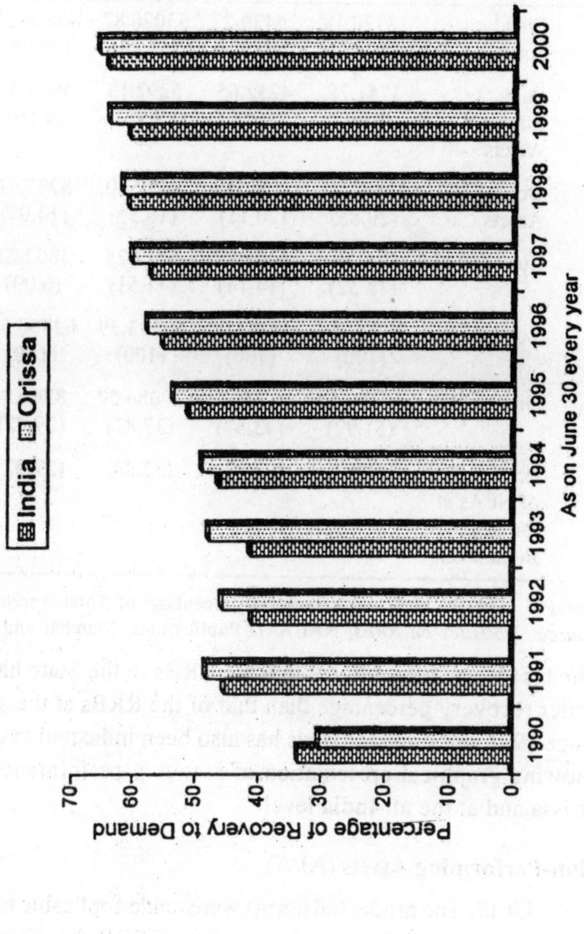

Table 5.15

Assets Classification of RRBs in Orissa
(From 1995-96 to 1999-2000)

(Rs. in Lakhs)

Sl. No.	*Particulars*	*1995-96*	*1996-97*	*1997-98*	*1998-99*	*1999-2000*
1.	Standard Assets	18720.18 (48.03)	25439.22 (56.33)	33026.82 (62.18)	43856.18 (70.28)	59048.74 (78.40)
2.	Sub-Standard Assets	3741.28 (9.60)	4252.65 (9.42)	5292.13 (9.96)	5964.60 (9.56)	5028.36 (6.72)
3.	Doubtful Assets	11637.18 (29.85)	9080.26 (20.11)	8682.20 (16.35)	8777.51 (14.07)	8514.87 (11.36)
4.	Loss Assets	4881.00 (12.52)	6389.87 (14.14)	6112.24 (11.51)	3802.23 (6.09)	2621.97 (3.52)
5.	Total Assets	38979.64 (100)	45162.00 (100)	53113.39 (100)	62400.52 (100)	75313.94 (100)
6.	Gross NPA	20259.46 (51.97)	19722.78 (43.67)	20086.57 (37.82)	8544.34 (29.72)	16265.20 (21.60)
7.	Percentage of NPAs at the All India level.	(43.07)	(36.83)	(32.84)	(27.92)	(23.07)

Notes : Figures in brackets indicate percentage of Total Assets.
Source: Statistics on RRBs, NABARD Publications, Mumbai and Bhubaneshwar.

The table further highlights that the RRBs in the State have registered better recovery percentage than that of the RRBs at the all-India level since 1991 and onwards. This has also been indicated in the Figure 5.6 showing graphical presentation of recovery performance of RRBs in Orissa and at the all-India level.

Non-Performing Assets (NPA)

5.4.17. The prudential norms were made applicable to RRBs during 1995-96 and since then the asset quality of RRBs has shown significant improvement as may be seen from the Table 5.15. The share of standard assets in the total advances of RRBs steadily increased from 48.03 per cent in 1995-96 to 78.40 per cent in 1999-2000. The Gross NPA level

Fig. 5.7

Share of Standard Assets and NPAs to Total Assets of RRBs in Orissa and at all-India Level

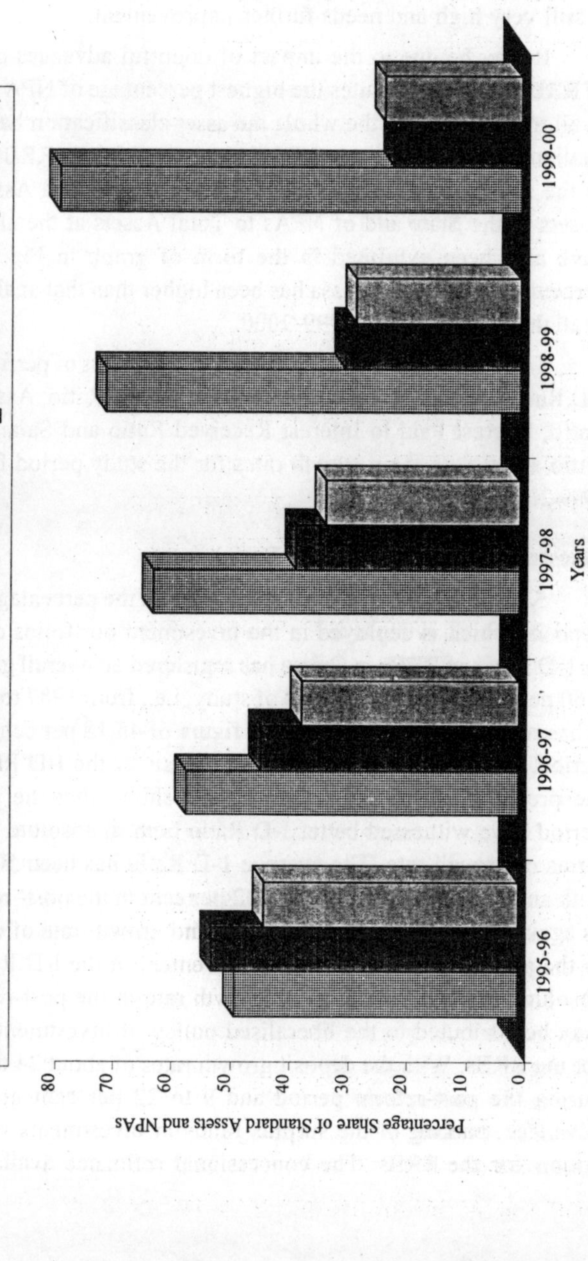

has declined from 51.97 per cent in 1995-96 to 21.60 per cent in 1999-2000. The level of NPAs at Rs. 16265.20 lakh constituting 21.60 per cent is still very high and needs further improvement.

It may be due to the impact of doubtful advances on the NPAs of RRBs which constitutes the highest percentage of NPA components in all these years. On the whole the asset classification have indicated qualitative improvement in NPA management by the RRBs. The trends of the shares of NPAs to Total Assets and Standard Assets to Total Assets in the State and of NPAs to Total Assets at the all-India level have also been exhibited in the form of graph in Fig. 5.7. RRBs' percentage of NPA in Orissa has been higher than that at all-India level in all these years except 1999-2000.

Table 5.16 presents the following 5 indicators of performance viz., I-D Ratio, Accumulated Losses to Total Assets Ratio, Assets per Staff Ratio, Interest Paid to Interest Received Ratio and Salary to Income Ratio along with their growth rates for the study period from 1986 to 1999-2000.

Investment-Deposit Ratio (I-D Ratio)

5.4.18. I-D Ratio of the RRBs indicates the percentage of the total deposits which is deployed in the investment portfolios of the RRBs. In 1-D Ratio of RRBs in Orissa has registered an overall growth rate of 1.60 per cent during the period of study, i.e., from 1987 to 1999- 2000. It has recorded an overall average figure of 45.18 per cent for the said period. However, the comparative analysis of the I-D Ratio between the pre-reform and post-reform period shows that the post- reform period have witnessed better I-D Ratio both in absolute terms and in terms of growth rate. The average 1-D Ratio has been 50.70 per cent with an average growth rate of 2.32 per cent in the post- reform period as against the ratio of 37.82 per cent and growth rate of 0.45 per cent in the pre-reform period. The improvement in the I-D Ratios both in absolute terms and in terms of growth rate in the post-reform period may be attributed to the liberalised policy of investment by the GOI for the RRBs. With the deposit growth rates of about 24 to 30 per cent during the post-reform period and 9 to 22 per cent growth rate in advances, parking of the surplus funds in investments was an easier option for the RRBs. The concessional refinance available to them

Table 5.16

Key Indicators of Performance of RRBs in Orissa (Total Sample): Period from 1986 to 1999-2000

(Rs. in Crore)

Sl. No.	*Efficiency Indicators*	*Pre-Reform Period*						
		1986	*1987*	*1988-89*	*1989-90*	*1990-91*	*1991-92*	*Avg.*
1.	I-D Ratios	-	47.94	41.24	42.02	47.63	48.11	37.82
	Growth	-	-	13.98	1.89	13.35	1.01	0.45
2	Accumulated Losses to Total Assets	3.97	4.75	7.10	8.36	9.32	12.86	7.73
	Growth	-	19.96	49.47	17.75	1148	37.98	27.27
3.	Assets per Staff (Rs. in lakhs)	5.96	6.15	7.19	8.27	9.29	9.67	7.76
	Growth	-	3.19	16.91	15.02	12.33	0.94	9.68
4.	Interest paid to Interest-received	85.12	86.39	99.36	100.61	103.36	118.24	95.85
	Growth	-	1.49	15.01	1.26	2.73	14.40	6.98
5.	Salary to Income	41.74	37.09	38.32	38.63	39.71	59.22	42.45
	Growth	-	-11.14	3.32	0.81	2.80	49.13	8.98

(Cont. Table 5.16)

(Cont. Table 5.13)

Sl. No.	Efficiency Indicators	Post-Reform Period									Overall Avg.
		1992-93	1993-94	1994-95	1995-96	1996-97	1997-98	1998-99	1999-2000	Avg.	
1.	I-D Ratios	51.29	52.12	42.45	45.65	56.21	50.50	52.58	54.83	50.70	45.18
	Growth	6.61	1.62	-18.55	7.54	23.13	-10.16	4.12	4.28	2.32	1.60
2	Accumulated Losses to Total Assets	16.47	17.56	20.91	22.02	23.97	23.80	17.29	17.08	19.89	14.22
	Growth	28.07	6.62	19.08	5.31	8.86	-0.71	-27.35	-1.21	0.21	11.81
3.	Assets per Staff (Rs. in lakhs)	10.42	12.57	14.52	17.27	21.71	25.09	40.56	43.76	23.24	16.02
	Growth	7.76	20.63	15.51	18.94	25.71	15.57	61.66	7.89	21.71	16.55
4.	Interest paid to Interest-received	155.03	155.84	179.74	219.27	215.95	195.64	190.62	182.47	186.82	158.39
	Growth	31.11	0.52	15.34	21.99	-1.51	-9.40	-2.57	-4.28	6.40	6.62
5.	Salary to Income	60.13	58.28	62.75	63.83	50.24	42.76	37.52	33.00	51.06	50.53
	Growth	1.54	-3.08	7.67	1.72	-21.29	-14.89	-12.25	-12.05	-7.65	-0.10

Note: I-D Ratio for 1986 could not be computed due to non-availability of data on investment for the year.
Source: Ratios are computed on the basis of data compled from *Statistics on RRBs*, NABARD Publications, Mumbai and Bhubaneswar.

further enhanced the investible surplus. The favourable market conditions and the sponsor banks paying a higher rate of interest, made the RRBs to prefer the investment route in their pursuit of performing a turnaround.

Accumulated Losses to Total Assets

5.4.19. This ratio has been steadily increasing in absolute terms during the study period up to the year 1996-97 at a considerably high annual average rate of 11.81 per cent which is a negative symptom of the financial health of the RRBs in the State. However, the rate of growth in this ratio is remarkably lower, i.e., only 0.21 per cent in the post-reform period against 27.27 per cent in the pre-reform period. It indicates that the restructuring measures have enabled the RRBs to reduce the growth rate of their accumulated losses. This is reflected also by the declining trend of this ratio in absolute terms and the negative growth rate in the post-reform period especially from 1997-98 onwards.

Assets per Staff

5.4.20. This ratio not only registers a steadily upward trend during the entire period of study but also records considerably higher magnitude in absolute terms as well as in terms of growth rate during the post-reform period. The average figure of Asset per Staff went up from Rs. 7.76 lakhs per annum in the pre-reform period to a high of Rs. 23.24 lakhs in the post-reform period i.e. an increase of nearly three times. Similarly, the growth rate went up from an average of 9.68 per cent to that of 21.71 per cent recording an increase of more than two times during the same period.

Interest Paid as Percentage to Interest Received

5.4.21. Interest paid as percentage to interest received ratio has been increasing at an overall annual rate of 6.62 per cent. The growth-rate of this ratio in the post-reform period is 6.40 per cent which is slightly lower than the growth rate in the pre-reform period. The ratio has been always more than cent per cent in the post-reform period implying thereby that the amount of interest paid by the RRBs has been more than the amount received. This shows the inefficiency of the RRBs.

Table. 5.17
Productivity Ratios of RRBs in Orissa (From 1986 to 1999-2000)

(Rs. in Lakhs)

Sl. No.	Efficiency Indicators	Pre-Reform Period						
		1986	*1987*	*1988-89*	*1989-90*	*1990-91*	*1991-92*	*Avg.*
1.	Branch Productivity	26.52	32.18	39.26	46.18	45.38	53.23	-
2.	Growth (%)	-	17.59	12.88	17.63	-1.73	17.30	10.61
3.	All-India	27.26	33.99	42.88	53.35	59.19	68.50	-
4.	Employee Productivity	6 70	7.36	9.00	10.25	9.85	11.08	-
5.	Growth (%)	-	9.85	32.55	13.89	-3.90	12.49	9.52
6.	All India	NA	NA	NA	NA	NA	NA	-

(Cont. Table 5.17)

(Cont. Table 5.17)

Sl. No.	*Particulars*	*Post-Reform Period*									*Overall Avg.*
		1992-93	*1993-94*	*1994-95*	*1995-96*	*1996-97*	*1997-98*	*1998-99*	*1999-2000*	*Avg.*	
1.	Branch Productivity	63.84	78.27	96.95	122.24	149.42	182.33	216.65	279.40	–	–
2.	Growth (%)	19.93	22.60	23.87	26.09	22.23	21.96	18.82	28.96	23.06	17.75
3.	All-India	79.52	95.52	118.04	146.47	183.83	221.42	262.32	312.62	–	–
4.	Employee Productivity	12.73	15.22	18.84	23.29	28.41	34.79	42.68	56.71	–	–
5.	Growth (%)	14.89	19.56	23.78	23.62	21.98	22.46	22.68	32.87	22.73	17.65
6.	All India	NA	20.02	24.69	29.92	37.56	45.28	53.75	64.56	–	–

Note: Employee productivity of RRBs at all-India level could not be computed for the period from 1986 to 1999-2000 due to non-availability of data regarding the number of RRB staff.

Source: Compute as per the data collected from *Statistics on RRBs*, NABARD Publications, Mumbai and Bhubaneswar.

Salary as Percentage to Income

5.4.22. The salary as a percentage to income ratio has registered a negative overall growth rate of -0.10 per cent per annum. This ratio have shown a higher average of 51.06 per cent in the post-reform period than the pre-reform period average figure of 42.45 per cent. However, the ratio has started declining from 63.83 per cent in 1995-96 to 33.00 per cent in 1999-2000 registering an average negative growth rate of -7.65 per cent in the post-reform period which is considerably lower than the pre-reform period average of 8.98 per cent. The years 1994-95 and 1995-96 witnessed the two highest figures of this ratio during the study period. This may be due to the payment of NIT arrears to the RRB employees. The favourable trend in this ratio, especially towards the latter years in the post-reform period may be due to the revamping measures initiated by the GOI on the RRBs. The low cost profile of the RRBs ceases to exist any longer in view of the implementation of the NIT award giving parity of pay to the RRB staff with the employees of the PSBs.

B. Analysis of Productivity: Branch and Employee Productivity

5.4.23. The branch and employee productivity of RRBs in Orissa are presented in Table 5.17. It is found that both the ratios, i.e., volume of business of RRBs per branch and per employee have shown upward trend during the entire period of study except in the year 1990-91 registering an average annual growth rate of around 18 per cent. The branch productivity has gone up from Rs. 26.52 lakhs in 1986 to a high of Rs. 279.40 lakhs in 1999-2000. The average growth rate of branch productivity in the post-reform period is 23.06 per cent which is more than two times higher than the pre-reform period average of 10.61 per cent. Similarly, the employee productivity has also increased from Rs. 6.70 lakhs in 1986 to Rs. 56.71 lakhs in 1999-2000 recording a higher average growth rate during the post-reform period. It is observed that the RRBs in the Stale have shown lower branch and employee productivity than those at the all-India level in all the years as presented in the Table 5.17.

Profitability Analysis of RRBs in Orissa

5.5.1. The profitability and viability of the financial institutions including RRBs have gained added significance on account of several monetary policy measures initiated by the GOI since 1991. As a result, profitability has become a new challenge before the banking sector in general and the RRBs in particular. The thrust has been on making the banks more competitive and profitable so as to improve their efficiency, productivity, quality of customer service and the range of services offered by them. Profitability in a financial organisation depends upon several factors such as yield on advances and investments, cost of funds in the form of deposits and borrowings and transaction costs comprising of the cost of management and administrative costs. The present section seeks to analyse the profitability of the RRBs in Orissa for the period from 1992-93 to 1999-2000.

Framework for Profitability Analysis

5.5.2. For analytical comparison of the profitability performance of the RRBs in Orissa, a framework developed by the Khusro Committee have been used. The Committee did detail analysis of the profitability aspects of rural lending in general. The framework requires working out of five key indicators derived by relating various components of profit and loss account statement to a common denominator, i.e., Working Funds (WFs). The indicators are scientific and practically useful. In this framework, the terms and concepts used by the Committee together with their definitions are explained below.[4]

(a) *Working Funds (WFs)* : Working Funds are the aggregate of Owned Funds, Deposits and Borrowings of RRBs.

(b) *Financial Costs* : These are the actual costs of raising the financial resources and include total interest payments on all categories of deposits and borrowings of the RRBs.

(c) *Transaction Costs* : The transaction costs are essentially the organisational costs for carrying out the day-to-day operations of the institutions. They comprise of the cost of management and the administrative costs of the RRBs.

(d) *Risk Costs* : These could be the actual write-offs or reserves created for bad and doubtful debts. The amount of claims paid by the Deposit Insurance and Credit Guarantee Corporation (DICGC) is used as an approximation to bad debts in RRBs.

(e) *Income* : The principal components of income of the RRBs are the interest earned on loans and advances, investments and inter-bank funds.

(f) *Miscellaneous Income* : The income of the RRBs in the form of commission and exchange is very small in amount. These banks have limited scope to increase such income in view of their limited area of operation confined to 3 districts on an average in Orissa. However, as per the recent policy initiatives, the RRBs have been allowed to undertake non-fund business like issue of demand drafts/traveller's cheques, discounting of cheques and bills, they can provide remittance and locker facilities also. Thus, the income from these sources are included in the category of miscellaneous incomes of the RRBs.

5.5.3. Indicators of Profitability :

The five key indicators of profitability are :

1. Average Return on Funds

$$= \frac{\text{Interest earned in Loans and Advances and Investments}}{\text{Working Funds}} \times 100$$

2. Average Cost of Funds

$$= \frac{\text{Interest paid on Deposits and Borrowings}}{\text{Working Funds}} \times 100$$

3. Financial Margin
   = Average Return on Funds – Average Cost of Funds
4. Transction Cost to WFs

$$= \frac{\text{Total Expenses} - (\text{Interest on Deposits and Borrowing} + \text{Provision and Contingency})}{\text{Working Funds}} \times 100$$

5. Net Margin = (Financial Margin + Miscellaneous Income to WFs) – (Transaction Cost to WFs + Risk Cost to WFs)

   Working Funds (WFs) = Owned Funds + Deposits + Borrowings

The Khusro Committee noted that profitability is a function of the spread available between the rates of income and expenses. The spread in turn depends upon : (a) the cost of raising resources comprising deposits and borrowings; the lower the cost, the higher will be the spread; and (b) the income earned on the investment and loans made out of the resources; the higher the income, the higher will be the spread. Table 5.18 shows the profitability ratios of RRBs in Orissa for the period from 1986 to 1999-2000.

Return on Investments (ROI) and Return on Advances (ROA)

5.5.4. Return on investments of RRBs in Orissa remained around 10 per cent during the post-reform period. Though, the overall average growth rate of ROI is 4.26 per cent per annum for the whole period of study, the RRBs in Orissa as a whole have registered lower growth rate of -0.22 per cent in the post-reform period against the pre-reform period average of 9.39 per cent indicating thereby a negative feature of the RRBs' performance in the State in this regard. Return on advances increased at an overall annual rate of 1.60 per cent during the study period. The growth rate of ROA is 0.95 per cent in the post-reform period which is lower than that of 2.35 per cent in the pre-reform period. However, ROA shows steady improvement from 8.08 per cent in 1995-96 to 9.93 per cent in 1999-2000. This may be attributed to the deregulation of interest rates on advances and receipt of cost-free funds from GOI and other stakeholders namely the Government of Orissa and the sponsor banks by way of recapitalisation support.

Cost of Deposits and Borrowings

5.5.5. Cost of deposits varied in the range of 4.95 per cent to 7.29 per cent in the pre-reform period and from 6.94 per cent to 8.64 per cent in the post-reform period. This shows that deposits have become costlier in the post-reform period. This may be due to predominance of term deposits in the deposit structure of RRBs in Orissa involving higher amount towards payment of interest on such deposits. However, the cost of deposits records a lower average growth rate of 5.48 per cent in the post-reform period in comparison to 5.80 per cent in the pre-reform period. Similarly, the borrowings have also become costlier, have remained around 7 per cent since last 7 years and have witnessed a fairly higher average growth rate of 7.78 per cent in the post-reform period than the pre-reform period average of 0.61 per cent.

Table 5.18

Profitability Ratios of RRBs in Orissa (From 1986 to 1999-2000)

(Figures in per cent)

Sl. No.	Ratios	Pre-Reform Period						
		1986	*1987*	*1989-90*	*1988-89*	*1990-91*	*1991-92*	*Avg.*
1.	Return on Investments	7.72	11.48	12.94	10.92	15.99	11.75	
	Growth Rate	–	48.70	12.72	-15.61	46.43	-26.52	9.39
2.	Return on Advances	848	8.47	10.19	7.98	9.74	9.34	
	Growth Rate	–	-0.12	20.31	-21.69	22.06	-4.12	2.35
3.	Cost of Deposits	4.95	5.19	7.29	5.46	5.37	6.56	
	Growth Rate	–	4.64	40.66	-25.21	-1.65	22.16	5.80
4.	Cost of Borrowings	6.30	5.82	8.30	6.53	6.85	5.87	
	Growth Rate	–	-7.62	42.61	-21.33	4.90	-14.31	0.61
5.	Average Return on Funds	7.75	8.58	10.10	8.15	8.85	8.19	
	Growth Rate	–	10.71	17.72	-19.31	8.59	7.46	3.60
6.	Average Cost of Funds	4.96	5.19	7.30	5.46	5.37	5.45	
	Growth Rate	–	4.64	40.66	-25.21	-1.65	1.49	2.85

(Cont. Table 5.18)

(Cont. Table 5.18)

Sl. No.	Ratios	Post-Reform Period									Overall Avg.
		1992-93	1993-94	1994-95	1995-96	1996-97	1997-98	1998-99	1999-2000	Avg.	
1.	Return on Investments	11.10	10.38	10.25	10.68	11.25	10.81	10.60	11.43		
	Growth Rate	-5.53	-6.49	-1.25	4.20	5.34	-3.91	-1.94	7.83	-0.22	4.26
2.	Return on Advances	9.25	8.83	8.87	8.08	8.12	9.19	9.53	9.93		
	Growth Rate	-0.96	-4.54	0.45	-8.91	0.50	13.18	3.70	4.20	0.95	1.60
3.	Cost of Deposits	7.52	6.94	7.62	7.40	8.64	8.51	8.32	8.56		
	Growth Rate	14.63	7.71	9.80	-2.89	15.41	-1.5	-2.23	2.88	5.48	5.63
4.	Cost of Borrowings	10.95	7.39	7.23	7.01	7.83	7.25	7.15	7.90		
	Growth Rate	86.54	-32.51	-2.17	-3.04	11.70	-7.41	-1.38	10.49	7.78	4.43
5.	Average Return on Funds	8.48	8.05	8.13	7.36	8.24	8.40	8.53	8.88		
	Growth Rate	3.54	-5.07	0.99	-9.59	12.11	1.94	1.55	4.10	0.86	2.14
6.	Average Cost of Funds	7.43	5.82	7.26	6.88	7.44	7.36	7.17	7.24		
	Growth Rate	36.33	-21.67	24.74	-5.23	8.14	-1.08	-2.58	0.98	5.66	4.35

(Cont. Table 5.18)

(Cont. Table 5.18)

Sl. No.	Ratios	Pre-Reform Period						
		1986	1987	1988-89	1989-90	1990-91	1991-92	Avg.
7.	Financial Margin (5 - 6)	2.79	3.39	2.80	2.69	3.48	2.74	
	Growth Rate	–	21.51	-21.07	-3.93	29.37	-21.26	0.65
8.	Misc. Income to Working Funds	0.25	0.12	0.08	0.10	0.08	0.21	
	Growth Rate	–	-52.0	-33.33	25.00	-20.00	162.5	11.74
9.	Transaction Cost to Working Funds	4.70	4.56	5.83	5.00	5.17	6.43	
	Growth Rate	–	-2.98	27.85	-14.24	3.4	24.37	5.49
10.	Risk Cost to Working Funds						0.95	
	Growth Rate							
11.	Net Margin (7+8)-(9+10)	-1.66	-1.05	-2.95	-2.21	-1.61	-4.43	
	Growth Rate	–	36.75	-180.95	25.08	27.15	-175.16	-38.16
12.	Average Working Funds (Monthly Averages) (Rs. in Crore)	15.22	17.63	19.64	25.43	29.22	31.65	
	Growth Rate	–	15.83		29.47	14.88	8.32	11.03

(Cont. Table 5.18)

(Cont. Table 5.18)

Sl. No.	Ratios	Post-Reform Period									Overall Avg.
		1992-93	1993-94	1994-95	1995-96	1996-97	1997-98	1998-99	1999-2000	Avg.	
7.	Financial Margin (5 - 6)	1.05	2.23	0.87	0.48	0.80	1.04	1.36	1.64		
	Growth Rate	-61.68	112.38	-60.99	-44.83	66.67	30.00	30.77	20.59	22.08	12.08
8.	Misc. Income to Working Funds	0.18	0.15	0.27	0.30	0.28	0.30	0.34	0.95		
	Growth Rate	-14.29	-16.67	80.00	11.11	-6.67	7.14	13.33	179.41	31.67	22.37
9.	Transaction Cost to Working Funds	6.48	6.09	7.03	5.98	5.16	4.38	2.83	3.63		
	Growth Rate	0.78	-6.02	15.44	-14.94	-13.71	-15.12	-35.39	28.27	-5.09	-0.15
10.	Risk Cost to Working Funds	0.52	0.64	2.77	1.45	4.63	1.36	0.54	0.27		
	Growth Rate	-45.26	23.08	332.81	-47.65	219.31	-70.63	-60.29	-50.00	37.67	37.67
11.	Net Margin (7+8)-(9+10)	-5.77	-4.35	-8.66	-6.65	-8.71	-4.40	-1.67	-1.31		
	Growth Rate	-30.25	24.61	-99.08	23.21	-30.98	49.48	62.05	21.56	2.94	-16.24
12.	Average Working Funds (Monthly Averages) (Rs. in Crore)	35.67	43.33	62.39	85.39	108.50	116.43	144.10	176.1		
	Growth Rate	12.70	21.48	44.00	36.86	27.07	7.31	23.76	22.22	24.43	18.18

Source: Ratios are computed on the basis of data compiled from *Statistics on RRBs*, NABARD Publications, Mumbai and Bhubaneswar.

Average Return on Funds, Average Cost of Funds and Financial Margin

5.5.6. The average return on funds has always been higher than the average cost of funds. Hence there has been positive financial margin all through the period of study. It has also recorded an overall growth rate of 12.08 per cent per annum during the study period. The overall growth rate of the average cost of funds is 4.35 per cent which is higher than that of the average return on funds, i.e., 2.14 per cent. In addition to this, the average cost of funds has recorded higher growth rate and average return on fund lower growth rate in the post-reform period in comparison to their respective growth rates in the pre-reform period. In spite of this, financial margin has recorded a higher growth rate of 22.08 per cent in the post-reform period against its growth rate of 0.65 per cent in the pre-reform period. The financial margin also increased continuously from 0.48 per cent in 1995-96 to 1.64 per cent in 1999-2000 in absolute terms. This was possible due to a consistent increase in the average return on funds from 7.36 per cent in 1995-96 to 8.88 per cent in 1999-2000 and decline in the average cost of funds from 7.44 per cent in 1996-97 to 7.24 per cent in 1999-2000 which may again be attributed to flow of cost free funds to the RRBs from their shareholders in the form of recapitalisation support.

Misc. Income to WFs, Transaction Cost to WFs and Risk Costs to WFs

5.5.7. Miscellaneous income as percentage to working funds of RRBs remained insignificant (less than 1 per cent) all through the period of study despite several relaxations accorded to RRBs in recent years. However, this ratio shows improvement from 0.28 per cent in 1996-97 to 0.95 per cent in 1999-2000. It is indeed a positive feature of the RRBs' performance especially in the post-reform period which is reflected in terms of a steady decline in the transaction cost to working funds ratio from 7.03 per cent in 1994-95 to 2.83 per cent in 1998-99 recording an overall negative growth rate of -5.09 per cent per annum during the post-reform period. Risk cost to the working funds ratio was the highest, i.e., 4.63 per cent in the year 1996-97. This may be due to creation of provisions by RRBs against their incremental NPAs in pursuance to the provisioning norms implemented on RRBs since this year, i.e., 1996-97. However, it started declining from 4.63 per cent in 1996-97 to 0.27 per cent in 1999-2000.

Fig. 5.8
Trends of Profitability Performance of RRBs in Orissa

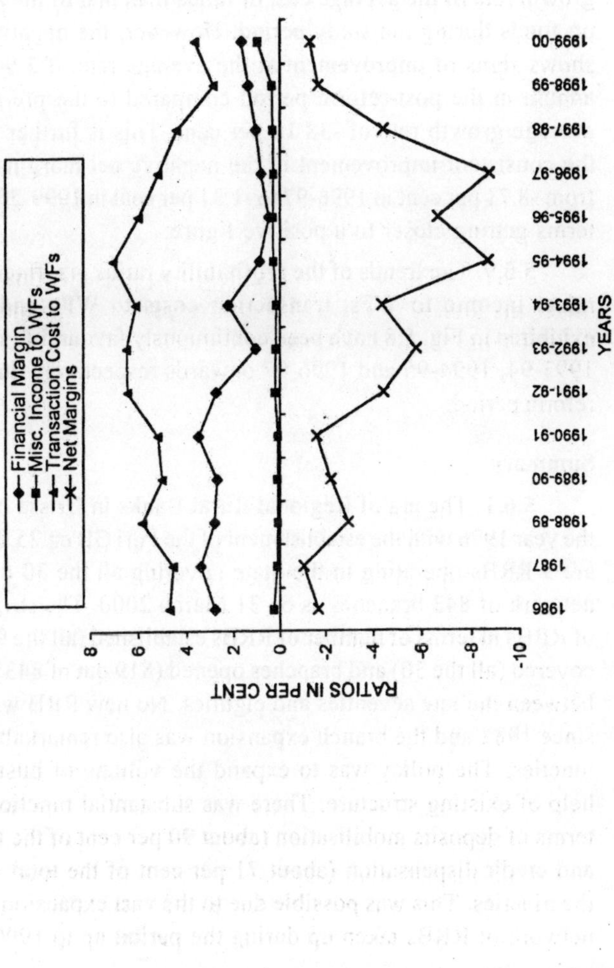

Net Margins

5.5.8. The net margins of the RRBs were found to be negative in all the years during the study period. It records the highest figure, i.e., -8.71 per cent in 1996-97. This was due to high increase in the risk cost (at a rate of 219.31 per cent over the previous year). This was also the year since which the provisioning norms became applicable on RRBs due to which the RRBs are required to make provisions as per the asset classification. The negative net margins may also be attributed to higher growth rate of the average cost of funds than that of the average return on funds during the study period. However, the negative net margin shows signs of improvement at the average rate of 2.94 per cent per annum in the post-reform period compared to the pre-reform period average growth rate of -38.16 per cent. This is further reinforced by the consistent improvement in the negative net margins of the RRBs from -8.71 per cent in 1996-97 to -1.31 per cent in 1999-2000 in absolute terms getting closer to a positive figure.

5.5.9. The trends of the profitability ratios viz. financial margins, misc. income to WFs, transaction costs to WFs and net margins exhibited in Fig. 5.8 have been continuously favourable since 1995-96, 1993-94, 1994-95 and 1996-97 onwards respectively during the post-reform period.

Summary

5.6.1. The era of Regional Rural Banks in Orissa commenced in the year 1976 with the establishment of the Puri GB on 25.02.1976. There are 9 RRBs operating in the State covering all the 30 districts with a network of 843 branches as on 31 March 2000. The structural growth of RRBs in terms of number of RRBs established (all the 9), the districts covered (all the 30) and branches opened (819 out of 843) concentrated between the late seventies and eighties. No new RRB was established since 1982 and the branch expansion was also remarkably slow in the nineties. The policy was to expand the volume of business with the help of existing structure. There was substantial functional growth in terms of deposits mobilisation (about 90 per cent of the total deposits) and credit dispensation (about 71 per cent of the total credit) during the nineties. This was possible due to the vast expansion of the branch network of RRBs taken up during the period up to 1990 in the State.

Out of the 9 RRBs, 3 have been sponsored by the SBI, 2 each by the IOB and the UCO Bank and 1 each by the BOI and the Andhra Bank.

5.6.2. Deposits constitute the major resource component which accounts for about 62 per cent of the total resources followed by borrowings with 35 per cent and owned funds with nearly 3 per cent during the period of study from 1986 to 1999-2000. The increase in the percentage share of owned funds mainly in the post-reform period was due to the re-capitalisation measures. The owned funds have registered the highest overall growth rate of 43.54 per cent per annum followed by deposits with 24.46 per cent and borrowings with 7.83 per cent during the study period. Owned funds and deposits of RRBs have displayed higher overall growth rate and percentage share whereas their borrowings have shown lower percentage share and growth rate in the post-reform period.

5.6.3. The pattern of composition of deposits reveals that all the three types of deposits have increased steadily in absolute terms during the period under study. The term deposits constitute the major component registering the highest average growth of 27.50 per cent and percentage share of 41.61 per cent during the period. Savings bank deposits followed the term deposits with overall growth rate and percentage share of 19.84 per cent and 43.41 per cent respectively. Current account deposits were the smallest deposit component of RRBs showing the lowest overall growth rate of 17.27 per cent and percentage share of 8.92 per cent during the study period.

5.6.4. RRBs' borrowings from NABARD has been showing an increasing trend both in absolute terms as well as in terms of percentage shares to the total borrowings. Borrowings from this source have increased from 64.62 per cent in 1986 to 89.15 per cent in 1999-2000. Thus, majority of the borrowings of RRBs come from NABARD. As against this, borrowings from sponsor banks have been steadily declining from 34.96 per cent to a mere 10.77 per cent during the same period. The borrowings from other sources are small in all terms.

5.6.5. The non-agricultural advances of RRBs have increased at a faster rate of 17.34 per cent against that of 10.14 per cent of advances to the agricultural sector taking the whole period of study into consideration. Similarly, the percentage share of agricultural advances to the total outstanding advances has been falling from an average of

52.02 per cent in the pre-reform period to 42.44 per cent in the post-reform period. On the other hand, the share of non-agricultural advances has gone up from 47.95 per cent to 57.56 per cent during the same period. Thus, there has been a clear shift in the credit policy of the RRBs to lay more emphasis on lending to the non-farm sector during the post-reform period. This is reflected through higher advances to the non-farm sector not only in absolute terms, but also in terms of growth rate and percentage share in the post-reform era.

5.6.6. The advances of RRBs to all the 3 categories under non-farm sector namely rural artisans, retail trade and miscellaneous purposes are increasing in absolute terms, but the former two categories have shown lower average growth rates and percentage shares in the post-reform period. Whereas advances for miscellaneous purposes have shown higher average growth rates and percentage shares during the post-reform period. Taking the whole period into consideration, advances under retail trade categories constitute the highest share of 30.80 per cent of the total advances followed by 13.85 per cent and 7.71 per cent of miscellaneous purposes and rural artisans category respectively. The increase in the advances for miscellaneous purposes especially in the post-reform period may be attributed to a shift in the policy whereby the RRBs are allowed to finance the Non-Target Group (NTG) of borrowers since September 1992.

5.6.7. The overdues of RRBs have increased in absolute terms at an overall rate of 12.56 per cent during the study period. However, the RRBs have witnessed a fall in the average growth rates from 19 per cent in the pre-reform period to 7.28 per cent in the post-reform period. In addition to this, percentage shares of overdues to total advances have registered a decline from 27.21 per cent in 1992-93 to 16.42 per cent in 1999-2000.

5.6.8. There has been improvement in the ground level disbursements of RRBs in absolute terms, in terms of growth rate, number of beneficiaries covered and average loan per account during the post-reform period. The NTG loan accounts for nearly 44 per cent of the total loans disbursed per annum during the period under review.

5.6.9. The SLR and non-SLR investments of the RRBs have registered higher growth rates in the post-reform period. The non- SLR investment have increased at a faster average rate of 172.45 per cent than that of 23.96 per cent of the SLR investment during the post-reform period. The low yield on loans and advances due to low recovery and high transaction cost led the RRBs to go for investment specifically for non-SLR investment in a big way which was allowed to RRBs by the RBI since 1994-95.

5.6.10. The working results of RRBs show indications of improvement especially in the post-reform period which is reflected in terms of the higher average growth rate of income and lower average growth rates of expenditure, operating losses and accumulated losses in the same period. It is observed that there has been have continuous rise in the income of the RRBs throughout the study period. Further, the annual losses of RRBs have shown a declining trend for the last 3 years viz. 1997-98, 1998-99 and 1999-2000 at Rs. 3834 lakhs, Rs. 3013 lakhs and Rs. 2150 lakhs respectively. The rates of growth of accumulated losses have been coming down gradually over the last 3 and years, i.e., from 38.68 per cent in 1996-97 to 5.94 per cent in 1999-2000. All these facts show indications of improvement in the working results of RRBs in the State during the post-reform period.

5.6.11. The findings of the analysis of the efficiency and 'the productivity of the RRBs in terms of 10 indicators may be summarised as follows: Their performance especially with regard to recovery, NPA management, assets per staff, branch and employee productivity has been very impressive in absolute terms, in terms of growth rate and consistency during the post-reform period. The higher average I-D Ratios in absolute terms and in terms of growth rate, the lower average growth rates of accumulated losses to total assets ratio and RBs salary to income ratio during the post-reform period, do reflect the improvement in the operational efficiency of RRBs during the said period. Further, accumulated losses to total assets ratio has shown reduction in absolute terms from 23.97 per cent in 1996-97 to 17.08 per cent in 1999-2000 and the Salary to Income Ratio from 63.83 per cent in 1995-96 to 33 per cent in 1999-2000. These are symptoms of improvement in the financial health of these banks. But, the progressive fall in the C-D Ratios from 173 per cent in December 1988 to 51 per cent in March 2000, NPAs still existing at the level of 21.60 per cent of the total advances, the unfavourable interest paid to interest received ratios etc., bring to the fore the inefficiencies of the RRBs. These are the areas which deserve special attention of the managements of RRBs to bring about improvement in their performance.

5.6.12. The profitability analysis leads to the inference that in spite of the dismal performance of the RRBs reflected through the negative net margins, unfavourable return on investments, higher growth rate of the average cost of funds than that of the average return on funds, they have started showing symptoms of improvement in their performance especially towards the later years in the post-reform period. These symptoms are evident in the form of improvement in the profitability ratios of the RRBs such as steady rise in the financial margins, steady decline in the amount of negative net margins, continuous decrease in the transaction costs to working funds etc. during the second half of the post-reform period.

5.6.13. A comparative analysis of the key indicators of performance of RRBs in the State and at the all- India level shows that C-D Ratios, percentage of recovery of RRBs in Orissa are better whereas the percentage shares of NPAs to total advances, Branch and Employee Productivity ratios are lower than those of RRBs at the all-India level. However, the NPAs of RRBs at 22 per cent in Orissa is better than 23 per cent of NPAs at the all-India level for the year 1999-2000. The analysis of all the basic operations of RRBs and variables indicating their efficiency, productivity and profitability indicates that the revamping initiatives taken by the NABARD in coordination with the RBI and GOI have positive impact on the working and financial health of RRBs in Orissa.

References

1. There were 196 RRBs covering 492 districts in India as on 31 March 2000.
2. *Performance of RRBs in Orissa as on 31 March 2000,* NABARD Publications, Regional Office, Bhubaneswar, p. 45.
3. Dubhashi, P.R., "Changing profile of banks in rural financing", *Kurushetra,* 49 (1) Oct. 2000 (Annual Issue), p. 7.
4. Reserve Bank of India. *Report of the Agricultural Credit Review Committee* (1989), (headed by Khusro, A.M.) pp. 663-664.

6

Analysis of the Progress and Performance of RRBs in Orissa (Variable Wise)

Introduction

6.1.1. The macro-analysis of the performance of RRBs in Orissa during the last one and half-decade of their operation revealed that these banks were successful in fulfilling some of the basic objectives underlying their establishment. In particular, their contribution in opening branches at unbanked and underbanked rural areas of the State and also in providing institutional credit to weaker sections for their productive endeavour are really praiseworthy. As a matter of fact, there exists a lot of diversities among these banks with regard to their age, size, area of operations, management etc. It may be expected that some operations which may be favourable for one RRB may be unfavourable and least choiceable option for another. Therefore, this chapter seeks to examine the performance of each individual RRB in the State throwing light on the following specific aspects of their operations :

(i) Decadal Analysis of the growth and progress of RRBs in Orissa;

(ii) Quantitative Analysis of their performance relating to the basic areas of operations viz. resource mobilisation, credit dispensation, investment and working results;

(iii) Qualitative Analysis of their performance in terms of some key parameters of efficiency and productivity; and

(iv) Analysis of their profitability.

The analysis mentioned in (iii) and (iv) above has been made so as to depict the impact, on the efficiency, productivity and profitability of the individual RRBs, of various policy initiatives implemented in the recent past especially during the period from 1992-93 to 1999-2000. Therefore, the data used for the purpose of qualitative analysis and profitability analysis relate to the said period, i.e., 1992-93 to 1999-2000.

Decadal Growth Analysis

Growth of the Structure

6.2.1. Table 6.1 presents the decadal growth and progress of individual RRBs in Orissa ever since their inception. The table reveals the trends in the progress of RRBs during the two and half decades of their operation. The table shows that 7 out of the total 9 RRBs in the State were established during the period from 1976 to 1980. The remaining 2 RRBs came up in 1981. Although, the establishment of RRBs totally dropped after 1981 in Orissa, the picture in respect of branches opened was quite different. The table indicates that the branch expansion of all the RRBs except that of Koraput GB was the highest during the eighties, i.e., from 1981 to 1990. Koraput GB has set up 35 branches in the eighties against 55 in the preceding five years period from 1976 to 1980. Similarly, the total number of branches of the Cuttack GB was almost equally divided between the two periods with 60 and 61 branches during seventies and eighties respectively. The number of branches established by Puri GB, Bolangir GB, Kalahandi GB, Baitarani GB, Balasore GB, Rushikulya GB and Dhenkanal GB during 1981-90 was substantially large. Thus, the structural growth in cases of 8 out of the 9 RRBs in the State was concentrated in the eighties.

Growth of Business

6.2.2. On the other hand, the level of business activities of all the RRBs was the highest in the nineties varying in the range of 74.27 per cent and 89.93 per cent of Cuttack GB and Rushikulya GB respectively. The Table 6.1 reveals that nearly 70.12 per cent of the total number of branches of RRBs in Orissa were established alone during 1981-90 and 83.22 per cent of their total business, was transacted during 1991-2000 only. The above analysis reflects the branch licensing policy of the RRBs followed between 1985 and 1990 which laid

Table 6.1

Decadal Analysis of the Growth and Progress of RRBs in Orissa

(Volume of Business Rs. in Crores)

Sl. No.	*RRBs/Date of Establishment*	*Indicators*	*1976-80*	*1981-90*	*1991-2000*	*Total*
1.	Puri GB	No. of	48	52	12	112
		Branches	(42.86)	(46.43)	(10.71)	(100)
	25.2.1976	Volume of	11.51	40.10	353.81	405.42
		Business	(2.84)	(9.89)	(87.27)	(100)
2.	Bolangir GB	No. of	52	103	01	156
		Branches	(2.84)	(66.03)	(0.64)	(100)
	10.04.1976	Volume of	13.01	46.86	207.73	267.60
		Business	(4.86)	(17.51)	(77.63)	(100)
3.	Cuttack GB	No. of	60	61	00	121
		Branches	(49.59)	(50.41)	(00)	(100)
	11.10.1976	Volume of	10.41	79.52	259.62	349.55
		Business	(2.98)	(22.75)	(74.27)	(100)
4.	Koraput GB	No. of	55	35	00	90
		Branches	(61.11)	(38.89)	(00)	(100)
	13.11.1976	Volume of	9.73	44.48	203.64	257.85
		Business	(3.77)	(17.25)	(78.98)	(100)
5.	Kalahandi GB	No. of	04	73	00	77
		Branches	(5.19)	(94.81)	(00)	(100)
	26.05.1980	Volume of	0.42	22.07	123.72	146.21
		Business	(0.29)	(15.09)	(84.62)	(100)
6.	Baitarani GB	No. of	05	85	01	91
		Branches	(5.49)	(93.41)27	(1.10)	(100)
	23.06.1980	Volume of	0.23	27.67	214.93	242.83
		Business	(0.09)	(11.40)	(88.51)	(100)
7.	Balasore GB	No. of	04	59	00	63
		Branches	(6.35)	(93.65)	(00)	(100)
	06.08.1980	Volume of	0.25	21.99	80.97	103.21
		Business	(0.24)	(21.31)	(78.45)	(100)
8.	Rushikulya GB	No. of	-	75	06	81
		Branches		(92.59)	(7.41)	(100)
	14.02.1981	Volume of		26.60	237.51	264.11
		Business		(10.07)	(89.93)	(100)
9.	Dhenkanal GB	No. of	-	48	04	52
		Branches		(92.31)	(7.69)	(100)
	12.08.1981	Volume of		23.37	185.09	208.46
		Business		(11.21)	(88.79)	(100)
10.	All RRBs in	No. of	228	591	24	843
	Orissa	Branches	(27.05)	(70.12)	(2.73)	(100)
		Volume of	45.56	332.66	1875.59	2253.81
		Business	(2.02)	(14.76)	(83.22)	(100)

Notes: Figures in brackets indicate the percentage of the Total.

Source: Statistics on RRBs, NABARD Publications, Mumbai and Bhubaneshwar.

emphasis on consolidation of the RRB system rather than further expansion and also the need to reduce the pace of branch expansion programme of RRBs in view of the rise in the number of loss-incurring RRBs.

Operational Analysis; Quantitative Aspects

6.3.1. This section attempts to make a quantitative analysis of the basic operations of individual RRBs in Orissa in the spheres of resource generation, credit dispensation, investment and working results. For this purpose, the average growth rates and/or percentage shares of the said variables have been computed for the pre-reform and post-reform period for each individual RRBs in the State and compared with a view to ascertaining the changes (favourable or adverse) in their performance during the post-reform period. Secondly, overall average figures of growth rates/percentage shares for the whole period of study from 1987 to 1999-2000 have been calculated to facilitate bank-wise comparison of their performance in the above said areas.

Resource Mobilisation

6.3.2. Table 6.2 and Table 6.3 present the average growth rates and percentage shares to total resources of the three resource components of the individual RRBs in Orissa respectively for the pre-reform period from 1987 to 1991-92, post-reform period from 1992-93 to 1999-2000 and the whole period from 1987 to 1999-2000 of study.

(a) Owned Funds

Owned funds of 8 out of the 9 RRBs show the higher growth rates in the post-reform period. Balasore GB deviates from this trend. The lowest and the highest overall growth rates of 13.92 per cent and 247.86 per cent were recorded by Balasore GB and Cuttack GB respectively. Seven RRBs display favourable trend in terms of higher post-reform period average share of Owned Funds. Koraput GB and Balasore GB did not adhere to this trend. The lowest and highest shares of 1.93 per cent and 6.68 per cent were shown by Puri GB and Cuttack GB respectively. Eight RRBs have shown highest overall growth rates and of all RRBs have shown lowest overall percentage share of owned funds during the period mentioned above.

(b) Deposits

Growth rates of deposits exhibit favourable trend in terms of higher growth rates and percentage shares in the post-reform period in cases of all the RRBs in the State. The highest and the lowest overall growth rates of 31.72 per cent and 19.36 per cent were shown by Rushikulya GB and Cuttack GB respectively. Similarly, the highest and the lowest average percentage shares of 69.88 per cent and 54.99 per cent were reported by Balasore GB and Kalahandi GB respectively. Deposits of all RRBs have shown the highest overall percentages and the second highest overall growth rates among the resource components during the period of study.

(c) Borrowings

Borrowings of 6 RRBs have shown favourable trend in terms of lower post-reform period average growth rates. The remaining 3 RRBs viz. Puri GB, Baitarani GB and Dhenkanal GB have deviated from the trend by showing higher post-reform period average growth rates. The overall growth rates of borrowings varied in the range of - 1.81 per cent (of Cuttack GB) to 18.12 per cent (of Dhenkanal GB). The borrowings of all individual RRBs have displayed lower percentage shares in the post-reform period. The highest and the lowest percentage shares of borrowings of 38.81 per cent and 24.43 per cent were recorded by Kalahandi GB and Cuttack GB respectively. Borrowings of all RRBs constitute the second largest resource component and records the lowest overall growth rates during the study period.

(d) The foregoing analysis shows that deposits constitute the largest resource component followed by borrowings and owned funds. Owned funds registers the highest overall growth rates followed by deposits and borrowings. Deposits and owned funds record upward trend and borrowings show downward trend in terms growth rates and percentage shares during the period of study from 1987 to 1999-2000 in cases of all or majority of the RRBs in Orissa.

Credit Dispensation

6.3.3. Table 6.4 presents the average growth rates of advances of Individual RRBs in Orissa for the pre-and post-reform periods and the whole period from 1987 to 1999-2000. Seven out of 9 RRBs have

Table 6.2

Growth Rates of Resources Components of Individual RRBs in Orissa

(Figures in per cent)

Sl. No.	RRBs	Owned Funds				Deposits				Borrowings			
		Pre-Reform Period Av. 1987-92	Post-Reform Period Av. 1993-00	Trend	Overall Average 1987-2000	Pre-Reform Period Av. 1987-92	Post-Reform Period Av. 1993-00	Trend	Overall Average 1987-2000	Pre-Reform Period Av. 1987-92	Post-Reform Period Av. 1993-00	Trend	Overall Average 1987-2000
1	Puri GB	10.00	162.15	F	103.63	13.54	34.03	F	26.15	12.02	17.54	A	16.70
2	Bolangir GB	18.74	195.66	F	127.61	19.35	26.50	F	25.80	21.30	-5.24 1	F	4.97
3	Cuttack GB	17.73	391.70	F	247.86	17.15	20.75	F	19.36	5.80	-6.57	F	-1.81
4	Koraput GB	22.24	46.91	F	37.42	22.19	22.84	F	22.59	10.93	4.88	F	7.21
5	Kalahandi GB	1.80	212.07	F	131.20	7.60	35.46	F	26.82	8.79	8.69	F	8.73
6	Baitarni GB	0.00	110.89	F	67.19	17.75	33.95	F	30.89	1.77	13.32	A	8.88
7	Balasore GB	30.00	3.87	A	13.92	19.30	22.63	F	21.35	15.65	-3.15	F	4.08
8	Rushikulya GB	0.00	197.24	F	121.38	24.17	32.49	F	31.72	14.42	9.58	F	11.44
9	Dhenkanal GB	0.27	138.60	F	85.40	22.27	29.90	F	26.97	11.48	22.27	A	18.12
10	All RRBs in Orissa	11.37	72.42	F	48.94	18.01	26.98	F	25.49	9.12	5.53	F	6.91

Note: 'F' favourable; 'A' Adverse.
Source: *Statistics on RRBs*, NABARD Publications, Mumbai and Bhubaneswar.

Table 6.3

Percentage Shares of Resource Components of Individual RRBs in Orissa

(Figures in per cent)

Sl. No.	RRBs	Owned Funds				Deposits				Borrowings			
		Pre-Reform Period Av. 1987-92	Post-Reform Period Av. 1993-00	Trend	Overall Average 1987-2000	Pre-Reform Period Av. 1987-92	Post-Reform Period Av. 1993-00	Trend	Overall Average 1987-2000	Pre-Reform Period Av. 1987-92	Post-Reform Period Av. 1993-00	Trend	Overall Average 1987-2000
1	Puri GB	1.46	2.25	F	1.93	50.16	74.68	F	65.27	48.38	23.07	F	32.82
2	Bolangir GB	0.83	1.51	F	0.99	37.70	74.47	F	60.32	61.47	24.02	F	38.42
3	Cuttack GB	0.77	10.42	F	6.68	58.07	75.60	F	68.90	41.16	13.98	F	24.43
4	Koraput GB	4.17	2.53	A	3.19	46.57	73.78	F	63.29	49.15	23.69	F	33.49
5	Kalahandi GB	2.34	9.26	F	6.59	35.49	66.36	F	54.49	61.91	24.38	F	38.81
6	Baitarni GB	2.38	4.61	F	3.76	53.26	77.60	F	68.23	44.36	17.79	F	28.01
7	Balasore GB	2.59	1.79	A	2.10	61.12	75.36	F	69.88	36.29	22.85	F	28.02
8	Rushikulya GB	2.52	6.07	F	4.36	55.85	75.00	F	67.64	41.63	18.93	F	27.66
9	Dhenkanal GB	3.39	4.82	F	4.27	61.32	70.17	F	66.76	35.16	25.01	F	28.91
10	All RRBs in Orissa	1.98	5.16	F	3.89	49.73	73.80	F	64.55	48.28	21.04	F	31.52

Note: 'F' favourable; 'A' Adverse.

Source: Statistics on RRBs, NABARD Publications, Mumbai and Bhubaneswar.

Table 6.4

Average Growth Rate of Advances of Individual RRBs in Orissa

(Figures in per cent)

Sl. No.	*RRBs*	*Pre-Reforms Period Av. 1987-92*	*Post-Reform Period Av. 1993-2000*	*Trend*	*Overall Avg. 1987-2000*
1.	Puri GB	5.77	24.99	F	17.60
2.	Bolangir GB	6.66	11.42	F	9.59
3.	Cuttack GB	8.12	10.23	F	9.42
4.	Koraput GB	8.14	16.95	F	14.47
5.	Kalahandi GB	4.48	17.69	F	12.61
6.	Baitarani GB	2.94	22.46	F	14.96
7.	Balasore GB	18.64	10.27	A	13.49
8.	Rushikulya GB	20.30	19.28	A	19.67
9.	Dhenkanal GB	17.19	26.22	F	22.75
10.	All RRBs in Orissa	8.00	16.87	F	15.19

Notes: 'F' Favourable; 'A' Adverse.
Source: *Statistics on RRBs*, NABARD Publications, Mumbai and Bhubaneshwar.

conformed to the general trend of having higher post-reform period average growth rates of advances than pre-reform period average growth rates.

However, the trends in case of the two RRBs viz. Balasore GB and Rushikulya GB have deviated from the general trend as mentioned above. Whereas in case of Balasore GB, the pre-reform period average growth rate was fairly lower than the post-reform period average, Rushikulya GB has displayed slightly lower average growth rate in the post-reform period than its pre-reform period average. The overall growth rates of advances for the study period varied in the range of 9.42 per cent in case of Cuttack GB to 22.75 per cent in case of Dhenkanal GB. 3 RRBs viz. Puri GB, Rushikulya GB and Dhenkanal GB have registered higher growth rates than the State's average of 15.19 per cent. The remaining 6 RRBs have lower average growth rates than the State's average during the period.

Table 6.5

Average Growth Rate of Investments of Individual RRBs in Orissa

(Figures in per cent)

Sl. No	*RRBs*	*Pre-Reform Period Av. 1987-92*	*Post-Reform Period Av. 1993-2000*	*Trend*	*Overall Avg. 1987-2000*
1.	Puri GB	15.96	48.98	F	36.28
2.	Bolangir GB	22.69	24.44	F	23.78
3.	Cuttack GB	23.53	28.70	F	26.71
4.	Koraput GB	26.35	20.92	A	23.00
5.	Kalahandi GB	2.40	51.19	F	31.50
6.	Baitarani GB	40.38	42.00	F	41.38
7.	Balasore GB	9.12	43.56	F	30.31
8.	Rushikulya GB	17.46	42.07	F	32.61
9.	Dhenkanal GB	18.82	30.16	F	25.80
10.	All RRBs in Orissa	18.36	30.36	F	25.75

Notes: 'F' Favourable; 'A' Adverse.
Source: *Statistics on RRBs*, NABARD Publications, Mumbai and Bhubaneshwar.

Investments

6.3.4. The average growth rates of investment of all the individual RRBs for the pre- and post-reform period have been shown in Table 6.5. All the RRBs have shown tangible improvement in their investment in the post-reform period which is reflected in terms of higher average growth rates of investment in the said period in cases of all the RRBs except Koraput GB. The same trend is also observed in respect of all the RRBs in the State as a whole. The overall growth rate of investment per annum was the highest in case of Baitarani GB with 41.38 per cent and was the lowest in case of Koraput GB with 23 per cent during the period of study, as shown in the table. The overall growth rates of investments of Puri GB, Cuttack GB, Kalahandi GB, Balasore GB and Rushikulya GB were higher than the State's average of 25.96 per cent and those of the remaining three RRBs viz. Bolangir GB, Koraput GB and Dhenkanal GB were lower than the State's average growth rate.

Working Results

6.3.5. Table 6.6 displays the working results of individual RRBs in the form of average growth rates of operating profit/losses and accumulated losses for the pre-reform, post-reform periods and the whole period from 1987 to 1999-2000.

(a) Operating Profits/Losses

The operating losses of all the individual RRBs in Orissa exhibit favourable trend as is evidenced by the lower average growth rates in the post-reform period. Even 6 of them, namely Puri GB, Koraput GB, Kalahandi GB, Baitarani GB, Rushikulya GB and Dhenkanal GB have shown negative growth rates in the post-reform period implying thereby progressive reduction in the amount of their operating losses. The remaining 3 RRBs have shown positive but lower growth rates in the said period. The highest and the lowest overall growth rates of 550.02 per cent and -197.34 per cent of operating losses were registered by Bolangir GB and Koraput GB respectively during the period of study from 1987 to 1999-2000.

(b) Accumulated Losses

The Table 6.6 reveals that Koraput GB has recorded the highest average growth rate of 217.81 per cent in the post-reform period. The analysis of overall average growth rate of accumulated losses shows that it was the lowest in case of Dhenkanal GB with 19.96 per cent followed by Rushikulya GB with 25.36 per cent and Balasore GB with 28.63 per cent. On the other hand, the three highest growth rates were registered by Koraput GB (217.81 per cent), Cuttack GB (67.43 per cent) and Bolangir GB (39.93 per cent). Their overall growth rates of accumulated losses were also higher than the State's average of 33.73 per cent. The comparative analysis of the growth rates of accumulated losses of RRBs between the pre-reform and post-reform period shows that all except Koraput GB and Balasore GB, have shown lower average growth rates in the post-reform period.

Operational Analysis; Qualitative Aspects

Working Results

6.4.1. Table 6.7 presents the working results in terms of operating losses/profits of individual RRBs in Orissa during the period from 1992-

Table 6.6
Average Growth Rates of Working Results of Individual RRBs in Orissa

(Figures in per cent)

Sl. No.	RRBs	Growth Rates of Operating Losses				Growth Rates of Accumulated Losses			
		Pre-Reform Period Av. 1987-92	Post-Reform Period Av. 1993-00	Remarks	Overall Average 1987-2000	Pre-Reform Period Av. 1987-92	Post-Reform Period Av. 1993-00	Remarks	Overall Average 1987-2000
1.	Puri GB	80.07	-7.61	F	26.11	49.54	22.63	F	32.98
2.	Bolangir GB	1382.43	29.77	F	550.02	57.64	28.86	F	39.93
3.	Cuttack GB	281.15	95.86	F	167.13	94.28	50.66	F	67.43
4.	Koraput GB	-117.93	-246.97	F	-197.34	-	217.81	A	217.81
5.	Kalahandi GB	95.43	-19.97	F	24.41	38.92	26.98	F	31.57
6.	Baitarani GB	50.88	-0.58	F	-19.22	49.95	21.90	F	32.69
7.	Balasore GB	27.41	26.59	F	26.91	25.48	30.61	A	28.63
8.	Rushikulya GB	47.85	-257.54	F	-140.09	33.66	20.17	F	25.36
9.	Dhenkanal GB	47.15	-119.54	F	-55.43	20.33	19.73	F	19.96
10.	All RRBs in Orissa	74.29	12.07	F	36.00	42.58	28.20	F	33.73

Note: 'F' favourable; 'A' Adverse.
Source: *Statistics on RRBs*, NABARD Publications, Mumbai and Bhubaneswar.

93 to 1999-2000. It is observed that all RRBs in the State except Bolangir GB and Balasore GB have improved their working results during the said period especially from 1996-97 onwards which is evidenced by the declining trend of their operating losses in absolute terms. This finding is further reinforced by the fact that, out of these 7 RRBs, all except Cuttack GB, have also recorded negative overall average growth rates of operating losses for the said period. The remaining three banks, namely, Cuttack GB, Bolangir GB, and Balasore GB have shown the highest average growth rates of operating losses of 95.86 per cent, 29.77 per cent and 26.59 per cent respectively, which are considerably higher than the State's average of 12.07 per cent during the period. The aggregate operating losses of these three banks were averaged to Rs. 2612 lakh, which constitutes nearly 64 per cent of the total average operating losses of all the RRBs in the State. On the other hand, Koraput GB has recorded the lowest average amount of operating losses to the extent of Rs. 41.48 lakh and Rushikulya GB has shown the lowest average growth rate of -257.54 per cent during the study period. The overall improvement in the working results position of the RRBs in the State is evident from the data figured in the Table 6.8, which presents the abstracts of the working results during the period from 1995-96 to 1999-2000.

The table reveals that the number of profit-making RRBs has increased from 0 to 5 and the amount of annual profit earned by them has increased from Rs. 3.52 crore in 1997-98 to Rs. 4.62 crore in 1999-2000. The net operating losses have continuously decreased from Rs. 82.18 crore in 1996-97 to Rs. 21.50 crore in 1999-2000. The 5 profit-making RRBs as on 31 March 2000 are Puri GB, Koraput GB, Kalahandi GB, Rushikulya GB and Dhenkanal GB. Besides this, 2 out of the remaining 4 loss incurring RRBs namely Cuttack GB and Baitarani GB have been showing reduction in their operating losses since 1997-98 onwards. Thus, the operating losses of the rest two RRBs viz. Bolangir GB and Balasore GB does not follow any specific trend either in absolute terms or in terms of growth rate during the said period from 1992-93 to 1999-2000.

Accumulated Losses

6.4.2. Table 6.9 presents the accumulated losses of the individual RRBs in Orissa for the period from 1992-93 lo 1999-2000. As on 31

Table 6.7
Working Results [Operating Losses (-) / Profits (+)] of RRBs in Orissa

(Figures in per cent)

Sl. No.	RRBs	1992-93	1993-94	1994-95	1995-96	1996-97	1997-98	1998-99	1999-2000	Average
1.	Puri GB	-510.19	-586.53	-514.50	-628.69	-789.28	-933.33	-572.42	+ 19.33	-564.44
	Growth (%)	12.51	14.96	12.28	22.19	25.54	18.25	-38.67	-103.38	-7.61
2.	Bolangir GB	-639.51	-497.91	-1068.59	-1470.70	-1607.56	-1105.71	-1074.55	-1405.46	-1108.75
	Growth (%)	102.00	-22.14	114.62	37.63	9.31	-31.22	-2.82	30.80	29.77
3.	Cuttack GB	-353.88	-350.32	-2259.69	-548.07	-2286.34	-735.65	-459.17	-209.36	-897.96
	Growth (%)	72.87	-1.03	545.20	-75.75	390.15	-72.62	-37.58	-54.40	95.86
4.	Koraput GB	+4.86	+112.57	-145.43	-464.42	-309.90	+325.49	+42.79	+ 102.19	-41.48
	Growth (%)	82.21	-2216.26	229.19	219.34	-33.27	-205.03	86.85	-138.82	-246.97
5.	Kalahandi GB	-219.68	-238.55	-310.10	-299.53	-652.59	-195.10	+ 11.23	+28.05	-234.53
	Growth (%)	12.82	8.59	29.99	-3.41	117.87	-70.10	-105.76	-149.78	-19.97
6.	Baitarani GB	-377.79	-389.98	-412.95	-374.07	-691.11	-421.59	-402.94	-164.75	-403.90
	Growth (%)	12.38	4.33	5.89	-9.42	84.75	-39.00	-4.42	-59.11	-0.58
7.	Balasore GB	-232.50	-282.85	-300.55	-476.17	-964.83	-735.59	-954.82	-833.50	-604.85
	Growth (%)	33.87	21.66	6.26	58.43	102.62	-17.75	20.32	-12.71	26.59
8.	Rushikulya GB	-224.52	-226.21	-283.32	-345.48	-351.14	+11.45	+251.55	+ 132.73	-129.37
	Growth (%)	43.03	0.75	25.25	21.94	1.64	-103.26	-2096.94	47.24	-257.54
9.	Dhenkanal GB	-140.38	-203.97	-194.23	-189.30	-165.12	+14.02	+145.37	+ 180.44	-69.15
	Growth (%)	87.98	45.30	-4.78	-2.54	-12.77	-108.49	-936.88	-24.12	-119.54
10.	All RRBs in Orissa	-2689.59	-2663.65	-5489.36	-4796.43	-8217.87	-3834.01	-3012.96	-2150.33	-4106.78
	Growth (%)	36.11	-0.96	106.08	-12.62	71.33	-53.35	-21.41	-28.63	12.07

Source: All Ratios are computed as per the data contained in *Statistics on RRBs*, NABARD Publications, Mumbai and Bhubaneswar.

Table 6.8

Abstracts of Working Results of Individual RRBs in Orissa

(Figures in per cent)

Sl. No.	*RRBs Working Results*	*1995-96*		*1996-97*		*1997-98*		*1998-99*		*1999-2000*	
		No.	*Amount*	*No.*	*Amount*	*No.*	*Amount*	*No.*	*Amount*	*No.*	*Amount*
1	Profit making RRBs	0	-	0	-	2	3.52	4	4.51	5	4.62
2	Loss-Incurring RRBs	9	47.96	9	82.18	7	41.86	5	34.64	4	26.12
3	Total	9	47.96	9	82.18	9	38.34	9	30.13	9	21.50

Source: Based on the data figured in Table 6.2.

March 2000, Bolangir GB has shown the largest amount of accumulated losses of Rs. 10269.72 lakh followed by that of Rs. 8093.83 lakh of Cuttack GB. On the lower end, Koraput GB has the lowest amount of Rs. 331.85 lakh. This has been shown in Fig. 6.1. The trend analysis reveals that there is reduction in the accumulated losses in absolute terms for the last one year 1999-2000 in case of Puri GB, for 2 years, i.e., 1998-99 and 1999-2000 in case of Kalahandi GB, for 3 years from 1997-98 to 1999-2000 in case of Koraput GB, Rushikulya GB and Dhenkanal GB. The remaining 4 RRBs have shown declining growth rates of accumulated losses; the growth rates of Bolangir GB have reduced from 42.12 per cent in 1994-95 to 31.67 per cent in 1996-97 and have remained around 15 per cent from 1997-98 onwards. The growth rates of accumulated losses have sharply and steadily reduced from 67.10 per cent to 2.66 per cent in case of Cuttack GB, from 28.51 per cent to 4.22 per cent in case of Baitarani GB, from 49.41 per cent to 17.86 per cent in case of Balasore GB during the period from 1996-97 to 1999-2000. Thus, the position of all the RRBs with regard to their accumulated losses has been improving which becomes evident from the negative/declining growth rates of their accumulated losses during the period under review.

The Viability Aspect

6.4.3. As on 31 March 2000, 5 out of the 9 RRBs in Orissa have reported operating profits and hence, have attained current viability. But, none of the RRBs in the State including the profit-making ones, have been able to wipe out accumulated losses from their balance sheet. Therefore, none of the RRBs in the State have attained sustainable viability by the end of March 2000.

Credit-Deposit Ratio (C-D Ratio)

6.4.4. Table 6.10 presents the Credit-Deposit Ratios of the individual RRBs in Onssa for the period from 1992-93 to 1999-2000. It is found that 6 out of the 9 RRBs viz. Puri GB, Cuttack GB, Koraput GB, Kalahandi GB, Balasore GB and Dhenkanal GB have higher overall C-D Ratios than the State's average of nearly 64 per cent in the said period. The remaining 3 RRBs such as Bolangir GB, Baitarani GB and Rushikulya GB have displayed lower overall C-D Ratios than the State's

Table 6.9
Accumulated Losses of RRBs in Orissa

(Rs. in Lakhs)

Sl. No.	RRBs	1992-93	1993-94	1994-95	1995-96	1996-97	1997-98	1998-99	1999-2000	Average
1.	Puri GB	-1668.92	-2255.44	-2769.94	-3398.63	-4187.91	-5121.24	-5693.66	-5674.33	
	Growth (%)	44.03	35.14	22.81	22.70	23.22	22.29	11.18	-0.34	22.63
2.	Bolangir GB	-2039.24	-2537.15	-3605.74	-5076.44	-6684.00	-7789.71	-8864.26	-10269.72	
	Growth (%)	45.69	24.42	42.12	40.79	31.67	16.54	13.79	15.86	28.86
3.	Cuttack GB	-845.32	-1195.55	-3455.24	-4003.31	-6689.65	-7425.30	-7884.47	-8093.83	
	Growth (%)	72.01	41.43	189.01	15.86	67.10	11.00	6.18	2.66	50.66
4.	Koraput GB	-	117.43	-28.00	-492.42	-802.32	-476.83 -	-434.04	-331.85	
	Growth (%)		–	-123.84	1658.64	62.93	40.57	-8.97	-23.54	217.81
5.	Kalahandi GB	-592.72	-831.29	-1141.39	-1440.92	-2093.51	-2288.61	-2277.38	-2257.18	
	Growth (%)	58.89	40.25	37.30	26.24	45.29	9.32	-0.49	-0.98	26.98
6.	Baitarani GB	-1246.94	-1636.92	-2049.87	-2423.94	-3115.05	-3536.64	-3939.58	-4066.57	
	Growth (%)	42.81	31.27	25.23	18.25	28.51	13.53	11.39	4.22	21.90
7.	Balasore GB	-893.31	-1176.16	-1476.71	-1952.88	-2917.71	-3711.30	-4666.12	-5499.63	
	Growth (%)	35.18	31.66	25.55	32.25	49.41	27.20	25.73	17.86	30.61
8.	Rushikulya GB	-777.21	-867.92	-1151.24	-1496.72	-1847.86	-1836.41	-1584.86	-1452.13	
	Growth (%)	86.30	11.67	32.64	30.01	23.46	-0.62	-13.70	-8.37	20.17
9.	Dhenkanal GB	-372.19	-576.16	-770.39	-959.69	-1124.81	-1110.79	-965.42	-784.98	
	Growth (%)	60.56	54.80	33.71	24.57	17.21	-1.25	-13.09	-18.69	19.73
10.	All RRBs in Orissa	-8435.85	-10959.16	-16448.52	-21244.95	-29462.82	-33296.83	-36309.79	-38430.22	
	Growth (%)	50.48	29.91	50.09	29.16	38.68	13.01	9.05	5.94	28.20

Source: *Statistics on RRBs*, NABARD Publications, Mumbai.

Fig. 6.1
Accumulated Losses of Individual RRBs in Orissa (As on 31 March 2000)

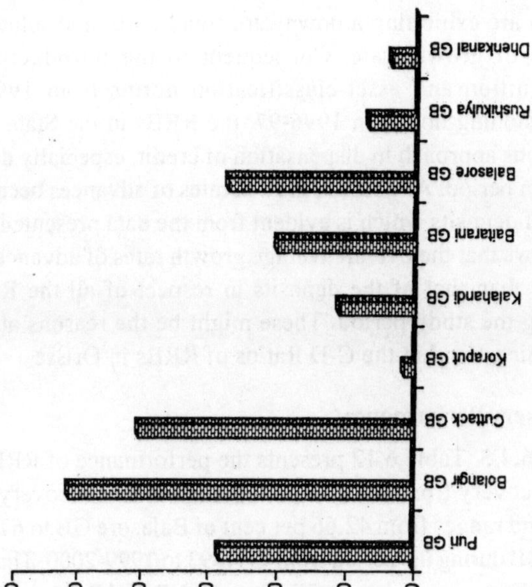

average. The overall negative growth rates in the C-D Ratios of all the 9 RRBs reveal that there has been an overall declining trend in the C-D Ratios of all RRBs in Orissa. The Balasore GB has registered the highest overall rate of decline at -11.96 per cent followed by that of Kalahandi GB at -11.89 per cent. On the other hand, the C-D ratios of Dhenkanal GB and Koraput GB have declined at the lowest rate of around -3 per cent during the period of study. The highest and lowest overall C-D Ratios of 75 per cent and 45.49 per cent were reported by Balasore GB and Baitarani GB respectively during the period under review. This analysis reveals that the C-D Ratios of all the individual RRBs are exhibiting a downward trend both in absolute terms and in terms of growth rate. Consequent to the introduction of income recognition and asset-classification norms from 1995-96 and the provisioning norms in 1996-97, the RRBs in the State had adopted a cautious approach in dispensation of credit, especially during the post-reform period. As a result, growth rates of advances became lower than that of deposits which is evident from the data presented in Table 6.11. It shows that the overall average growth rates of advances were always lower than that of the deposits in respect of all the RRBs in Orissa during the study period. These might be the reasons attributed to the declining trend in the C-D Ratios of RRBs in Orissa.

Recovery Performance

6.4.5. Table 6.12 presents the performance of RRBs in Orissa in the recovery front. It is found that the average recovery percentage to demand ranges from 42.66 per cent of Balasore GB to 67.96 per cent of Puri GB during the period from 1992-93 to 1999-2000. Three of the RRBs in the State viz. Bolangir GB, Cuttack GB and Balasore GB have lower and the remaining 6 have higher recovery percentage than the State's average of 57.34 per cent. All RRBs except Cutlack GB have registered improvement in their recovery performance as is reflected in terms of their overall positive growth rates. Whereas the overall negative growth rate of -3.20 per cent in case of Cuttack GB, shows its poor recovery performance during the period under review. The rate of improvement in the recovery performance was the highest in case of Kalahandi GB with 10.87 per cent followed by Puri GB with growth of 9.88 per cent. On the other hand, Balasore GB has recorded a very slow but positive average growth rate of 0.02 per cent during the study period. The table

Table 6.10

Credit-Deposit Ratios of Individual RRBs in Orissa

(Figures in per cent)

Sl. No.	*RRBs*	*1992-93*	*1993-94*	*1994-95*	*1995-96*	*1996-97*	*1997-98*	*1998-99*	*1999-2000*	*Average*
1.	Puri GB	87.71	72.36	73.28	67.06	54.61	48.59	54.47	59.77	64.73
	Growth (%)	-15.03	-17.50	1.27	-8.49	-18.57	11.02	12.10	9.73	-5.94
2.	Bolangir GB	82.43	70.33	60.03	56.66	47.59	46.17	41.93	39.27	55.55
	Growth (%)	-18.09	-14.68	-14.22	-5.61	-16.01	-2.98	-9.18	-6.34	-10.89
3.	Cuttack GB	93.54	88.99	81.67	77.56	67.56	58.91	47.14	46.39	70.22
	Growth (%)	-8.36	-4.86	-8.23	-5.03	-12.89	-12.80	-19.98	-1.59	-9.22
4.	Koraput GB	97.11	64.41	56.87	54.87	63.41	67.16	69.69	66.35	67.48
	Growth (%)	3.02	-33.67	-11.71	-3.52	15.56	5.91	3.78	-4.79	-3.18
5.	Kalahandi GB	139.82	84.52	61.99	64.47	59.68	58.35	59.66	64.37	74.12
	Growth (%)	-33.37	-39.55	-26.66	4.00	-7.43	-2.23	2.25	7.89	-11.89
6.	Baitarani GB	58.27	45.73	44.23	44.23	46.15	43.15	40.74	41.44	45.49
	Growth (%)	34.13	-21.52	-3.28	–	4.34	-6.50	-5.59	1.72	-8.12
7.	Balasore GB	96.02	90.37	92.55	87.86	80.36	64.11	53.81	34.93	75.00
	Growth (%)	-7.23	-5.88	2.41	-5.07	-8.54	-20.22	-16.07	-35.09	-11.96
8.	Rushikulya GB	80.57	63.37	56.46	57.73	51.86	50.46	42.68	40.96	55.51
	Growth (%)	-19.13	-21.35	-10.90	2.25	-10.17	-2.70	-15.42	-4.03	-10.18
9.	Dhenkanal GB	89.67	76.29	63.49	72.67	74.04	75.30	71.33	71.00	74.22
	Growth (%)	-3.96	-14.92	-16.78	14.46	1.89	1.70	-5.27	-0.46	-2.92
10.	All RRBs in Orissa	88.78	72.36	66.70	63.81	58.83	55.91	51.99	50.48	63.61
	Growth (%)	-13.39	-18.50	-7.82	-4.33	-7.80	-4.96	-7.01	-2.90	-8.35

Source: *Statistics on RRBs,* NABARD Publications, Central Office, Mumbai and Regional Office, Bhubaneswar.

Table 6.11

Overall Average Growth Rates of Advances and Deposits of RRBs in Orissa (For the period from 1992-93 to 1999-2000)

(Figures in per cent)

Sl. No.	*RRBs*	*Growth Rate of Advances*	*Growth Rate of Deposits*	*Remarks*
(1)	(2)	(3)	(4)	(5)
1.	Puri GB	24.99	34.03	(4) > (3)
2.	Bolangir GB	11.42	26.50	-do-
3.	Cuttack GB	10.23	20.75	-do-
4.	Koraput GB	16.95	22.84	-do-
5.	Kalahandi GB	17.69	35.46	-do-
6.	Baitarani GB	22.46	33.95	-do-
7.	Balasore GB	10.27	22.63	-do-
8	Rushikulya GB	19.28	32.49	-do-
9.	Dhenkanal GB	26.22	29.90	-do-
10.	All RRBs in Orissa	16.87	26.98	-do-

Source: Computed from the data collected from the *Statistics on RRBs*, NABARD Publications, Mumbai and Bhubaneswar.

further reveals that, as on 30 June 2000, 2 RRBs viz. Puri GB and Dhenkanal GB have shown more than 70 per cent of recovery against the recovery percentage in the range of 60 to 70 in case of 5 RRBs namely Rushikulya GB, Kalahandi GB, Koraput GB, Baitarani GB and Bolangir GB. The remaining 2 RRBs namely, Balasore GB and Cuttack GB have shown very poor recovery performance of 44.20 per cent and 33.80 per cent respectively as on the said date. The recovery performance of the RRBs in the State as at the end of June 2000 has been exhibited in graphical form in Fig. 6.2. The Puri GB has shown a recovery percentage of more than 81 per cent. The disquieting feature was that of Cuttack GB where the recovery percentage has not only shown a declining trend since 1996-97 but has dipped from a level of 51.78 per cent as at the end of June 99 to 33.80 per cent at the end of June 2000. Incidentally, the areas under Cuttack GB were affected severely by the Super Cyclone in October 1999.

Table 6.12

Recovery Performance of Individual RRBs in Orissa (Percentage of Recovery to Demand) (Year: July to June)

(Figures in per cent)

Sl. No.	*RRBs*	*1992-93*	*1993-94*	*1994-95*	*1995-96*	*1996-97*	*1997-98*	*1999-99*	*1999-2000*	*Average*
1.	Puri GB	55.83	60.78	60.29	60.55	72.16	74.08	78.63	81.36	67.96
	Growth (%)	39.09	8.87	-0.81	0.43	19.17	2.66	6.14	3.47	9.88
2.	Bolangir GB	41.69	44.21	47.26	43.79	49.78	56.11	58.60	60.62	50.26
	Growth (%)	-29.11	6.04	6.90	-7.34	13.68	12.72	4.46	3.45	1.35
3.	Cuttack GB	53.37	40.16	50.43	58.19	53.38	53.26	51.78	33.80	49.29
	Growth (%)	4.18	-24.75	25.57	15.39	-8.27	-0.22	-2.78	-34.72	-3.20
4.	Koraput GB	45.14	60.01	59.62	63.94	64.66	64.72	65.52	66.58 1.62	61.28
	Growth (%)	-24.58	32.94	-0.65	7.25	1.13	0.09	1.24		2.38
5.	Kalahandi GB	40.08	53.67	62.59	65.04	56.32	61.95	64.92	67.71 4.30	59.03
	Growth (%)	26.76	33.91	16.62	3.91	-13.41	10.00	4.79		10.87
6.	Baitarani GB	56.90	58.36	64.45	68.32	54.10	55.03	58.52	63.19 7.98	59.86
	Growth (%)	3.61	2.57	10.44	6.00	-20.81	1.72	6.34		2.23
7.	Balasore GB	40.04	40.88	41.80	47.35	47.05	41.69	38.21	44.20	42.66
	Growth (%)	-12.71	2.10	2.25	13.28	-0.63	-11.39	-8.35	15.68	0.02
8.	Rushikulya GB	46.49	47.00	50.49	60.60	71.08	70.01	70.50	67.78	60.50
	Growth (%)	17.22	1.10	7.43	20.02	17.29	-1.51	0.70	-3.86	7.30
9.	Dhenkanal GB	40.44	50.54	59.85	65.76	69.40	73.41	72.34	77.71 7.42	63.68
	Growth (%)	-3.04	24.98	18.42	9.87	5.54	5.78	-1.46		8.44
10.	All RRBs in Orissa	47.72	48.80	53.39	57.57	60.07	61.62	63.85	65.64	57.34
	Growth (%)	4.63	2.26	9.41	7.83	4.34	2.58	3.62	2.80	4.68

Source: *Statistics on RRBs,* NABARD Publications, Central Office, Mumbai and Regional Office, Bhubaneswar.

Fig. 6.2
Recovery Performance of Individual RRBs in Orissa (As on 31 March 2000)

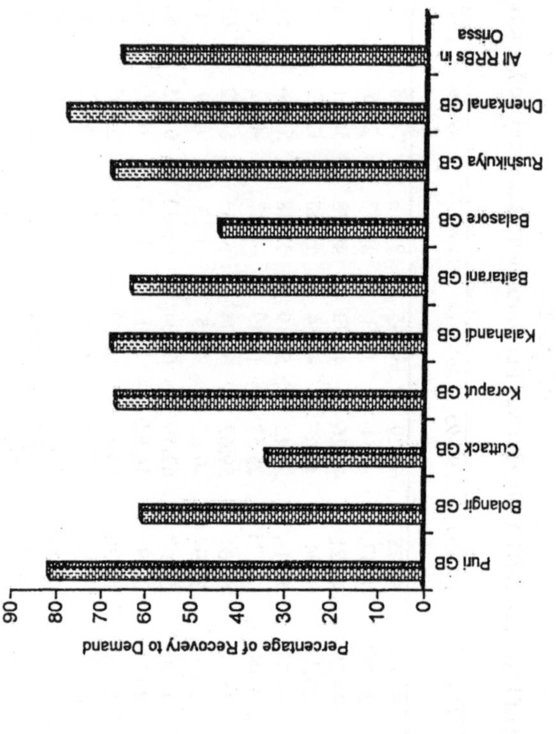

Non-Performing Assets to Total Advances

6.4.6. With the introduction of the asset classification norms, the RRBs were advised to arrest the fresh inflows of NPAs, to reduce the magnitude of the existing NPAs, and to bring about a culture of doing away with NPAs. Table 6.13 presents the bank-wise position of the NPAs of the RRBs in Orissa since the asset classification norms were implemented in 1995-96. It is observed that asset classification of 7 RRBs namely Puri GB, Cuttack GB, Koraput GB, Kalahandi GB, Baitarani GB, Rushikulya GB and Dhenkanal GB have shown qualitative improvement in NPA management. This becomes evident from the declining trend of the NPAs as percentage to the total advances of the said RRBs. The analysis of the growth rates of NPAs of RRBs reveals that Puri GB and Koraput GB had the lowest and the highest average growth rate of NPAs at -13.77 per cent and 6.88 per cent respectively. Similarly, Balasore GB, Cuttack GB and Bolangir GB have recorded the three highest average ratios of NPAs to total assets at 57.17 per cent, 52.79 per cent and 49.43 per cent respectively and are considerably higher than the State's average of nearly 37 per cent. On the other hand, Puri GB, Baitarani GB, Rushikulya GB and Dhenkanal GB have this ratio at 27.42 per cent, 24.8 per cent, 23.21 per cent and 16.3 per cent respectively which are lower than the State's average during the period under review. The 2 RRBs namely Bolangir GB and Balasore GB have shown very poor NPA management as is evidenced by their positive average growth rates of NPAs and the fluctuating trend of the NPAs to total assets ratio. The NPAs as percentage of total advances of RRBs in Orissa for the year ending on 31 March 2000 have been exhibited in pictorial form in Fig. 6.3.

Investment to Deposit Ratio (I-D Ratio)

6.4.7. I-D Ratios of individual RRBs in Orissa arc shown in Table 6.14 for the period from 1992-93 to 1999-2000. It is observed that Koraput GB has I-D Ratios varying between 63 per cent and 92 per cent. The I-D Ratios of Cuttack GB, Rushikulya GB and Dhenkanal GB have been more than 50 per cent since 1995-96 onwards. This ratio, in the cases of Puri GB, Bolangir GB, Kalahandi GB and Baitarani GB, has shown variation in the range of 32 per cent and 61 per cent during the last 3 to 4 years. However, that of the Balasore GB remained very low and varied between 5 per cent to 24 per cent recording the lowest overall

Table 6.13

NPAs Position of RRBs in Orissa

(Rupees in Lakhs)

Sl. No	*RRBs*	*1995-96*	*1996-97*	*1997-98*	*1998-99*	*1999-2000*	*Average*
1.	Puri GB	2462.26	2326.31	1500.15	1588.85	1268.88	
		(49.26)	(41.86)	(22.49)	(15.11)	(8.37)	(27.42)
	Growth (%)		-5.52	-35.51	5.91	-20.14	-13.77
2.	Bolangir GB	3410.34	2381.90	3047.99	3379.96	3543.45	
		(62.01)	(41.92)	(47.88)	(48.37)	(46.96)	(49.43)
	Growth (%)		-30.22	27.96	10.89	4.84	3.19
3.	Cuttack GB	5786.00	5911.67	6027.00	4727.11	2833.66	(52.79)
		(63.70)	(62.55)	(59.80)	(51.29) -	(27.01) –	-9.99
	Growth (%)		2.17	19.51	21.57	40.06	
4.	Koraput GB	2576.00	2694.89	2484.00	3074.37	3264.14	
		(52.50)	(40.98)	(33.25)	(31.68)	(31.74)	(38.03)
	Growth (%)		4.62	-7.83	23.77	6.17	6.68
5.	Kalahandi GB	1530.00	1610.93	1654.74	1395.50	1366.58	
		(61.10)	(52.14)	(44.25)	(30.00) -	(23.57)	(42.27)
	Growth (%)		5.29	2.72	15.67	-2.07	-2.43
6.	Baitarani GB	906.00	1014.15	1201.00	1245.34	1079.27	
		(32.59)	(27.31)	(26.51)	(22.42)	(15.17)	(24.8)
	Growth (%)		11.94	18.42	3.69	-13.34	5.18
7.	Balasore GB	1398.86	1585.29	1822.31	1992.68	1552.74	
		(46.69)	(52.50)	(61.69)	(66.87)	(58.11)	(57.17)
	Growth (%)		13.33	14.95	9.35	-22.08	3.89
8.	Rushikulya	1346.00	1357.64	1425.38	483.12	675.78	
	GB	(40.29)	(32.15)	(26.78)	(8.01)	(8.81)	(23.21)
	Growth (%)		0.86	4.99	-66.11	39.88	-5.10
9.	Dhenkanal GB	844.00	840.00	724.00	657.41	680.70	
	Growth (%)	(29.40)	(21.04)	(13.46)	(9.72)	(7.88)	(16.3)
			-0.47	-13.81	-9.20	3.54	-4.99
10.	All RRBs in	20259.46	19722.78	20086.57	18544.34	16265.20	
	Orissa	(51.97)	(43.67)	(37.82)	(29.72)	(21.60)	(36.96)
	Growth (%)		-2.65	1.84	-7.68	-12.29	-5.20

Notes: Figures in brackets indicate the NPAs as percentage to the total advances of RRBs.

Source: *Statistics on RRBs*, NABARD Publications, Mumbai and Bhubaneshwar.

Fig. 6.3

NPAs Level of Individual RRBs in Orissa (As on 31 March 2000)

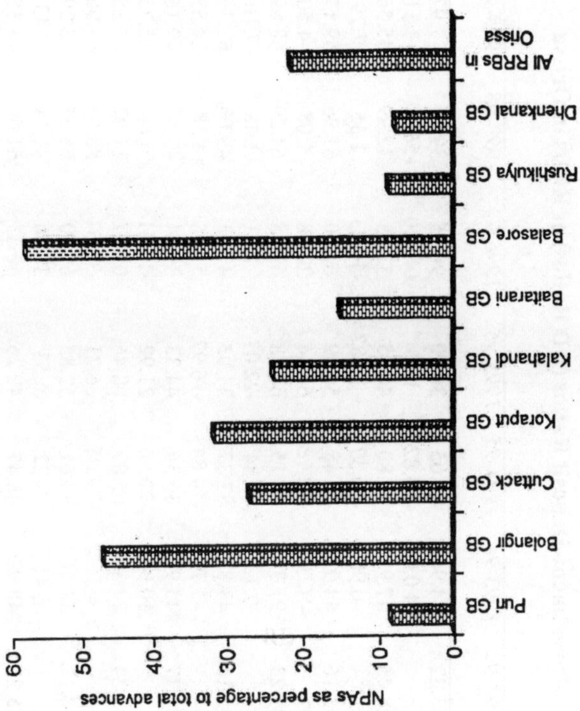

Table 6.14

Investment-Deposit Ratios (I-D Ratios) of RRBs in Orissa

(Figures in per cent)

Sl. No.	*RRBs*	*1992-93*	*1993-94*	*1994-95*	*1995-96*	*1996-97*	*1997-98*	*1998-99*	*1999-2000*	*Average*
1.	Puri GB	43.22	44.96	36.05	36.70	90.35	39.27	37.97	42.54	39.46
	Growth (%)		4.03	-19.82	1.80	146.10	-56.54	-3.31	12.04	12.06
2.	Bolangir GB	48.45	47.97	35.80	40.05	32.35	32.99	35.56	43.06	39.53
	Growth (%)		-0.99	-25.37	+ 11.87	-19.23	1.35	7.79	21.09	-0.50
3.	Cuttack GB	53.16	44.93	30.48	50.09	61.30	61.96	59.17	61.45	52.82
	Growth (%)		-16.31	-32.16	64.34	22.38	1.08	-4.50	3.85	5.53
4.	Koraput GB	85.23	91.31	84.15	68.58	63.35	64.29	68.89	70.56	74.55
	Growth (%)		7.13	-7.84	-22.07	-7.63	1.48	7.16	2.42	-2.76
5.	Kalahandi GB	45.14	43.88	37.37	31.03	47.03	49.09	61.14	60.53 -	46.90
	Growth (%)		-2.79	-14.84	-16.97	51.56	4.38	24.55	1.00	6.41
6.	Baitarani GB	41.77	45.97	36.36	44.33	39.84	42.47	49.16	52.50	44.05
	Growth (%)		10.06	-20.90	21.92	-12.41	6.60	15.75	6.79	3.97
7.	Balasore GB	23.24	24.30	05.09	08.46	05.87	11.07	18.15	22.26	14.91
	Growth (%)		4.56	-79.05	66.21	-30.61	88.59	63.96	22.64	19.47
8.	Rushikulya GB	48.17	51.26	49.61	52.85	69.50	68.57	72.29	70.68	60.37
	Growth (%)		6.41	-3.22	6.53	31.50	-1.34	5.43	-2.23	6.15
9.	Dhenkanal GB	45.28	48.92	48.47	49.26	66.33	61.00	63.35	61.42 -	55.51
	Growth (%)		8.04	-0.92	1.63	34.65	-8.04	3.85	3.05	5.17
10.	All RRBs in Orissa	51.29	52.12	42.45	45.65	56.21	50.50	52.58	54.83	50.7
	Growth (%)	6.61	1.62	-18.55	7.54	23.13	-10.16	4.12	4.28	2.32

Source: All Ratios are computed as per the data contained in the *Statistics on RRBs,* NABARD Publications, Mumbai and Bhubaneswar.

average of 14.91 per cent during the period of study. The table further shows that Koraput GB has registered the highest overall average I-D Ratio of 74.55 per cent followed by Rushikulya GB with 60.37 per cent and Dhenkanal GB with 55.51 per cent. The growth rate of this ratio has varied between -2.76 per cent of Koraput GB and 19.47 per cent of Balasore GB. Three RRBs viz. Cuttack GB, Rushikulya GB and Dhenkanal GB have better average I-D Ratios both in absolute terms as well as in terms of growth rate than the State's average of 50.70 per cent and 2.32 per cent respectively. It is observed from the table that the I-D Ratios of Bolangir GB, Cuttack GB, Koraput GB, Kalahandi GB, Baitarani GB and Balasore GB shows upward trend during the last 3 to 4 years of the study period. The ratios in cases of Rushikulya GB and Dhenkanal GB have remained above 68 per cent and 61 per cent respectively in the last four years of the study period. The lone RRB, i.e., Puri GB does not show any trend with regard to this ratio.

Accumulated Losses to Total Assets

6.4.8. Table 6.15 presents the accumulated losses as percentage to total assets of the RRBs for the period from 1992-93 to 1999-2000. The average amount of the accumulated losses to total assets for the study period was the highest in case of Balasore GB at 40.41 per cent followed by the Bolangir GB at 38.72 per cent and Baitarani GB at 27.43 per cent. This reflects the unhealthy financial position of these RRBs. On the other hand, this ratio was the lowest in case of the Dhenkanal GB at 11.49 per cent followed by Rushikulya GB at 14.09 per cent and Cuttack GB at 19.88 per cent implying their better position than that of other RRBs in the State. Koraput GB, Rushikulya GB and Dhenkanal GB have better ratios in absolute terms and in terms of growth rate than the State's average of 19.89 per cent and 0.21 per cent respectively during the study period. The trend analysis of the growth rates reveals that 5 out of the 9 RRBs in the State namely Koraput GB, Kalahandi GB, Baitarani GB, Rushikulya GB and Dhenkanal GB have shown declining accumulated losses to total assets and hence negative growth rates consecutively at least for 3 years since 1997-98 onwards. This ratio for 3 RRBs viz. Puri GB, Bolangir GB and Cuttack GB have recorded negative growth rates for the last two years of the study period. Even the Balasore GB, though have shown increasing trend of this ratio, but at a steadily declining growth rate from 30.27 per cent in 1996-97

Table 6.15

Accumulated Losses to Total Assets Ratios of RRBs in Orissa

(Figures in per cent)

Sl. No.	*RRBs*	*1992-93*	*1993-94*	*1994-95*	*1995-96*	*1996-97*	*1997-98*	*1998-99*	*1999-2000*	*Average*
1.	Puri GB	22.23	29.76	25.97	26.32	25.82	26.95	19.70	15.02	23.97
	Growth (%)	-	33.87	-12.74	1.35	-1.90	4.38	-26.90	-23.76	-3.67
2.	Bolangir GB	24.39	25.96	30.63	74.73	40.18	41.05	36.52	36.29	38.72
	Growth (%)	-	6.44	17.99	143.98	-46.23	2.17	-11.04	-0.63	16.10
3.	Cuttack GB	7.49	9.09	20.64	18.97	25.09	29.47	25.49	22.81	19.88
	Growth (%)	-	21.36	127.06	-8.09	32.26	17.46	-13.51	-10.51	23.71
4.	Koraput GB	0	0	0.27	3.87	5.00	2.52	1.87	01.33	2.48
	Growth (%)	-	-	-	1333.33	29.20	-49.6	-25.79	-28.88	-9.38
5.	Kalahandi GB	25.81	23.40	25.25	27.44	27.18	24.55	17.87	15.53	23.38
	Growth (%)	-	-9.34	7.91	8.67	35.50	-9.68	-27.21	-13.09	-1.03
6.	Baitarani GB	34.84	33.47	29.36	28.31	27.94	25.70	21.74	18.11	27.43
	Growth (%)	-	-3.93	-12.28	-3.58	-1.31	-8.02	-15.41	-16.70	-8.75
7.	Balasore GB	27.20	28.77	31.76	34.99	45.58	49.31	51.88	53.82	40.41
	Growth (%)	-	5.77	10.39	10.17	30.27	8.18	5.21	3.74	10.53
8.	Rushikulya GB	19.55	17.15	17.17	17.99	14.64	11.90	8.25	6.10	14.09
	Growth (%)	-	-12.28	0.12	4.78	-18.62	-18.72	-30.67	-26.06	-14.49
9.	Dhenkanal GB	12.21	15.21	15.95	15.61	12.28	9.59	6.54	4.50	11.49
	Growth (%)	-	24.57	4.87	-2.13	-21.33	-21.91	-31.80	-31.19	-11.27
10.	All RRBs in Orissa	16.47	17.56	20.91	22.02	23.97	23.80	17.29	17.08	19.89
	Growth (%)	28.07	6.62	19.08	5.31	8.86	-0.71	-27.35	-1.21	0.21

Note: While calculating average growth rate for Koraput GB, the growth rate for the year 1994-95 has been ignored, as it is expectionally high.

Source: All Ratios are computed as per the data contained in the *Statistics on RRBs,* NABARD Publications, Mumbai and Bhubaneswar.

to 3.74 per cent in 1999-2000. Thus, on the whole all the RRBs in Orissa have shown improvement in this ratio either in absolute terms or in terms of the growth rate during the study period, especially in its later half.

Assets per Staff

6.4.9. Assets per staff is yet another indicator of operational efficiency of RRBs and have been shown in the Table 6.16 for the said period. All the RRBs in Orissa have exhibited steadily increasing trend and positive growth rates of assets per staff. Balasore GB has registered the lowest overall growth rate of 12.42 per cent and the lowest average assets per staff ratio of Rs. 11.92 lakhs during the period mentioned above. This is the only bank which has shown negative growth rates of -18.32 per cent and -3.90 per cent in the year 1994-95 and 1996-97 respectively. Bolangir GB followed the Balasore GB in this respect recording the second lowest growth rate of 14.75 per cent, the second lowest average ratio and Rs. 14.41 lakhs during the said period. On the upper side, the top two positions with regard to this ratios have been occupied by Dhenkanal GB and Rushikulya GB with the highest average ratios of Rs. 37.31 lakhs and Rs. 31.88 lakhs and registering overall average growth rates of 30.72 per cent and 32.73 per cent respectively during the period under review.

Interest-paid to Interest-received Ratio

6.4.10. Table 6.17 presents the Interest-paid to Interest-received on loans and advances of individual RRBs in Orissa from 1992-93 to 1999-2000. The larger the interest paid on deposits and borrowings, the higher will be the ratio. Similarly, the larger the interest received on loans and advances, the lower will be the ratio. Therefore, in common parlance, a lower ratio is desirable. The most noticeable feature the table brings out is that this ratio has been always more than 100 per cent in cases of all the RRBs indicating thereby the fact that interest paid by the RRBs was always higher than the interest received.

This may be due to the higher proportion of term deposits in the total deposit structure of the RRBs in the State which require higher debt servicing cost in the form of interest payment in comparison to those of current and savings deposits. The analysis of this ratio reveals that the average figure of this ratio for the said period was the highest

Table 6.16
Assets per Staff of RRBs in Orissa

(Rupees in Lakhs)

Sl. No.	*RRBs*	*1992-93*	*1993-94*	*1994-95*	*1995-96*	*1996-97*	*1997-98*	*1998-99*	*1999-2000*	*Average*
1.	Puri GB	9.25	11.57	12.46	15.00	19.04	23.17	37.14	51.44	22.38
	Growth (%)	-	25.08	7.69	20.39	26.93	21.69	60.29	38.50	28.65
2.	Bolangir GB	9.01	10.38	11.68	12.15	12.70	16.50	19.71	23.18	14.41
	Growth (%)	-	15.21	12.52	4.02	4.53	29.92	19.45	17.61	14.75
3.	Cuttack GB	12.08	16.12	17.89	23.05	26.88	30.38	31.03	37.06	24.31
	Growth (%)	-	33.44	10.98	28.84	16.62	13.02	2.14	19.43	17.78
4.	Koraput GB	15.12	18.07	20.59	24.15	30.47	36.73	45.13	49.17	29.93
	Growth (%)	-	19.51	13.95	17.29	26.17	20.54	22.87	8.95	18.47
5.	Kalahandi GB	6.97	7.90	9.85	11.14	16.45	24.81	30.77	36.11	18.00
	Growth (%)	-	13.34	24.68	13.10	47.67	50.82	24.02	17.35	27.28
6.	Baitarani GB	5.45	7.57	11.50	14.31	18.51	23.76	32.68	42.38	19.52
	Growth (%)	-	38.90	51.92	24.43	29.35	28.36	37.54	29.68	34.31
7.	Balasore GB	7.76	12.61	10.30 -	11.55	11.10 -	12.43	14.10	15.47	11.92
	Growth (%)	-	62.5	18.32	12.14	3.90	11.98	13.44	9.72	12.42
8.	Rushikulya GB	9.57	12.59	16.67	20.62	32.65	41.34	53.58	67.99	31.88
	Growth (%)	-	31.56	32.41	23.70	58.34	26.62	29.61	26.89	32.73
9.	Dhenkanal GB	12.28	14.72	18.63	23.92	37.36	48.70	64.73	78.14	37.31
	Growth (%)	-	19.87	26.56	28.40	56.19	30.35	32.92	20.72	30.72
10.	All RRBs in Orissa	10.42	12.57	14.52	17.27	21.71	25.09	40.56	43.76	23.24
	Growth (%)	7.76	20.63	15.51	18.94	25.71	15.57	61.66	7.89	21.71

Source: Figures are computed on the basis of the data collected from *Statistics on RRBs*, NABARD Publications, Mumbai and Bhubaneswar.

Table 6.17
Interest Paid to Interest Received on Loans and Advances of RRBs in Orissa

(Figures in per cent)

Sl. No.	RRBs	1992-93	1993-94	1994-95	1995-96	1996-97	1997-98	1998-99	1999-2000	Average
1.	Puri GB	233.95	260.24	182.10	202.20	225.93	177.02	144.58	126.40	194.05
	Growth (%)		11.24	-30.03	11.04	11.74	-21.65	-18.33	-12.57	-6.94
2.	Bolangir GB	256.56	196.34	237.48	292.94	256.45	232.81	247.28	283.69	250.44
	Growth (%)		-23.47	39.29	23.35	-12.46	-9.22	6.22	14.72	5.49
3.	Cuttack GB	135.14	122.07	188.94	223.53	274.96	297.95	349.32	307.41	237.42
	Growth (%)		-9.67	54.78	18.31	23.01	8.36	17.24	-12.00	14.29
4.	Koraput GB	103.94	136.32	150.81	225.93	154.79	139.41	139.72	147.36	149.79
	Growth (%)		31.15	10.63	49.81	-31.49	-9.94	0.22	5.47	7.98
5.	Kalahandi GB	110.16	133.62	134.56	164.29	179.38	142.61	124.76	116.36	138.22
	Growth (%)		21.30	0.70	22.09	9.18	-20.50	-12.52	-6.73	1.93
6.	Baitarani GB	339.69	339.97	306.02	232.41	225.93	207.48	214.13	208.62	259.28
	Growth (%)		0.08	-9.78	-24.05	-2.79	-8.17	3.21	-2.57	-6.30
7.	Balasore GB	140.42	140.05	128.47	196.35	247.73	302.04	405.36	334.27	236.84
	Growth (%)		-0.26	-8.27	52.84	26.17	21.92	34.21	-17.53	15.58
8.	Rushikulya GB	126.51	137.25	147.53	220.32	225.59	213.44	191.75	209.48	183.98
	Growth (%)		8.49	7.49	49.34	2.39	-5.39	-10.16	9.25	8.77
9.	Dhenkanal GB	109.13	134.63	153.55	180.88	146.75	121.40	129.24	132.40	138.50
	Growth (%)		23.37	14.05	17.80	-18.87	-17.27	6.46	2.45	4.00
10.	All RRBs in Orissa	155.03	155.84	179.74	219.27	215.95	195.64	190.62	182.47	186.82
	Growth (%)	31.11	0.52	15.34	21.99	-1.51	-9.40	-2.57	-4.28	6.40

Source: All Ratios are computed as per the data contained in the *Statistics on RRBs,* NABARD Publications, Mumbai and Bhubaneswar.

at 259.28 per cent in case of Baitarani GB, followed by 250.44 per cent of Bolangir GB and 237.42 per cent of Cuttack GB. On the other hand, the two lowest average figures of this ratio were 138.22 per cent and 138.50 per cent being recorded by the Kalahandi GB and Dhenkanal GB respectively. The average growth rate of this ratio has shown a variation between -6.94 per cent and 15.58 per cent registered by Puri GB and Balasore GB respectively during the study period. This ratio exhibits very erratic trend in cases of 7 RRBs. However, the remaining 2 RRBs namely Puri GB and Kalahandi GB have shown an initial upward trend and then have started showing downward trend in the last 3 to 4 years of the study period implying thereby some improvement.

Salary to Income Ratio

6.4.11. Table 6.18 presents the salary to income ratios of the RRBs in Orissa from the year 1992-93 to 1999-2000. This ratio indicates the percentage of income of the RRBs that is used for meeting the wage bill. The average figures for this ratio given in the table reveal that this ratio in case of 5 RRBs viz. Puri GB, Bolangir GB, Kalahandi GB, Baitarani GB and Balasore GB varied between 74.99 per cent (Puri GB) and 104.56 per cent (Balasore GB). It implies that major portion of the income of these RRBs have been spent towards the payment of salary of their staff.

On the other hand, this ratio was comparatively low in case of the remaining 4 RRBs and varied between 32.22 per cent (Dhenkanal GB) and 41.71 per cent (Cuttack GB). Notwithstanding the comparatively high figures of this ratio in case of 5 RRBs as stated above, all RRBs except Bolangir GB and Balasore GB have shown negative average growth rates which implies improvement in this ratio. This finding is further reinforced by the declining trend of this ratio from 1995-96 onwards in case of all the RRBs except these two RRBs. Even in the cases of these two RRBs, the ratio shows indication of improvement. The ratio of Bolangir GB has been showing continuously downward trend during ihe period of study from 104.83 per cent in 1995-96 to 71.59 per cent in 1998-99 with a slight increase to 76.07 per cent in 1999-2000. Balasore GB has shown negative growth rales in the last two years. The declining trend of this ratio revealed that almost all the RRBs have been showing improvement. The rate of improvement was the highest at -18.36 per cent in case of Baitarani GB, followed by Puri

Table 6.18
Salary to Income Ratio of RRBs in Orissa

(Figures in per cent)

Sl. No.	*RRBs*	*1992-93*	*1993-94*	*1994-95*	*1995-96*	*1996-97*	*1997-98*	*1998-99*	*1999-2000*	*Average*
1.	Puri GB	95.12	101.98	85.27	77.39	55.07	50.11	35.30	24.70	74.99
	Growth (%)		7.21	-16.39	-0.09	-28.84	-9.01	-29.55	-30.02	-15.24
2.	Bolangir GB	71.25	69.61	104.83	91.71	83.39	72.18	71.59	76.07	80.08
	Growth (%)		-2.30	50.60	-12.52	-9.07	-13.44	-0.82	6.26	2.67
3.	Cuttack GB	38.76	37.03	54.58	56.62	41.61	39.38	35.12	30.66	41.71
	Growth (%)		-4.46	47.12	3.93	-26.51	-5.36	-10.82	-12.70	-1.26
4.	Koraput GB	37.48	34.56	37.03	44.63	36.49	29.47	33.68	29.18	35.32
	Growth (%)		-7.79	7.15	20.52	-18.24	-19.24	14.29	-13.36	-2.38
5.	Kalahandi GB	97.24	100.85	112.39	108.89	98.35	59.32	46.77	39.63	82.93
	Growth (%)		3.71	11.44	-3.11	-9.68	-39.68	-21.16	-15.27	-10.54
6.	Baitarani GB	164.96	131.29	70.92	73.00	50.79	50.83	42.46	34.72	77.37
	Growth (%)		-20.41	-45.98	2.93	-30.42	0.08	-16.47	-18.23	-18.36
7.	Balasore GB	86.44	78.54	81.39	106.84	114.61	133.79	130.71	104.13	104.56
	Growth (%)		-9.14	3.63	31.27	7.27	16.74	-2.30	-20.34	3.88
8.	Rushikulya GB	53.45	49.06	46.84	38.59	27.01	24.49	20.18	17.53	34.64
	Growth (%)		-8.21	-4.53	-17.61	-30.01	-9.33	-17.60	-13.13	-14.35
9.	Dhenkanal GB	43.24	46.01	43.18	42.10	33.66	19.07	16.13	14.33	32.22
	Growth (%)		6.41	-6.15	-2.50	-20.05	-43.34	-15.42	-11.16	-13.17
10.	All RRBs in Orissa	60.13	58.28	62.75	63.83	50.24	42.76	37.52	33.00	51.06
	Growth (%)	1.54	-3.08	7.67	1.72	-21.29	-14.89	-12.25	-12.05	-7.65

Source: All Ratios are computed as per the data contained in the *Statistics on RRBs*, NABARD Publications, Mumbai and Bhubaneswar.

GB at -15.24 per cent and Rushikulya GB at -14.35 per cent during the period. The initial upward trend in this ratio was due to the implementation of the NIT Award giving RRB staff parity of pay with those of the sponsor banks since 1987 onwards.

Branch Productivity

6.4.12. Branch productivity or volume of business per branch of the individual RRBs in Orissa are presented in Table 6.19. The table shows that the per branch productivity of all the RRBs have displayed increasing trend during the period of eight years under review. Average branch productivity of the Dhenkanal GB was the highest with Rs. 196.36 lakh followed by that of Cuttack GB with Rs. 188.40 lakh and Koraput GB with Rs. 177.25 lakh.

On the other hand, the branch productivity of Kalahandi GB was the lowest with Rs. 103.41 lakh followed by that of Balasore GB with Rs. 104.37 lakh and Bolangir GB with Rs. 106.06 lakh. The ratios of 5 RRBs viz. Puri GB, Cuttack GB, Koraput GB, Rushikulya GB and Dhenkanal GB are higher and those of the remaining 4 RRBs viz. Bolangir GB, Kalahandi GB, Baitarani GB and Balasore GB are lower than the State's average of Rs. 148.69 lakh during the period under review. The overall annual growth rate of the branch productivity of the RRBs in the State varied from 18.16 per cent of Balasore GB to 30.96 per cent of Baitarani GB during the period. Five RRBs viz. Puri GB, Kalahandi GB, Baitarani GB, Rushikulya GB and Dhenkanal GB have registered higher growth rates, whereas, the remaining 4 RRBs such as Bolangir GB, Cuttack GB, Koraput GB and Balasore GB have recorded lower growth rates of branch productivity than the State's average of 23.51 per cent.

Employee Productivity

6.4.13. Table 6.20 presents the employee productivity or volume of business per employee of the RRBs in Orissa from 1992-93 to 1999-2000. All the RRBs in Orissa have witnessed an increasing trend in their employee productivity ratio during the period under review. But, Bolangir GB recorded a decline in this ratio in the year 1999-2000 with a negative growth rate of -27.44 per cent over the previous year. The average employee productivity ratio of Dhenkanal GB was the highest

Table 6.19

Branch Productivity of RRBs in Orissa (Business per Branch)

(Rs. in Lakhs)

Sl. No.	*RRBs*	*1992-93*	*1993-94*	*1994-95*	*1995-96*	*1996-97*	*1997-98*	*1998-99*	*1999-2000*	*Average*
1.	Puri GB	64.73	75.84	99.11	124.54	157.33	203.96	266.23	361.98	169.22
	Growth (%)		17.16	30.68	25.66	26.33	29.64	30.53	35.97	28.00
2.	Bolangir GB	51.46	59.58	73.28	98.10	113.69	129.18	151.61	171.54	106.06
	Growth (%)		15.78	22.99	33.87	15.89	13.62	17.36	13.15	18.95
3.	Cuttack GB	106.89	124.25	149.69	171.86	193.69	224.68	237.74	298.43	188.40
	Growth (%)		16.24	20.47	14.81	12.70	16.00	21.84	25.53	18.23
4.	Koraput GB	79.34	104.31	123.94	153.88	184.25	223.24	262.51	286.50	177.25
	Growth (%)		31.47	18.82	24.16	19.74	21.16	17.59	9.14	20.30
5.	Kalahandi GB	41.00	46.76	65.86	82.95	107.36	131.80	161.66	189.88	103.41
	Growth (%)		14.05	40.85	25.95	29.43	22.76	22.66	17.46	24.74
6.	Baitarani GB	40.35	55.77	76.59	100.72	132.13	165.19	210.85	266.85	131.06
	Growth (%)		37.47	37.33	31.51	31.19	25.02	27.64	26.56	30.96
7.	Balasore GB	51.96	70.58	84.08	101.67	107.58	120.04	135.21	163.83	104.37
	Growth (%)		35.84	19.13	20.92	5.81	11.58	12.64	21.17	18.16
8.	Rushikulya GB	60.47	76.42	96.02	121.71	171.72	229.98	248.78	366.82	171.49
	Growth (%)		26.38	25.65	26.75	41.09	33.93	8.17	47.45	29.92
9.	Dhenkanal GB	72.71	84.73	101.88	142.12	191.56	250.50	318.66	408.74	196.36
	Growth (%)		16.53	20.24	39.50	34.79	30.77	27.21	28.27	28.19
10.	All RRBs in Orissa	64.24	78.27	96.95	122.24	149.42	182.33	216.65	279.40	148.69
	Growth (%)	19.93	22.60	23.87	26.09	22.23	21.96	18.82	28.96	23.51

Source: Figures are computed on the basis of the data collected from *Statistics on RRBs*, NABARD Publications, Mumbai and Bhubaneswar.

Table 6.20

Employee Productivity of RRBs in Orissa (Business per Employee)

(Rs. in Lakhs)

Sl. No.	RRBs	1992-93	1993-94	1994-95	1995-96	1996-97	1997-98	1998-99	1999-2000	Average
1.	Puri GB	10.26	15.22	18.84	23.29	28.41	34.79	42.68	64.97	25.31
	Growth (%)		48.34	23.78	23.62	21.98	22.46	22.68	52.23	30.73
2.	Bolangir GB	11.46	11.98	15.63	19.64	24.89	32.48	47.71	34.40	24.84
	Growth (%)		4.54	31.25	25.66	26.73	30.49	46.89	-27.44	19.73
3.	Cuttack GB	19.27	20.26	23.69	28.03	31.54	36.59	38.72	48.85	30.87
	Growth (%)		5.14	16.93	18.32	12.52	16.01	5.82	26.16	14.41
4.	Koraput GB	15.00	18.55	22.05	27.37	32.84	40.02	46.97	51.36	31.77
	Growth (%)		23.67	18.87	24.13	19.99	21.86	17.37	9.35	19.32
5.	Kalahandi GB	9.15	10.47	14.78	18.68	24.24	29.76	36.61	43.00	23.34
	Growth (%)		14.43	41.17	26.39	29.76	22.77	23.02	17.45	25.00
6.	Baitarani GB	8.48	11.67	16.07	20.89	27.16	34.80	44.41	55.95	27.43
	Growth (%)		37.62	37.70	29.99	30.31	28.13	27.61	25.99	31.01
7.	Balasore GB	10.63	14.44	17.20	20.80	22.00	24.63	27.75	33.73	21.40
	Growth (%)		35.84	19.11	20.93	5.77	11.95	12.67	21.55	18.26
8.	Rushikulya GB	13.58	17.21	21.63	27.58	37.47	48.09	61.25	80.28	38.39
	Growth (%)		26.73	25.68	27.51	35.86	28.34	27.37	31.07	28.94
9.	Dhenkanal GB	16.01	18.66	22.43	31.44	43.66	58.26	76.30	97.87	46.83
	Growth (%)		16.55	20.20	40.17	38.87	33.44	30.96	28.27	29.78
10.	All RRBs in Orissa	12.81	15.22	18.84	23.29	28.41	34.79	42.68	56.71	29.09
	Growth (%)		18.81	23.78	23.62	21.98	22.46	22.68	32.87	23.74

Source: Figures are computed on the basis of the data collected from *Statistics on RRBs*, NABARD Publications, Mumbai and Bhubaneswar.

at Rs. 46.83 lakhs followed by that of Rushikulya GB with Rs. 38.39 lakhs. On the other hand, Balasore GB recorded the lowest average employee productivity of Rs. 21.40 lakhs followed by Kalahandi GB with Rs. 23.34 lakhs during the said period. Four RRBs viz. Cuttack GB, Koraput GB, Rushikulya GB and Dhenkanal GB have shown higher and the remaining 3, lower average employee productivity than the State's average of Rs. 29.09 lakhs. In terms of growth rate of the employee productivity ratio of the RRBs in Orissa, it is the Cuttack GB which showed the lowest growth rate of 14.41 per cent. Balasore GB and Koraput GB followed the Cuttack GB with growth rates of 18.26 per cent and 19.32 per cent respectively. At the upper end, Baitarani GB had the highest growth rate of 31.01 per cent followed by that of Puri GB with a growth rate of 30.73 per cent and Dhenkanal GB with 29.78 per cent. Thus, 5 RRBs viz. Puri GB, Kalahandi GB, Baitarani GB, Rushikulya GB and Dhenkanal GB have higher growth rates and 4 RRBs such as Bolangir GB, Cuttack GB, Koraput GB and Balasore GB have lower growth rates than the State's average of 23.74 per cent during the period under review.

Profitability Analysis of Individual RRBs in Orissa

6.5.1. This section deals with the profitability analysis of individual RRBs in Orissa. For analytical comparison of the profitability performance of the RRBs in Orissa, the same framework developed by the Khusro Committee has been used. For this purpose, the key indicators of profitability namely, average return on funds, average cost of funds, financial margins, miscellaneous income to WFs, transaction costs to WFs, risk costs to WFs and net margins, as defined earlier, have been computed for each of the individual RRBs for the period from 1992-93 to 1999-2000. The trend of these ratios and their growth rates have been studied.

Average Return on Funds

6.5.2. Table 6.21 presents the average return on funds of the RRBs for the period from 1992-93 to 1999-2000. The table reveals that the Dhenkanal GB has shown the highest average return on funds of 11.13 per cent followed by Koraput GB and Rushikulya GB with 10.62 per cent and 9.76 per cent respectively. Viewing from the bottom, the three lowest average figures of 6.03 per cent, 6.17 per cent and 7.54 per cent have been registered by Bolangir GB, Balasore GB and Puri GB respectively. The overall annual growth rate of average return on funds has varied between 9.54 per cent (Puri GB) and -7.83 per cent (Balasore GB). It is further observed from the table that Bolangir GB, Cuttack GB and Balasore GB have registered negative overall growth rates of-0.86 per cent, -4.84 per cent and -7.83 per cent respectively. The average return on funds of Puri GB, Kalahandi GB, Rushikulya GB and Dhenkanal GB have shown improvement towards the later part of the period referred to above.

Average Cost of Funds

6.5.3. Table 6.22 presents the average cost of funds of the individual RRBs in Orissa from 1992-93 to 1999-2000. Baitarani GB has shown consecutively declining ratio from 7.86 per cent to 6.50 per cent and Dhenkanal GB from 8.86 per cent to 8.35 per cent during the period from 1996-97 to 1999-2000. The average cost of funds of the remaining 7 RRBs does not follow any trend during the period covered under study. The overall average cost of funds was the highest at 9.03 per cent in case of Balasore GB followed by 8.06 per cent and 7.47 per cent in cases of Dhenkanal GB and Puri GB respectively. Bolangir GB, Cuttack GB, Kalahandi GB, Baitarani GB and Rushikulya GB have registered negative overall growth rates and the rest 4 RRBs in the State have shown positive overall growth rates of average cost of funds during the period under review. The lowest overall average cost of funds at 5.57 per cent and the lowest growth rate thereof at -3.26 per cent were witnessed by the Kalahandi GB and Cuttack GB respectively.

Financial Margins

6.5.4. Table 6.23 presents the financial margins of the RRBs in Orissa from 1992-93 to 1999-2000. In spite of the erratic trends of the average return on funds and the average cost of funds during the period referred to above, barring two viz., Bolangir GB and Balasore GB, the rest 7 RRBs in the State have positive financial margins. The overall average financial margin for the period was the highest in case of Koraput GB with 4.65 per cent followed by Dhenkanal GB at 3.07 per cent and Rushikulya GB at 2.34 per cent. The lowest financial margin of -2.86 per cent was recorded by Balasore GB. There is steady

Table 6.21
Profitability Analysis of RRBs in Orissa: Average Return on Funds

(Figures in per cent)

Sl. No.	RRBs	1992-93	1993-94	1994-95	1995-96	1996-97	1997-98	1998-99	1999-2000	Average
1.	Puri GB	6.12	5.79	7.09	6.55	7.78	7.21	8.88	10.90	7.54
	Growth (%)		-5.35	22.45	-7.62	18.78	-7.33	23.16	22.75	9.54
2.	Bolangir GB	6.49	6.95	7.37	4.78	5.48	5.59	6.07	5.51	6.03
	Growth (%)		7.09	6.04	-35.14	14.64	2.01	8.59	-9.23	-0.86
3.	Cuttack GB	10.74	10.69	8.63	7.89	8.51	6.65	6.66	7.21	8.37
	Growth (%)		-0.47	-19.27	-8.57	7.86	-21.87	0.15	8.26	-4.84
4.	Koraput GB	11.03	9.68	11.00	9.40	11.34	10.97	10.81	10.73	10.62
	Growth (%)		-12.24	13.64	-14.55	20.64	-3.26	-1.46	-0.74	0.29
5.	Kalahandi GB	8.58	7.96	7.44	6.84	6.77	8.01	8.47	8.85	7.87
	Growth (%)		-7.23	-6.53	-8.06	-1.02	18.32	5.74	4.49	0.82
6.	Baitarani GB	6.52	6.70	6.53	7.47	8.93	8.39	8.37	8.29	7.65
	Growth (%)		2.76	-2.54	14.40	19.54	-6.05	-0.24	-0.96	3.84
7.	Balasore GB	9.48	9.13	7.56	5.22	4.45	4.29	4.29	4.95	6.17
	Growth (%)		-3.69	-17.20	-30.95	-14.75	-3.60	-	15.38	-7.83
8.	Rushikulya GB	10.23	10.13	8.03	8.52	9.77	10.11	10.78	10.52	9.76
	Growth (%)		-0.98	-20.73	6.10	14.67	3.48	6.63	-2.41	0.97
9.	Dhenkanal GB	11.58	9.51	9.10	9.52	11.10	12.69	12.50	13.00	11.13
	Growth (%)		-17.88	-4.31	4.62	16.60	14.32	1.50	4.00	2.69
10.	All RRBs in Orissa	8.48	8.05	8.13	7.36	8.24	8.40	8.53	8.88	8.25
	Growth (%)		-5.07	0.99	-9.59	12.11	1.94	1.55	4.10	0.86

Source: All Ratios are computed as per the data figured in the *Statistics on RRBs*, NABARD Publications, Mumbai and Bhubaneswar.

Table 6.22

Profitability Analysis of RRBs in Orissa: Average Cost of Funds

(Figures in per cent)

Sl. No.	*RRBs*	*1992-93*	*1993-94*	*1994-95*	*1995-96*	*1996-97*	*1997-98*	*1998-99*	*1999-2000*	*Average*
1.	Puri GB	7.91	7.12	7.09	7.04	7.95	6.93	7.35	8.38	7.47
	Growth (%)		-9.36	-0.42	-0.71	12.93	-12.83	6.06	14.01	1.38
2.	Bolangir GB	8.58	6.91	7.17	5.74	6.18	6.16	6.51	6.55	6.73
	Growth (%)		-19.46	3.76	-19.94	7.67	-0.32	5.68	0.61	-3.14
3.	Cuttack GB	9.44	8.58	9.31	6.20	7.28	5.88	6.16	6.67	7.44
	Growth (%)		-9.11	8.51	-33.40	17.42	-19.23	4.76	8.28	-3.26
4.	Koraput GB	5.65	5.66	5.78	5.21	5.99	6.25	6.42	6.78	5.97
	Growth (%)		0.18	2.12	-9.86	14.97	4.34	2.72	5.61	3.58
5.	Kalahandi GB	5.71	5.32	6.01	6.10	6.29	5.44	4.66	4.97	5.57
	Growth (%)		-6.83	12.97	1.50	3.11	-13.51	-14.34	6.65	-1.49
6.	Baitarani GB	7.78	6.42	7.24	7.70	7.86	7.74	7.08	6.50	7.29
	Growth (%)		-17.48	12.77	6.35	2.08	-1.53	-8.53	-8.19	-2.08
7.	Balasore GB	8.02	7.91	8.14	8.46	9.26	10.38	10.87	9.18	9.03
	Growth (%)		-1.37	2.91	3.93	9.46	12.10	4.72	-15.55	2.32
8.	Rushikulya GB	8.06	7.31	6.90	7.54	7.28	7.28	7.21	7.81	7.43
	Growth (%)		-9.31	-5.61	9.28	-3.45	0.00	-0.96	8.32	-0.25
9.	Dhenkanal GB	7.47	7.26	7.70	7.90	8.86	8.54	8.40	8.35	8.06
	Growth (%)		-2.81	6.06	2.60	12.15	-3.61	-1.64	-0.60	1.74
10.	All RRBs in Orissa	7.43	5.82	7.26	6.88	7.44	7.36	7.17	7.24	7.08
	Growth (%)	36.33	-21.67	24.74	-5.23	8.14	-1.08	-2.58	0.98	5.66

Source: All Ratios are computed as per the data figured in the *Statistics on RRBs*, NABARD Publications, Mumbai and Bhubaneswar.

Table 6.23
Profitability Analysis of RRBs in Orissa: Financial Margins

(Figures in per cent)

Sl. No.	RRBs	1992-93	1993-94	1994-95	1995-96	1996-97	1997-98	1998-99	1999-2000	Average
1.	Puri GB	-1.79	-1.33	0	-0.49	-0.17	0.28	1.53	2.52	0.07
	Growth (%)		25.70	0.00	00	-65.31	264.71	446.43	107.65	146.53
2.	Bolangir GB	-2.09	0.04	0.20	-0.96	-0.70	-0.57	-0.44	-1.04	-0.70
	Growth (%)		101.91	400.00	-580.00	27.08	18.57	22.81	-136.36	-20.86
3.	Cuttack GB	1.30	2.11	1.32	1.69	1.23	0.77	0.50	0.54	1.18
	Growth (%)		62.31	-37.44	28.03	-27.22	-37.40	-35.06	8.00	-5.54
4.	Koraput GB	5.38	4.02	5.22	4.19	5.35	4.72	4.39	3.95	4.65
	Growth (%)		-25.28	29.85	-19.73	27.68	-11.78	-6.99	-10.02	-2.32
5.	Kalahandi GB	2.87	2.64	1.43	0.74	0.48	2.57	3.81	3.88	2.30
	Growth (%)		-8.01	-45.83	-48.25	-35.14	435.42	48.25	1.84	49.75
6.	Baitarani GB	-1.26	0.28	-0.71	-0.23	1.07	0.65	1.29	1.80	0.36
	Growth (%)		122.22	-353.57	67.61	565.22	-39.25	98.46	39.53	71.46
7.	Balasore GB	1.46	1.22	-0.58	-3.24	-4.81	-6.09	-6.58	-4.23	-2.86
	Growth (%)		-16.44	-147.54	-458.62	-48.46	-26.61	-8.05	35.71	-95.72
8.	Rushikulya GB	2.17	2.82	1.13	0.98	2.49	2.83	3.58	2.71	2.34
	Growth (%)		29.95	-59.93	-13.27	154.08	13.65	26.50	-24.30	18.10
9.	Dhenkanal GB	4.11	2.25	1.40	1.62	2.24	4.15	4.10	4.65	3.07
	Growth (%)		-45.25	-37.78	15.71	38.27	85.27	-1.20	13.41	9.78
10.	All RRBs in Orissa	1.05	2.23	0.87	0.48	0.80	1.04	1.36	1.64	1.18
	Growth (%)		112.38	-60.99	-44.83	66.67	30.00	30.77	20.59	22.08

Source: All Ratios are computed as per the data figured in the *Statistics on RRBs*, NABARD Publications, Mumbai and Bhubaneswar.

improvement in the financial margins of 5 RRBs during the said period. These RRBs are: Puri GB from -1.79 per cent in 1992-93 to 2.52 per cent in 1999-2000, Kalahandi GB from 0.48 per cent in 1996-97 to 3.88 per cent in 1999-2000; Baitarani GB from 1.07 per cent in 1996-97 to 1.80 per cent in 1999-2000; Rushikulya GB from 0.98 per cent in 1995-96 to 3.58 per cent in 1998-99 with a slight fall to 2.71 per cent in 1999-2000 and Dhenkanal GB from 1.40 per cent in 1994-95 to 4.65 per cent in 1999-2000. Out of the remaining 4 RRBs, 2 RRBs have shown positive financial margins but have displayed declining trend during the period under review. They are Cuttack GB with its financial margin declining from 1.69 per cent in 1995-96 to 0.54 per cent in 1999-2000 and Koraput GB with that declining from 5.35 per cent in 1996-97 to 3.95 per cent in 1999-2000. The remaining 2 RRBs, namely, Bolangir GB and Balasore GB have been displaying negative financial margins since last 5 and 6 years respectively. The positive financial margins of 7 RRBs as stated above may be attributed to the flow of cost-free funds to these RRBs by way of recapitalisation support. Out of the remaining 2 RRBs with negative financial margin Bolangir GB was brought only in 1999-2000 and Balasore GB is yet to be covered under the restructuring programme under which recapitalisation support is provided to the RRBs by GOI and other stakeholders.

Miscellaneous Income to Working Funds

6.5.5. Miscellaneous income as percentage to the working funds of the RRBs have been presented in the Table 6.24 shows that the overall average of this ratio for the period is the highest at 0.47 per cent in case of Cuttack GB followed by 0.43 per cent and 0.40 per cent by Kalahandi GB and Puri GB respectively. At the lower end, the Baitarani GB, Bolangir GB and Dhenkanal GB recorded the lowest overall average amount of this ratio at 0.09 per cent and 0.11 per cent respectively during the period. The overall average growth rate has fluctuated between -14.17 per cent (Dhenkanal GB) and 104.80 per cent (Baitarani GB). It is observed from the table that this ratio has always remained constant at less than 1 per cent in cases of all the RRBs during all these years. However, Cuttack GB has shown this ratio at 1.19 per cent in 1999-2000. The small figures of this ratio were due to the miscellaneous income of the RRBs remaining very insignificant in cases of almost all of them in Orissa despite the several relaxations accorded to these banks in recent years.

Table 6.24

Profitability Analysis of RRBs in Orissa: Miscellaneous Income to Working Funds

(Rs. in Lakhs)

Sl. No.	*RRBs*	*1992-93*	*1993-94*	*1994-95*	*1995-96*	*1996-97*	*1997-98*	*1998-99*	*1999-2000*	*Average*
1.	Puri GB	0.18	0.17	0.39	0.33	0.37	0.52	0.31	0.94	0.40
	Growth (%)		-5.56	129.41	-15.38	12.12	40.54	-40.38	203.23	46.28
2.	Bolangir GB	0.003	0.004	0.08	0.08	0.11	0.12	0.30	0.15	0.11
	Growth (%)		33.33	1900.00	00.00	37.5	9.09	150.00	-50.00	29.99
3.	Cuttack GB	0.12	0.12	0.37	0.35	0.30	0.32	0.99	1.19	0.47
	Growth (%)		00.00	208.33	-5.41	-14.29	6.67	209.38	20.20	60.70
4.	Koraput GB	0.32	0.25	0.52	0.47	0.38	0.29	0.24	0.19	0.33
	Growth (%)		-21.88	108.00	-9.62	-19.15	-23.68	-17.24	-20.83	-0.63
5.	Kalahandi GB	0.40	0.34	0.58	0.90	0.22	0.25	0.20	0.56	0.43
	Growth (%)		-15.00	70.59	55.17	-75.56	13.64	-20.00	180.00	29.76
6.	Baitarani GB	0.07	0.01	0.09	0.12	0.12	0.12	0.09	0.10	0.09
	Growth (%)		-85.71	800.00	33.33	0.00	0.00	-25.00	11.11	104.80
7.	Balasore GB	0.41	0.33	0.24	0.21	0.32	0.51	0.41	0.40	0.35
	Growth (%)		-19.51	-27.27	-12.50	52.38	59.38	-19.61	-2.44	4.35
8.	Rushikulya GB	0.23	0.12	0.17	0.23	0.74	0.39	0.28	0.92	0.39
	Growth (%)		-47.83	41.67	35.29	221.74	-47.30	-28.21	228.57	57.70
9.	Dhenkanal GB	0.06	0.03	-	-	-	0.20	0.25	0.35	0.11
	Growth (%)		-50.00	-100.00			-	25.00	40.00	-14.17
10.	All RRBs in Orissa	0.18	0.15	0.27	0.30	0.28	0.30	0.34	0.95	0.35
	Growth (%)	-14.29	-16.67	80.00	11.11	-6.67	7.14	13.33	179.41	31.67

Source: Figures are computed on the basis of the data collected from *Statistics on RRBs*, NABARD Publications, Mumbai and Bhubaneswar.

Table 6.25

Profitability Analysis of RRBs in Orissa: Transaction Costs to Working Funds

(Figures in per cent)

Sl. No.	*RRBs*	*1992-93*	*1993-94*	*1994-95*	*1995-96*	*1996-97*	*1997-98*	*1998-99*	*1999-2000*	*Average*
1.	Puri GB	7.29	7.52	7.16	5.97	5.27	4.95	3.64	3.40	5.65
	Growth (%)	-	3.16	-4.79	-16.62	-11.73	-6.07	-26.46	-6.59	-9.87
2.	Bolangir GB	6.01	5.91	9.09	5.00	5.13	4.40	4.85	4.57	5.62
	Growth (%)	-	-1.66	53.81	-44.99	2.6	-14.23	10.23	-5.77	-0.001
3.	Cuttack GB	5.63	5.49	8.24	5.75	4.66	3.09	3.04	3.20	4.89
	Growth (%)	-	-2.49	50.09	-30.22	-18.96	-33.69	-1.62	5.26	-4.52
4.	Koraput GB	4.99	4.61	4.93	5.21	5.02	4.18	4.00	4.31	4.54
	Growth (%)	-	-7.62	6.94	5.68	-3.65	-16.73	3.37	-15.75	-5.06
5.	Kalahandi GB	7.65	7.55	9.67	9.08	7.60	5.32	3.41	3.96	6.78
	Growth (%)	-	-1.31	28.08	-6.10	-16.30	-30.00	-35.90	16.13	-6.49
6.	Baitarani GB	8.21	6.32	6.70	5.96	5.05	4.57	4.14	2.55	5.44
	Growth (%)	-	-23.02	6.01	-11.04	-15.27	-9.50	-9.41	-38.41	-14.38
7.	Balasore GB	7.94	8.14	7.81	7.86	6.67	6.99	6.67	6.14	7.28
	Growth (%)	-	2.52	-4.05	0.64	-15.14	4.80	-4.58	-7.95	-2.97
8.	Rushikulya GB	6.77	7.73	5.18	4.44	4.17	2.56	2.34	2.19	4.42
	Growth (%)	-	14.18	-32.99	-14.29	-6.08	-38.61	-8.59	-6.41	-13.26
9.	Dhenkanal GB	5.44	5.10	4.50	4.53	3.76	2.53	2.31	2.25	3.92
	Growth (%)	-	-6.25	-11.76	0.67	-17.00	-32.71	-8.70	-2.60	-11.56
10.	All RRBs in Orissa	6.48	6.09	7.03	5.98	5.16	4.38	2.83	3.63	5.20
	Growth (%)	0.78	-6.02	15.44	-14.94	-13.71	-15.12	-35.39	28.27	-5.09

Source: Figures are computed on the basis of the data collected from *Statistics on RRBs*, NABARD Publications, Mumbai and Bhubaneswar.

Transaction Costs to Working Funds

6.5.6. The transaction costs as percentage to the working funds of the individual RRBs in Orissa have been exhibited in the Table 6.25 for the study period. The analysis of the overall average growth rate for the period reveals that all the RRBs in the State have registered overall negative growth rates which varied between –0.001 per cent of Bolangir GB and -14.38 per cent of Baitarani GB.

The negative growth rate is due to the declining trend of this ratio in cases of all the RRBs especially during the later half of the period under study. Even in the case of Bolangir GB exhibiting a very slow overall decline rate of this ratio at 0.001 per cent, the transaction costs to working funds ratio has remained almost constant and hovered around 5 per cent during the years from 1995-96 and onwards. Thus, it is indeed a significant and positive feature that all the RRBs in Orissa could reduce the transaction cost as was reflected by the analysis of this ratio.

Risk Costs to Working Funds

6.5.7. Risk costs as percentage to the working funds of the RRBs have been shown in Table 6.26 for the period from 1992-93 to 1999-2000. The overall average amount of risk costs to working funds was the highest in case of Cuttack GB at 3.12 per cent followed by Bolangir GB and Balasore GB with 2.30 per cent and 1.84 per cent respectively. The lowest risk cost to working fund ratio was recorded by Rushikulya GB (0.82 per cent) and Puri GB (0.96 per cent) during the period. The trend analysis of this ratio reveals that the ratio was the highest in cases of almost all the RRBs mainly in three years, i.e., from 1995-96 to 1997-98 of the study period. This may be in view of the adoption of the provisioning norms by the RRBs on account of which they are required to create provisions against their incremental non-performing assets. The downward trend in this ratio observed towards the last two to three years of the study period was a positive development for the RRBs in the post-reform period.

Net Margins

6.5.8. Table 6.27 presents the net margins of the RRBs in Orissa during the period from 1992-93 to 1999-2000. This is the most important

Table 6.26

Profitability Analysis of RRBs in Orissa: Risk Costs to Working Funds

(Figures in per cent)

Sl. No.	*RRBs*	*1992-93*	*1993-94*	*1994-95*	*1995-96*	*1996-97*	*1997-98*	*1998-99*	*1999-2000*	*Average*
1.	Puri GB	0.97	0.81	0.57	0.77	1.68	2.18	0.66	-	0.96
	Growth (%)		-16.49	-29.63	35.09	118.18	29.76	-69.72		
2.	Bolangir GB		-	1.13	5.39	4.16	3.54	1.61	0.26	2.30
	Growth (%)	-			376.99	-22.82	-14.90	-54.52	-83.85	
3.	Cuttack GB	0.20	0.19	13.33	0.03	11.34	0.65	-	0.82	3.12
	Growth (%)		-5.00	6915.79	-99.77	37700.00	-94.27		-182.93	
4.	Koraput GB	0.10	1.56	2.25	3.92	3.18	-	0.10	0.01	1.39
	Growth (%)		1460.00	44.23	74.22	-18.88		-96.86	-90.00	
5.	Kalahandi GB	1.40	0.48	2.34	-	5.53	0.59	-	0.25	1.32
	Growth (%)		-65.71	387.5		136.32	-89.33		-57.63	
6.	Baitarani GB	0.01	0.002	1.78	-	4.26	1.78	0.30	0.19	1.04
	Growth (%)		-80	88900.00		193.33	-58.22	-83.15	-36.67	
7.	Balasore GB	0.18	0.40	0.51	0.51	8.01	1.92	2.12	1.06	1.84
	Growth (%)		122.22	27.5	0.00	1470.59	-76.03	10.42	-50.00	
8.	Rushikulya GB	1.27	0.53	0.86	1.25	2.27	0.27	0.10	-	0.82
	Growth (%)		-58.27	62.26	45.35	81.60	-88.11	-62.96		
9.	Dhenkanal GB	2.22	2.42	2.20	1.17	1.26	1.33	1.30	1.09	1.62
	Growth (%)		9.01	-9.09	-46.82	7.69	5.56	-2.26	-16.15	
10.	All RRBs in Orissa	0.52	0.64	2.77	1.45	4.63	1.36	0.54	0.27	1.52
	Growth (%)		23.08	332.81	-47.65	219.31	-70.63	-60.29	-50.00	

Source: Figures are computed on the basis of the data collected from *Statistics on RRBs*, NABARD Publications, Mumbai and Bhubaneswar.

Table 6.27
Profitability Analysis of RRBs in Orissa: Net Margins

(Figures in per cent)

Sl. No.	*RRBs*	*1992-93*	*1993-94*	*1994-95*	*1995-96*	*1996-97*	*1997-98*	*1998-99*	*1999-2000*	*Average*
1.	Puri GB	-9.87	-9.49	-7.34	-6.90	-6.75	-6.33	-2.46	0.06	-6.14
	Growth (%)		3.85	22.66	05.99	2.17	6.22	61.14	102.44	29.21
2.	Bolangir GB	-8.10	-5.87	-9.94	-11.27	-9.88	-8.39	-6.60	-5.73	-6.60
	Growth (%)		27.53	-69.34	-13.38	12.33	15.08	21.33	13.18	-76.45
3.	Cuttack GB	-4.41	-3.45	-21.88	-3.74	-14.47	-2.65	-1.55	-0.65	-8.22
	Growth (%)		21.77	-534.20	82.91	-286.90	81.69	41.51	58.06	0.96
4.	Koraput GB	0.61	-1.90	-1.44	-4.47	-2.47	0.83	0.53	0.76	-0.94
	Growth (%)		-411.47	24.21	-210.42	44.74	133.60	-36.14	43.40	-58.87
5.	Kalahandi GB	-5.78	-5.05	-10.00	-7.44	-12.43	-3.09	0.60	0.23	-5.37
	Growth (%)		12.63	-98.02	25.6	-67.07	75.14	119.42	-61.67	0.86
6.	Baitarani GB	-9.41	-6.03	-9.10	-6.07	-8.12	-5.58	-3.06	-0.84	-6.03
	Growth (%)		35.92	-50.92	33.30	-33.77	31.28	45.16	72.55	19.07
7.	Balasore GB	-6.25	-6.99	-8.66	-11.40	-19.17	-14.49	-14.96	-11.04	-11.62
	Growth (%)		-11.84	-23.89	-31.64	-68.16	24.41	-3.24	26.20	-12.59
8.	Rushikulya GB	-5.64	-5.32	-4.74	-4.48	-3.21	0.39	1.42	1.45	-2.52
	Growth (%)		5.67	10.90	5.49	28.35	112.15	264.10	2.11	61.25
9.	Dhenkanal GB	-3.49	-5.24	-5.30	-4.08	-2.78	0.49	0.74	1.66	-2.25
	Growth (%)		-50.14	-1.15	23.02	31.86	117.63	51.02	124.32	42.37
10.	All RRBs in Orissa	-5.77	-4.35	-8.66	-6.65	-8.71	-4.40	-1.67	-1.31	-5.19
	Growth (%)	-30.25	24.61	-99.08	23.21	-30.98	49.48	62.05	21.56	2.94

Source: Figures are computed on the basis of the data collected from *Statistics on RRBs*, NABARD Publications, Mumbai and Bhubaneswar.

indicator for ascertaining the profitability performance of the RRBs in Orissa. The analysis of the overall average figures of net margins of the RRBs during the period reveals that all these banks in the State have recorded negative net margins. Koraput GB, Dhenkanal GB and Rushikulya GB are in a better position than other RRBs in the State in view of these three banks recording the three lowest average negative net margins of -0.94 per cent, -2.25 per cent and -2.52 per cent respectively. On the other hand, the three highest average net margins of -11.62 per cent, -8.22 per cent and -6.60 per cent of Balasore GB, Cuttack GB and Bolangir GB respectively indicate the poorer profitability performance of these RRBs than others in the State. Existence of a large number of accounts with small amount of loan per account and lower lending rate which after providing the DICGC premium, was hardly adequate to cover the cost of raising the RRBs' resources (not to speak of their transaction costs), are factors attributed to the RRBs' working with negative margins on their lending portfolio after meeting the establishment management cost and risk cost. However, it is observed from the table that Puri GB have shown positive net margins for the last year, Kalahandi GB for the last two years, Koraput GB, Rushikulya GB and Dhenkanal GB for the last three years during the period of study. Thus, the number of RRBs registering positive net margins as on 31 March 2000 is 5.

The trends of the net margins during the period from 1992-93 to 1999-2000 and net margins on 31 March 2000 of individual RRBs in Orissa have been exhibited in the form of graphs in Fig. 6.4 and Fig. 6.5 respectively. The trend analysis of the net margins of RRBs shows that Puri GB and Rushikulya GB have shown consistent improvement throughout the period of study. The net margins of Puri GB have increased from -9.87 per cent in 1992-93 to 0.06 per cent in 1999-2000 and that of Rushikulya GB from -5.64 per cent to 1.45 per cent during the same period. Between these two RRBs, the pace of improvement of net margins in case of Rushikulya GB was much faster, i.e., 61.25 per cent than 29.21 per cent Puri GB. Dhenkanal GB has witnessed steady improvement in its net margin from -5.30 per cent in 1994-95 to 1.66 per cent in 1999-2000. Two RRBs viz., Bolangir GB and Koraput GB have shown improvement from 1995-96 onwards continuously. Three RRBs, namely, Cuttack GB, Kalahandi GB and Baitarani GB have also recorded steadily improving trend in their respective net margins from

Fig. 6.4 : Trends of Net Margins of Individual RRBs in Orissa (From 1992-93 to 1999-2000)

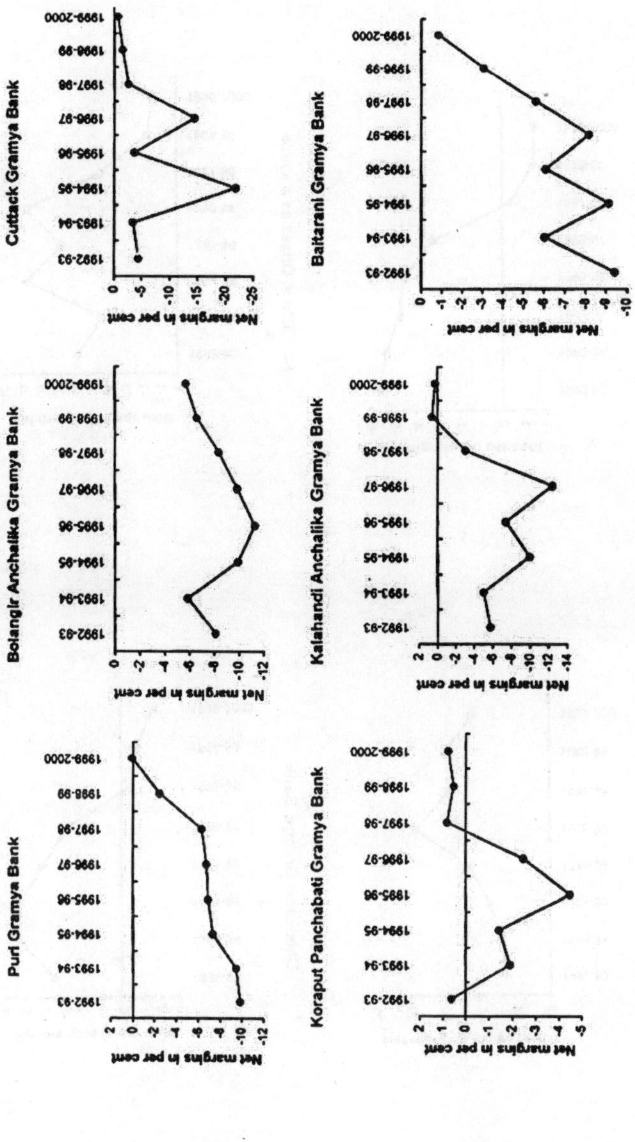

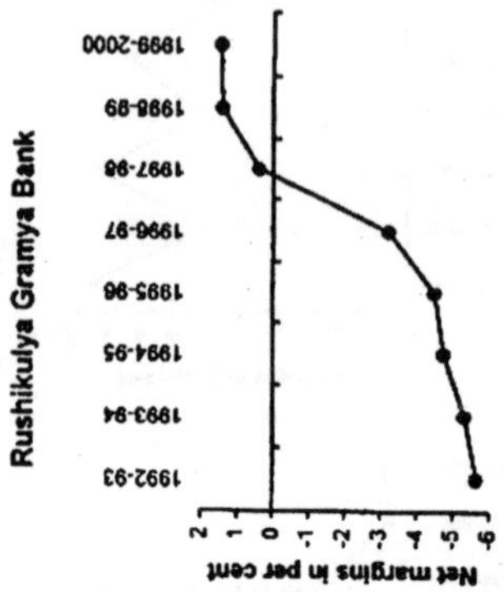
Rushikulya Gramya Bank
Net margins in per cent
1992-93
1993-94
1994-95
1995-96
1996-97
1997-98
1998-99
1999-2000

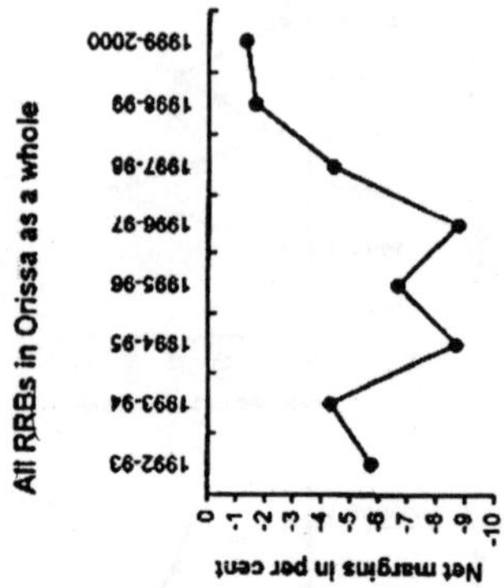
All RRBs in Orissa as a whole
Net margins in per cent
1992-93
1993-94
1994-95
1995-96
1996-97
1997-98
1998-99
1999-2000

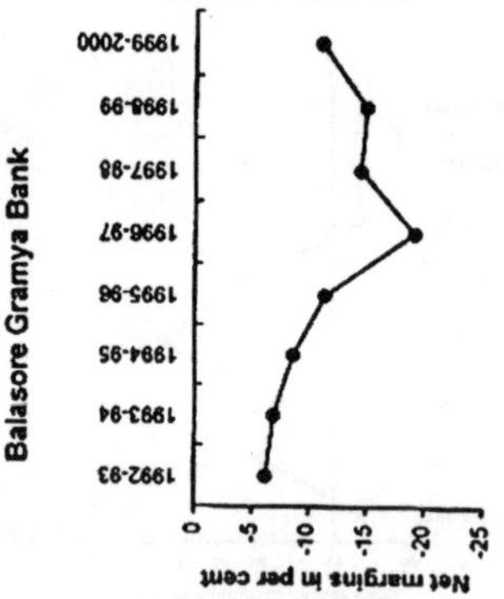
Balasore Gramya Bank
Net margins in per cent
1992-93
1993-94
1994-95
1995-96
1996-97
1997-98
1998-99
1999-2000

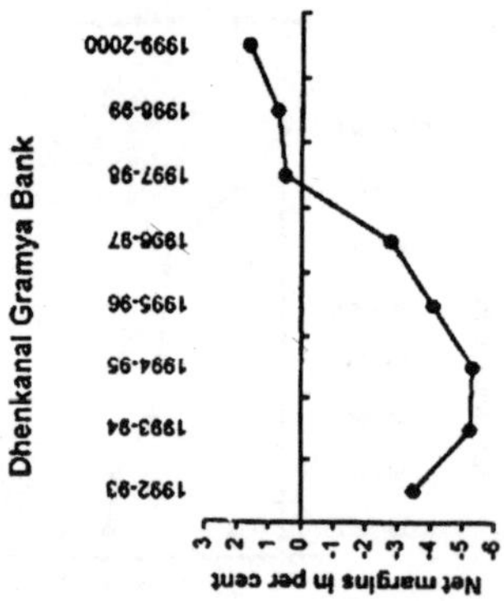
Dhenkanal Gramya Bank
Net margins in per cent
1992-93
1993-94
1994-95
1995-96
1996-97
1997-98
1998-99
1999-2000

Fig. 6.5
Net Margins of Individual RRBs in Orissa
(As on 31 March 2000)

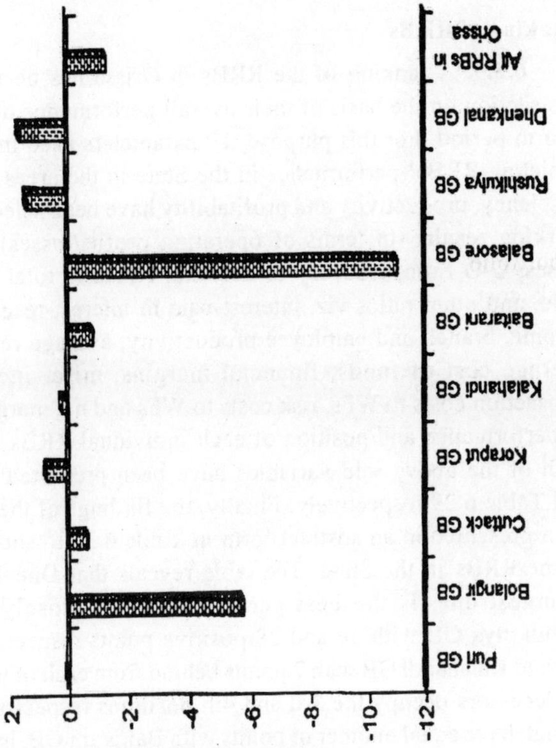

1997-98 to 1999-2000. Even the Balasore GB, which has been lagging behind other RRBs, also seems to be on the path of profitability improvement. This is evident from the fact that the net margin recorded at -19.17 per cent in 1996-97, remained around -14 per cent in the subsequent two years and was further reduced to -11.04 per cent in 1999-2000. The above analysis shows that the profitability of all the RRBs are showing indications of improvement.

Ranking of RRBs

6.5.9. A ranking of the RRBs in Orissa has been attempted in this section on the basis of their overall performance during the post-reform period. For this purpose, 19 parameters used in the study and depicting RRBs' performance in the State in the areas of operational efficiency, productivity and profitability have been selected. They are: working results (in terms of operating profits/losses), accumulated losses, C-D ratio, recovery to demand, NPAs to total advances, I-D ratio, and other ratios viz. interest-paid to interest-received, salary to income, branch and employee productivity, average return on funds, average cost of funds, financial margins, misc. income to WFs, transaction costs to WFs, risk costs to WFs and net margins. The trend of performance and position of each individual RRBs with regard to each of the above said variables have been presented in Table 6.28 and Table 6.29 respectively. Finally, the findings of these tables have been presented in an abstract form in Table 6.30 to show the ranking of the RRBs in the State. The table reveals that Dhenkanal GB, the youngest one, is the best performing RRB closely followed by Rushikulya GB with 30 and 28 positive points respectively. Koraput GB and Kalahandi GB with 7 points behind from each of their respective predecessors occupy the 3rd and 4th positions respectively. Puri GB, though have equal number of points with Baitarani GB, has been placed ahead of the latter in the 5th position in view of its operating profit and positive net margin in the year 1999-2000. Baitarani GB and Cuttack GB with 9 and 3 positive points, have occupied the 6th and 7th place respectively. This obviously, leaves the remaining two RRBs viz. Bolangir GB and Balasore GB with negative points of-13 and -23, to be positioned in the 8th and 9th places respectively. The difference between these two banks and others including the loss-making ones is that the latter, showing symptoms of improvement in their financial

Table 6.28

Variable-wise Trend Analysis of the Performance of Individual RRBs in Orissa

(Period from 1992-93 to 1999-2000)

Sl. No.	RRBs	Working Results	Acc. Losses	C-D Ratio	I-D Ratio	Recovery to Demand Ratio	NPAs to Total Advances	Acc. Losses to Total Assets	Assets per Staff	Int. paid to Int. Received	Salary to Income	Branch Productivity	Employee Productivity	Avg. Return on Funds	Avg. Cost of Funds	Financial Margin	Misc. Income to WFs	Transaction Cost to WFs	Risk Cost to WFs	Net Margins	Total F	Total A	Total
1.	Puri GB	F	F	A	A	F	F	F	F	F	F	F	F	F	A	F	F	F	A	F	15	4	19
2.	Bolangir GB	A	F	A	F	F	A	F	F	A	A	F	F	A	A	A	F	F	F	F	11	8	19
3.	Cuttack GB	F	F	A	F	A	F	F	F	A	F	F	F	A	A	A	F	F	F	F	13	6	19
4.	Koraput GB	F	F	A	F	F	A	F	F	A	F	F	F	A	A	A	A	F	F	F	12	7	19
5.	Kalahandi GB	F	F	A	F	F	F	F	F	F	F	F	F	F	F	F	F	F	F	F	18	1	19
6.	Bitarani GB	F	F	A	F	F	F	F	F	A	F	F	F	A	F	F	A	F	F	F	15	4	19
7.	Balasore GB	A	F	A	F	A	A	A	F	A	A	F	F	A	A	A	A	F	A	A	6	13	19
8.	Rushikulya GB	F	F	A	F	F	F	F	F	A	F	F	F	F	F	F	F	F	F	F	17	2	19
9.	Dhenkanal GB	F	F	A	F	F	F	F	F	F	A	F	F	F	F	F	F	F	F	F	17	2	19
10.	All RRBs in Orissa	F	F	A	F	F	F	F	F	F	F	F	F	F	F	F	F	F	F	F	18	1	19

Note: F: Favourable Trend; A: Adverse Trend.

Source: Based on the findings of the data figured in the Tables from 6.7 to 6.27.

Table 6.29

Position of the Individual RRBs on tbe Basis of their Variable-wise Performance (Period from 1992-93 to 1999-2000)

Sl. No.	RRBs	Working Results as on 31.3.2000	Acc. Losses as on 31.3.2000	C-D Ratio (Avg. Rate of Decline)	I-D Ratio	Recovery to Demand Ratio	NPAs to Total Advances	Acc. Losses to Total Assets	Assets per Staff	Int. paid to Int. Received	Salary to Income	Branch Productivity	Employee Productivity	Avg. Return on Funds	Avg. Cost of Funds	Financial Margin	Misc. Income to WFs	Transaction Cost to WFs	Risk Cost to WFs	Net Margins as on 31.3.2000	Total: No. of first 3 positions (+)	Total: No. of Last 3 Positions (-)
1.	Puri GB	5	7	3	8	1	4	6	5	5	5	5	6	7	7	7	3	7	2	5	4	6
2.	Bolangir GB	9	9	7	7	7	7	8	8	8	7	7	8	9	3	8	8	6	8	8	1	17
3.	Cuttack GB	7	8	5	4	8	8	4	4	7	4	2	4	4	6	5	1	4	9	6	2	6
4.	Koraput GB	3	1	2	1	3	5	1	3	3	3	3	3	2	2	1	6	3	5	3	16	0
5.	Kalahandi GB	4	4	8	5	6	6	5	7	1	8	9	7	5	1	4	2	8	4	4	3	6
6.	Bitarani GB	6	5	4	6	5	3	7	6	9	6	6	5	6	4	6	9	5	3	7	2	4
7.	Balasore GB	8	6	9	9	9	9	9	9	6	9	8	9	8	9	9	5	9	7	9	0	16
8.	Rushikulya GB	2	3	6	2	4	2	3	2	4	2	4	2	3	5	3	4	2	1	2	13	0
9.	Dhenkanal GB	1	2	1	3	2	1	2	1	2	1	1	1	1	8	2	7	1	6	1	16	2

Notes: (i) Figures represent position of RRBs; 1: The First Position, 9: The last position and so on.

(ii) Three variables viz. working results, accumulated losses and net margins relate to the year 1999-2000, whereas the remaining 16 variables are the average figure for the period from 1992-93 to 1999-2000.

Table 6.30

Ranking of RRBs in Orissa on the basis of their overall performance (During the period from 1992-93 to 1999-2000)

Sl. No.	*RRBs*	*Trends*		*Positions*		*Net Points*	*Overall Position*
		Favourable (+)	*Adverse (-)*	*No. of First 3 positions (+)*	*No. of Last 3 positions (-)*		
1.	PuriGB	+15	-4	+4	-6	+9	V
2.	Bolangir GB	+11	-8	+1	-17	-13	VIII
3.	Cuttack GB	+ 13	-6	+2	-6	+3	VII
4.	Koraput GB	+ 12	-7	+ 16	0	+21	III
5.	Kalahandi GB	+ 18	-1	+3	-6	+14	IV
6.	Baitarani GB	+15	-4	+2	-4	+9	VI
7.	Balasore GB	+6	-13	0	-16	-23	IX
8.	Rushikulya GB	+ 17	-2	+13	0	+28	II
9.	Dhenkanal GB	+ 17	-1	+16	-2	+30	I

Notes: Net Points = [The number of variables showing favourable trend + The number of variables showing the first three positions] – [The number of variables showing adverse trend + The number of variables showing the last three positions].

Source: *Statistics on RRBs*, NABARD Publications, Mumbai and Bhubaneshwar.

position, are on the path of recovery, whereas, the former two banks' positions are deteriorating. It can be concluded that the reform measures initiated by NABARD, RBI and GOI and applied on RRBs since early nineties and onwards seem to have left positive impact on the performance of majority of the RRBs in Orissa.

Summary

6.6.1. This chapter presents the variable-wise analysis of the performance of RRBs in Orissa. Microanalysis of the performance of the RRBs in the State was justified in view of the lot of diversities existing among the RRBs in the State with regard to their age, size, area of operation etc. It was also necessary with a view to highlighting certain issues of RRBs which could not be given focussed attention in macro analysis. Quantitative Analysis of the basic operations of RRBs are based on the data for the period from December 1987 to March 2000. Whereas the data on the qualitative aspects of the performance of RRBs and profitability analysis relate to the period from 1992-93 to 1999-2000. The reform measures of the RRBs were initiated in the year 1991-92. Hence, the implications emerging from the analysis of the data relating to the period from 1992-93 to 1999-2000 were expected to reflect the impact of banking sector reforms on the performance of RRBs. The general picture that emerges from the discussions in the foregoing sections can be summarised as follows.

6.6.2. The decadal analysis of the growth and progress of RRBs in Orissa reveals that the structural growth of RRBs was concentrated mainly in the eighties as is evident from the fact that nearly 70 per cent of the branches were established during this period i.e. from 1981 to 1990. All RRBs in the State except Koraput GB have their largest number of branches coming into existence during this period. As against this, the functional growth of all the RRBs occurs mainly during nineties, as more than 83 per cent of the business was transacted only during the period from 1991 to 2000.

6.6.3. Deposits constitute the major resource component followed by borrowings and owned funds in cases of all the individual RRBs during the period from 1987 to 2000. Deposits and owned funds show upward trend which is reflected in terms of their higher average growth rates and percentage shares in the post-reform period. As against this Borrowings show declining trend as is evident by their lower average growth rates and percentage shares in the post-reform period in case of majority of the RRBs in the State. This finding implies the too much dependence of RRBs on deposit component for their resources and the gradually declining dependence on borrowings during the period under review. Credit dispensation and investment of individual RRBs adhere to the general upward trend which becomes evident from their higher post-reform period average growth rates. Operating losses of all RRBs have shown symptoms of improvement in terms of lower average growth rates in the post-reform period. Even 6 of them viz.,

Puri GB, Koraput GB, Kalahandi GB, Baitarani GB, Rushikulya GB and Dhenkanal GB have registered negative overall growth rates in the post-reform period implying reduction of their operating losses. Accumulated losses of RRBs have also shown favourable trend as indicated by the lower average growth rates in the post-reform period in cases of all except Balasore GB. Thus, all the RRBs show quantitative improvement in their basic operations relating to resource mobilisation, credit dispensation, investment and working results during the post-reform period.

6.6.4. The functioning of RRBs has shown signs of improvement which is reflected in terms of the number of RRBs posting operating profits that has increased from none in 1995-96 to 5 in 1999-2000. Thus, these 5 RRBs, namely, Puri GB, Koraput GB, Kalahandi GB, Rushikulya GB and Dhenkanal GB have attained current viability.

Besides this, 2 RRBs viz., Cuttack GB and Baitarani GB have shown continuous reduction in their operating losses since last three years. However, the position of the remaining 2 RRBs, namely, Bolangir GB and Balasore GB in this regard is far from satisfactory. The RRBs have accumulated losses to the tune of Rs. 384.30 crore as on 31 March 2000. The accumulated losses position of all the RRBs is showing indications of improvement as is evident by the decreasing amount of accumulated losses in cases of the above said 5 RRBs and by the declining growth rates thereof in cases of the remaining 4 RRBs, i.e., Bolangir GB, Cuttack GB, Baitarani GB and Balasore GB.

6.6.5. The C-D ratios of all the individual RRBs have shown downward trend which is evidenced by their negative overall growth rates during the period of study. Balasore GB has recorded the highest decline rate of -11.96 per cent against the lowest rate of decline of-2.92 per cent in case of Dhenkanal GB during the period. The growth rates of advances of the RRBs have been lower than that of their deposits. The lower rates of advances of RRBs may be due to the adoption of cautious approach in extension of credit during the post-reform period as a sequel to the introduction of income recognition and asset classification norms.

6.6.6. The performance of all the RRBs except Cuttack GB in the recovery front has been improving which is reflected in terms of their positive overall growth rates during the period of study. Seven out of the 9 RRBs have shown more than 60 per cent recovery during the period. The remaining 2 RRBs viz. Balasore GB and Cuttack GB have been lagging behind other RRBs both in terms of percentage of recovery and growth rates. Puri GB has reported the highest overall recovery percentage of 67.96 per cent during the period of study. Its recovery percentage has been more than 81 per cent in the year ending on 30 June 2000. The sharp decline in the recovery percentage of Cuttack GB from 52 per cent in 1999 to 34 per cent in 2000 was due to the fact that the areas under its jurisdiction were badly hit by the Super Cyclone in October 1999.

6.6.7. The overall decline in the level of the NPAs position of the RRBs in Orissa reflected an welcome trend in their efficiency. However, the Balasore GB and the Bolangir GB were not keeping pace with other RRBs in Orissa in this respect. The favourable trend in the NPAs management of most of the RRBs in the State may be attributed to the strengthening of the credit appraisal system and credit monitoring measures by the RRBs and to the improvement of their recovery performance especially during the post-reform period. However, the level of NPAs of all the RRBs as a whole in the State was 21.60 per cent against 23 per cent at the all-India level in 1999-2000.

6.6.8. The I-D Ratios of all RRBs except Balasore GB have remained in the range of 30 per cent to 90 per cent whereas that of Balasore GB varied between 5 per cent to 23 per cent during the period from 1992-93. The increase in the I-D Ratio may be attributed to increase in the investment portfolios of the RRBs in the State. RRBs preferred to park the surplus fund, emanating from lower growth of credits than deposits, in investment avenues for increasing their profitability.

6.6.9. The Assets per Staff of all the RRBs have shown upward trend during the period of study. The accumulated losses to total assets ratio and the salary to income ratios have also shown improvement in the second half of the study period, i.e., from 1992-93 to 1999-00. The initial upward trend in the salary to income ratio was due to the increase in the wage bill of the RRBs due to the implementation of the National Industrial Tribunal (NIT) award. The analysis of interest-paid to interest-received ratio shows that only 2 RRBs namely Puri GB and Kalahandi GB have displayed a steadily declining trend since last four years. The ratio has always been more than 100 per cent in cases of all the RRBs out of which 4 RRBs, namely, Bolangir GB, Baitarani GB, Cuttack GB and Balasore GB showing this ratios at more than 200 per cent during the study period. This directly affects the income of the RRBs and hence, reflects a negative feature of their performance.

6.6.10. All RRBs in Orissa have shown steady upward trend in their branch as well as employee productivity during the study period. Dhenkanal GB has registered the highest average branch and employee productivity of Rs. 196.36 lakh and Rs. 46.83 lakh respectively. On the other hand, the lowest average branch productivity of Rs. 103.41 lakh and employee productivity of Rs. 21.40 lakh have been reported by Kalahandi GB and Balasore GB respectively during the period of study.

6.6.11. A framework developed by the Khusro Committee has been used for profitability analysis of RRBs in Orissa. The bank-wise profitability analysis reveals that 7 out of 9 RRBs in the State have recorded positive financial margins. The remaining 2 RRBs, namely, Bolangir GB and Balasore GB have shown negative financial margins throughout the period of study. A remarkable feature of the performance of RRBs in Orissa is that the ratios of their transaction cost to WFs have registered downward trend in cases of all the RRBs during the study period. The number of RRBs recording positive net margins have increased from none in 1996-97 to 5 in 1999-2000. These 5 banks are Puri GB, Koraput GB, Kalahandi GB, Rushikulya GB and Dhenkanal GB. Even 3 out of the remaining 4 RRBs with negative net margins (namely, Bolangir GB, Cuttack GB and Baitarani GB) have registered steady decline in the second half of the study period. But in spite of these welcome trends, the profitability performance of Balasore GB and Bolangir GB are disturbing in view of the spread between the cost of funds and the yield on funds, i.e., financial margin was negative in cases of these two banks. Thus, positive net margins of 5 RRBs and steady improvement in negative net margins of the remaining 4 RRBs are indications of improvement in their profitability. With the misc. income to working funds of the RRBs being insignificant (less than 1 per cent) and remaining almost constant, the decline in the risk costs and transaction costs especially during the later half of the study period, was largely attributed to improvement in the profitability performance of RRBs in Orissa.

6.6.12. The ranking of the RRBs on the basis of their overall performance reflected in terms of parameters used in the study during the period from 1992-93 to 1999-2000 reveals that Dhenkanal GB, Rushikulya GB, Koraput GB and Kalahandi GB are the four best performing RRBs in the State and are placed in Ist, 2nd , 3rd and 4th positions respectively. Whereas, Bolangir GB and Balasore GB are the worst performing rural banks in the State and have occupied the 8th and 9th positions respectively. The remaining 3 RRBs viz., Puri GB, Baitarani GB and Cuttack GB have been positioned in the 5th, 6th and 7th places respectively.

7
Summary of the Findings and Conclusions

Introduction

7.1.1. The study entitled "Operational Analysis of Regional Rural Banks in Orissa" is divided into two parts. The first part comprising of four chapters includes introduction, objectives and methodology of the study and a review of the relevant literature on the subject. It also deals with the theoretical discussion on the significance and sources of rural credit, the emerging scenario of rural banking in India, evolution, growth and development of RRBs at all-India level. This part also covers the socio-economic profile of Orissa and the imperatives for RRBs in the State. The second part, which is the core of the study, consists of three chapters. It encompasses an empirical analysis of the progress and performance of the RRBs in Orissa both at the macro and micro level. In the macro level study covering the period from 1986 to 1999-2000, an attempt has been made to make a comparative analysis of the operations of RRBs between the pre- and post-reform period. The micro-level study seeks to make an exhaustive analysis of the performance of individual RRBs in Orissa during the period from 1992-93, the year in which banking sector reforms were launched, to 1999-2000, the latest year up to which data were available. The objective was to ascertain the impact of the banking sector reforms, initiated in the early nineties, on the operational efficiency, productivity and profitability of the RRBs in terms of a number of selected parameters. The major findings of the study are summarised in the following paragraphs.

Significance and Sources of Rural Credit and Emerging Scenario of Rural Banking in India

7.2.1. The sharp fall in the agricultural prices the world over during the depression of 1930, left its impact on India due to which most of the villagers in general and the cultivators in particular had to incur huge amount of debt to meet their ends. The cumulative growth of debt resulted eventually in loss of land, gold or whatever other assets they had initially offered by way of security. Thus, Indian economy was characterised by massive accumulation of rural debt in the pre-independence era. This also becomes evident from the findings of the All-India Rural Credit Survey Committee, 1951. The report of the Committee published in 1954 revealed that in 1951, only 7.1 per cent of the cash-debt of all rural households was met by the formal agencies like cooperatives, government and bank against 92.9 per cent from non-institutional sources especially the private moneylenders. Naturally, it was incumbent on the nationalist government, which came to power in 1947, to adopt various measures and policies effective enough to deal not only with the rural debt accumulated over the years but also, more basically, with the current credit requirements of the rural population.

7.2.2. Indian economy is rural and agrarian in character. Agriculture sustains a large section of the community in the country. After the introduction of modern technology, agriculture has become a costly proposition. Further, farm sector development is only a part of the rural development which means improvement in the quality of the life of the rural society as a whole including the weaker sections of development of the rural area. Besides this, studies have shown that the private and public investment in agriculture and rural sector has been slowing down in recent years. It is in these contexts that the significance of the rural credit is to be considered.

7.2.3. The thrust of the rural credit policy in India has been to provide funds to the rural poor for productive purposes irrespective of the size and social status of the borrower. At the same time, credit, which has been recognised as an important tool to improve the lot of the rural masses should be utilised according to the national priorities. Therefore, keeping these broad purposes in view, the banking system was chosen as the institutional mechanism for implementation of the policy through a three-pronged strategy: (i) broadening of the institutional base; (ii) directed lending, (iii) concessional or subsidised credit. The ultimate objective was to displace the moneylenders from the rural credit scene. This approach has resulted in a rapid growth of the rural banking system over the last fifty years.

7.2.4. The foundation of the rural banking system in India was laid by the All India Rural Credit Survey Committee (AIRCSC) constituted by RBI in 1951. The survey report published in 1954 was the first of its kind to provide the database for framing policies and measures to make adequate credit available to the rural areas of the country. Since the days of AIRCSC (1954), India has come a long way in its search for an appropriate rural banking set-up. Since then one committee after another has examined this problem. Over the years, the approach has been to create new institutions if the old ones do not work satisfactorily. It is along such lines that the rural credit cooperatives came up followed by the commercial banks' diversification into rural banking after their nationalisation in two phases. The cooperative sector expanded vastly under State patronage to cover the entire village population while nationalised banks opened branches in rural areas at an unprecedented rate to improve access of rural areas to banking facilities. The country's largest bank the State Bank of India (SBI) was formed in 1955 in place of the Imperial Bank of India and was asked to undertake rural banking through its wide network of branches. Since, the commercial banks, too did not perform as expected, the institution of Regional Rural Banks (RRBs) was created in 1975 to meet the special needs of rural banking. A specialised organ, NABARD was carved out of the Reserve Bank of India in 1982 to support the activities of the various rural credit institutions through refinancing and other measures. Even then banking progress in the rural sector was not able to take care of the growing credit needs of the agriculture and the rural poor. Therefore, some innovations like micro Finance (mF), Rural Infrastructure Development Fund (RIDF), Local Area Banks (LABs), Kishan Credit Cards (KCCs), etc. have been introduced in the nineties in the sphere of rural banking. The search for evolving an effective rural banking system is still going on.

7.2.5. Thus, since 1975 a multi-agency approach has been adopted to meet the growing credit requirements of the rural area of the country. While cooperative credit institutions as an integral part of the Rural

Credit System have completed 95 years, the CBs and RRBs have been for almost 31 and 25 years respectively in the rural credit scene. As a result, while the share of informal rural credit has declined from nearly 90 per cent in 1951 to a mere 17 per cent in 1991, in case of institutional credit, it has increased from about 7 per cent to 64 per cent during the same period.

7.2.6. The sources of rural credit as it exists today in India can be broadly divided into two sectors viz. the formal sector and informal sector. The formal sector has a multi-agency character and includes the Cooperatives, Public Sector Commercial Banks (CBs) and the Regional Rural Banks (RRBs). On the other hand, the informal sector in its purview encompasses the Rotating Savings and Credit Associations (ROSCA), traders, landlords, merchants, contractors, commission agents, friends and relatives and local moneylenders. The formal sector's operation falls within the framework of the rules and regulations of the financial sector. On the other hand, the informal sector has its own norms, rules and operates in an autonomous fashion.

7.2.7. The share of formal agencies in the cash debt of rural households has substantially increased especially during the period from the late 70s to early 80s from nearly 29.2 per cent to 61.2 per cent. This development may be attributed to the exercise of Social Control on Banks in 1967, the nationalisation of major CBs in 1969 and 1980, and the establishment of RRBs in 1975. This reflects the multi-agency approach to the rural credit system in India. In the formal sector, the Cooperatives and the CBs have been playing a very crucial role in meeting the credit requirements of the rural area both in terms of structure and operations. The short-term cooperative credit structure as on 31 March 1999 consists of 92,000 primary units in the form of PACS, LAMPS and FSS, 367 DCCBS and 29 SCBs. On the other hand, the long-term structure encompasses within its purview 19 SCARDBs having 1154 branches and 745 Primary CARDBs with 686 branches.

7.2.8. The CBs including RRBs and nationalised banks have also created a strong base in rural area. The number of rural branches has increased from 8,187 in 1969 to 32,719 in 2000, which account for nearly 18 per cent and 50 per cent of the total number of bank branches respectively. There are 297 Scheduled CBs in the country out of which 196 are RRBs. The gross bank credit of all Scheduled CBs for agriculture and allied activities has increased from Rs. 938 crore in 1970-71 to Rs. 41,764 crore in 1999-2000. The combined reach broadly works out to 1 outlet for every 4.3 villages and about 20,000 rural population for each outlet. The Scheduled CBs have been able to mobilise Rs. 1204.5 crore worth of rural deposits and have deployed Rs. 473.96 crore of credit in rural areas at the end of March 2000 in the country. These figures constitute about 15 per cent of the total deposits and 10 per cent of the gross bank credit of these banks respectively.

7.2.9. The rural banking system stands today at an important stage of its evolution. It needs to meet the growing requirements of the agriculture which is becoming input intensive and getting diversified. At the same time, requirements of the poorer sections to create productive assets have to be met. The strategy and approach of the rural credit delivery system have undergone rapid changes in tune with the time and according to the changing needs of the various segments of the rural population in the country.

Evolution, Growth and Development of RRBs at All-India Level

7.3.1. In the wake of social control and nationalisation of major CBs in late sixties, a series of innovations in the form of Lead Bank Scheme, Service Area Approach, initiation of CBs in agriculture lending, setting up of FSS and LAMPS were brought in by the GOI and RBF for enhancing the flow of institutional credit to the rural areas. It was, however, observed that this approach could not make the expected headway in meeting the credit needs of the rural poor. This becomes evident from the report of the Narasimham Working Group on Regional Rural Banks, 1975 which reveals that the non-institutional credit was still two-third of the total credit to the agricultural and rural sector on the eve of the establishment of the RRBs in 1975.

7.3.2. This was also observed by the various committees probing into the problems of rural credit in India from time to time. The Rural Banking Enquiry Committee (1949) pointed out that the CBs had not shown much interest in agricultural and rural lending. The All India Rural Credit Survey Committee (AIRCSC), 1954 called for the strengthening of the cooperative credit movement through the development of a three-tier cooperative credit structure. The All India Rural Credit Review Committee (AIRCRC), 1969 observed that the CBs did not have the requisite expertise to deal with the problem of rural credit. Against the backdrop of such divergent views from different committees on the issue of rural credit, the Banking Commission (1972), after examining the strengths and weaknesses of the existing institutional agencies providing rural credit, i.e., cooperatives and CBs, recommended first time for the setting-up of "rural banks". The Narasimham Working Group on Rural Banks (1975), clearly spelt out the weaknesses of the cooperatives and commercial banks. According to the Committee, cooperatives suffered from inability to mobilise deposit resources, dominance of the vested interests, managerial and professional weaknesses etc. On the other hand, high-cost structure, urban orientation, lack of expertise to operate in rural areas were few weaknesses that came in the way of the efficient functioning of the commercial banks.

7.3.3. The Narasimham Working Group (1975), therefore, felt that in view of the rising demand for rural credit and the need to displace moneylenders, there existed scope for a third institutional agency in addition to the existing ones viz.- the cooperatives and commercial banks (CBs). The new agency would combine the local feel and familiarity of cooperatives and the business acumen and professional ability and modernised outlook of CBs leaving out the demerits of the both. Accordingly, the RRBs were established in 1975 in pursuance to the recommendations of the Narasimham Working Group on Rural Banks. The operations of the RRBs are governed according to the provisions of the RRB Act, 1976 and RRBs (Amendment) Act, 1987.

7.3.4. The various role expectations of RRBs have undergone change over a period of more than two and half decades of their operation as is evidenced by the reports of the various committees appointed by the GOI from time to time. Dantwala Committee (1978), CRAFTCARD (1981) and Kelkar Working Group (1986) were of the view that RRBs should continue their existence as the third arm of multi-agency approach and cater exclusively to the weaker sections. The RBI Study (1980) found that limited area of operation, unenterprising and financially weak clientele and keen competition from commercial banks and cooperatives are the causes that prevent RRBs from becoming viable. Agricultural Credit Review Committee (1989) under the Chairmanship of A.M. Khusro recommended the merger of RRBs with their sponsor banks. The Narasimham Committee on the Financial

System (1991), while making recommendations for the financial sector reforms in 1992, left the option to RRBs and their sponsor banks as to whether they should go for merger or retain their identity. The Committee also advocated for allowing the RRBs to carry out all types of businesses with a view to making them viable. The Bhandari Committee (1994) spearheaded the process of restructuring of the RRBs and laid down the norms for identification of RRBs for restructuring. The Thingalaya Expert Group on Policy Issues (1995) was formed to advise the RBI on policy issues relating to RRBs and to monitor the progress in this regard on an ongoing basis.

7.3.5. The RRBs, till recently, were mandated to confine their lending to weaker sections where the interest earned on loans was the lowest in the banking system. Low interest margins and the high cost of serving a large number of small accounts, coupled with the low volume of business on account of restricted clientele are some of the factors which contributed to the unprofitable working of these banks and are indeed endemic to the system as it was structured. The RRBs were expected to break even in the long run. But the volume of losses went on increasing. Therefore, notwithstanding the phenomenal progress of RRBs in terms of branch expansion, deposit mobilisation, credit deployment, they started facing several problems like sharply declining C-D ratios, poor performance in the recovery front, mounting overdues and huge amount of accumulated losses etc. The implementation of the NIT award since 1987 for the RRB staff giving remuneration package of staff of RRBs at par with those of the commercial banks, led to further deterioration in their financial position. Therefore, several reform and developmental measures were initiated on RRBs as a sequel to the banking sector reforms by the NABARD, RBI and GOI since 1992-93. The purpose was to make these banks operationally efficient, financially viable, organisationally sound and socially relevant.

7.3.6. The RRBs are now allowed to carry out all types of businesses including non-fund business in line with the commercial banks. Complete deregulation of interest rates, lending to Non-Target Group (NTG) of borrowers, broadening of the investment portfolios etc. are a few measures allowed to the RRBs with a view to improving their profitability. Capital base of the RRBs has been widened by enhancing their issued capital to Rs. 1 crore since 1995-96. Under the recapitalisation programme, RRBs selected for restructuring have been provided with additional share capital for strengthening of their financial position. Revamping measures of loss-incurring RRBs have been initiated by the RRBs since 1994-95 through the concept of Development Action Plan (DAP) coupled with Memorandum of Understanding (MoU). DAP is a comprehensive action plan for business improvement for attaining current viability in the short-run and sustainable viability in the long-run. MoU is a fresh commitment by RRBs on an annual basis to their sponsor banks for realisation of set objectives and targeted business levels through DAP implementation. RRBs can also open new branches and relocate their loss incurring branches subject to certain stipulations. They are now being treated on the same footing as the commercial banks with regard to priority sector discipline with effect from 1 April 1997. RRBs have been subjected to income recognition norms and asset classification norms since 1995-96 and provisioning norms since 1996-97. Introduction of these prudential norms aims at bringing transparency in the operations of RRBs by identifying their strengths and weaknesses. As a result of implementation of the measures mentioned above there has been perceptible improvement in the performance of the RRBs at the State and national level.

7.3.7. There were only 6 RRBs with 17 branches covering only 12 districts in the country in 1975, the year of their inception. Whereas, as on 31 March 2000, there are 196 RRBs operating through a branch network of 14517 covering 492 districts. Similarly, the deposits mobilised by these banks increased from Rs. 0.20 crore in 1975 to Rs. 32008.48 crore in March 2000 and their outstanding advances from Rs. 0.10 crore to Rs. 13102.47 crore during the same period. These figures indicate the overwhelming growth and progress of RRBs achieved over a period of two and half decades of their operation in the country.

7.3.8. An analysis of the basic operations of RRBs at the all-India level over the period from 1994-95 to 1999-2000 reveals that the resource base of the RRBs comprising of owned funds, deposits and borrowings has increased from Rs. 13668 crore to Rs. 39009 crore registering an average growth rate of around 23 per cent during the period. Deposit is the largest resource component constituting nearly 82 per cent of the total resources followed by borrowings and owned funds. The shares of owned funds and deposits in the total resources have recorded a steadily increasing trend against a sharply declining trend of the shares of borrowings during the said period. Deposit mobilisation have shown a continuously upward trend in absolute terms as well as in terms of number of accounts, deposit per account, average deposits per RRB and per branch. Major portion of the deposits were term deposits followed by savings bank deposits and current account deposits in the total deposit structure of RRBs at the all-India level during the period under review. RRBs deserve credit for their consistent improvement in their advances in absolute terms, in terms of advances per account, average advances per RRB and per branch during the said period. The farm-sector advances remain around 47 per cent of the total advances during this period. The percentage of recovery improved from 46.23 per cent in June 1994 to 64.09 per cent in June 2000. The level of NPAs has gone down from 43.07 per cent in 1995-96 to 23.07 per cent in 1999-2000. The working results position of the RRBs shows that the number of profit-making RRBs has increased from 32 to 162 and the amount of annual profits from Rs. 29 crore to Rs. 544 crore during the period from 1994-95 to 1999-2000. Out of the 162 profit-making RRBs as in March 2000, 56 have attained sustainable viability with no accumulated losses and 106 have attained current viability.

7.3.9. In the midst of these achievements, there are also some drawbacks. The fall in the C-D Ratios of RRBs from 56 per cent in 1994-95 to 41 per cent in 1999-2000, the high level of NPAs at 23 per cent of the total advances, huge amount of overdues, Rs. 113.55 crore of operating losses incurred by 34 RRBs, accumulated losses to the tune of Rs. 2979 crore of 140 RRBs as on 31 March 2000, are causes of growing concern for the management of these banks. The study also revealed that 77 per cent of the loss-incurring RRBs were concentrated in 5 States, namely, Bihar, Madhya Pradesh, Orissa, Rajasthan and West Bengal.

Socio-Economic Background of and Imperatives for RRBs in Orissa

7.4.1. The analysis of the socio-economic features of Orissa reveals that despite vast natural and human resources, the economy of Orissa is characterised by poverty, unemployment, low per capita income, low capital formation, inadequate exploitation of abundant natural resources, inadequate development of socio-economic infrastructure. The recent demographic profile of the State is marked by low levels of social development. Orissa is now the poorest State in the country according to the Planning Commission's latest estimates of poverty. People living below poverty line constitute 47.15 per cent in Orissa compared to the National average of 26 per cent. The rural urban break-up of population living below poverty line is 48.01 per cent in rural areas and 42.83 per cent in urban areas. Thus, incidence of poverty is more in rural areas of the State. The density of population in rural areas is the highest among the States in the country with nearly 87 per cent of people living in the rural areas of the State. 38 per cent of the State's population belong to SC/ST against 24 per cent at the all-India level.

7.4.2. The gap in the per capita income of the State and the national average in 1980-81 was Rs. 316/- and this gap has increased nearly four-fold to Rs. 1126/- in 1997-98. The Super Cyclone in October 1999 followed by a severe drought in 2000 and the unprecedented flood in July 2001 would make it difficult to bridge this gap in near future. The frequent occurrence of natural calamities like flood, cyclone and drought have all compounded the problems of underdevelopment in the State.

7.4.3. The growth of the State's economy depends to a considerable extent on the farm sector development, as agriculture contributes around 40 per cent to the NSDP. This sector provides employment to nearly 66 per cent of the workforce directly or indirectly. Out of the total number of 3948 operational holdings, nearly 80 per cent (3153) are occupied by small and marginal farmers and the remaining 20 per cent by the medium and large farmers. Only 37 per cent of the cultivable land was irrigated by the end of March 2000. In the absence of adequate irrigation facilities, agriculture depends largely on monsoon. As a result, agricultural production fluctuates. On account of the large linkages between this and other sectors of the economy, these fluctuations influence the overall growth rate of the State's economy to an appreciable degree. Besides, in the year ending on 31 March 2000, the total bank investment in agriculture is only Rs. 773.51 crore which was about 15 per cent of the total of Rs. 5062.15 crore by all Scheduled CBs in the State. Thus, there is over-dependence on agriculture on the one hand and agriculture is characterised by low investment, inadequate irrigation facilities etc. in the State on the other. Therefore, the rural and agrarian character of the State's economy calls for the need to give high priority to agriculture and rural development to alleviate poverty from the State and to bring about overall prosperity of the State's economy.

7.4.4. There is enough potential for development in the State in view of its varied agro-climatic conditions which are conducive to the promotion of agriculture and allied activities. There is also need for development of small-scale, village and cottage industries which will not only divert surplus labour from agriculture but will also help in income generation, creation of assets and employment opportunities in rural areas. The rate of exploitation of mineral and forest resources of the State needs to be enhanced to generate more income and to create more employment opportunities.

7.4.5. All these enterprises to be implemented require huge capital investment in the State. Bank credit has been recognised as an important means for sustaining the livelihood of the poor in a backward State like Orissa. But, the C-D Ratio of all Scheduled CBs in the State was 39.75 per cent against the all-India average of 57.05 per cent as on 31 March 2000. It is also lower than that of many other states in the country. Further, the population covered per office of a bank in Orissa was 17000 against 15000 at the all-India level on the said date. Therefore, there is need for enhancing banking facilities in the State by stimulating domestic savings and improving the volume of advances of all the Scheduled CBs in the State.

7.4.6. The socio-economic profile of Orissa being as highlighted in the foregoing discussion, the overall development of the State depends primarily on the development of rural area. The establishment of RRBs in Orissa was highly relevant and justified in view of the rural and agrarian feature of the State's economy with high incidence of poverty. These often being known as the 'Small Man's Bank', are the ideal banks to accelerate the pace of economic development of the State by supplementing the existing banking facilities especially in the rural areas.

7.4.7. RRBs occupy an important place in the banking scenario of Orissa in as much as they share nearly 38 per cent of the total bank offices, 11 per cent of the total deposits and 13 per cent of the total advances of all the Scheduled CBs in the State as on 31 March 2000. These percentages are fairly higher than those of 22 per cent, 4 per cent and 3 per cent respectively at the all-India level.

7.4.8. RRBs in Orissa have opened more than 90 per cent of their branches and have mobilised nearly 76 per cent of their deposits from and deployed 82 per cent of their credit in the rural areas of the State against 84 per cent, 70 per cent and 73 per cent respectively at the all-India level as on 31 March 2000. RRBs in Orissa have shared 47.34 per cent of rural branch network, 27.27 per cent of rural deposits and 34.04 per cent of rural credit of all Scheduled CBs as on the said date against these figures of 37.22 per cent, 18.60 per cent and 20.24 per cent respectively at the all-India level. The RRBs have shown better coverage of rural areas in terms of branch network and C-D Ratios than Nationalised Banks, SBI and its associates, but have reported lowest percentage share of deposits and business per branch in comparison to the said banks as on 31 March 2000. These findings lead to the conclusion that RRBs in Orissa stay ahead of those at the all-India level so far as coverage of rural areas is concerned. They deserve credit for fostering banking habits among the underprivileged in far flung rural areas of Orissa.

7.4.9. The farm and non-farm sector advances of RRBs constitute 36.09 per cent and 63.91 per cent of the total as on 31 March 2000. In the farm sector, the shares of short-term crop loan and long-term agricultural investments are 16.10 per cent and 19.99 per cent respectively. Similarly, in the non-farm sector, the miscellaneous category has received the largest chunk of 33.71 per cent followed by 24.51 per cent and 5.69 per cent of the retail trade, small business category and rural artisans category respectively.

7.4.10. RRBs have also provided huge sum of credit averaged at Rs. 37.61 crore per annum over the last six years. Under this scheme these banks have provided jobs on an average to nearly 36000 poor people belonging to SC/ST, minorities group, small and marginal farmers, landless agricultural labourers and to the IRDP beneficiaries.

7.4.11. RRBs in Orissa play an important role in the development of agriculture. The annual disbursal of agricultural loan has gone up from Rs. 42.47 crore in 1994-95 to Rs. 108.73 crore in 1999-2000. Agricultural loans have been provided to nearly 76000 farmers per annum and constitute on an average about 16 per cent of the total bank credit in Orissa. Similarly, the average contribution of RRBs in the total investment of funds for the development of village and cottage industries in Orissa is 23.09 per cent and in the employment generation in this sector is 10.32 per cent of the total in the State. On an average, the credit extended by the RRBs to this sector amounts to Rs. 1078 lakhs creating employment opportunities for more than 9000 people of rural area in the State per annum during the period under study.

Analysis of the Progress and Performance of RRBs in Orissa (Total Sample)

7.5.1. The establishment of all the 9 RRBs in Orissa took place in three phases. In the first phase Puri GB, Bolangir GB, Cuttack GB and Koraput GB were set up in 1976. Kalahandi GB, Baitarani GB and Balasore GB came into existence in 1980 in the second phase. The third phase witnessed the setting up of 2 RRBs viz., Rushikulya GB and Dhenkanal GB in 1981. Thus, there are 9 RRBs in the State with a network of 843 branches as on 31 March 2000. No new RRB has been set up since 1982. The branch expansion was also very slow. The policy was to expand the volume of business through the existing structural framework. Consequently, there was overwhelming growth in the volume of business of the RRBs during the nineties. This was possible due to their vast branch network which was already built up during the period from 1976 to 1990 in the State. The 9 RRBs are sponsored by 5 public sector banks viz. SBI, sponsoring three RRBs, U.Co. Bank and IOB two each and Allahabad Bank and Andhra Bank one each.

7.5.2. The analysis of the performance of the RRBs in Orissa as a whole covers the period from December 1986 to March 2000. The comparative analysis of the performance of the RRBs in Orissa between the pre-reform and post-reform period shows that these banks have displayed remarkable improvement in all important spheres of their basic operations like resource mobilisation, credit dispensation, investments and working results position. The deposits, advances and investments of RRBs in the State have registered not only consistently rising trend in absolute terms throughout the period of study but also higher average growth rates in the post-reform period. The overdues of RRBs have shown declining trend in terms of percentage shares to the total advances during the study period and lower average growth rates in the post-reform period. The operating losses of RRBs have shown reduction from Rs. 82 crore in 1996-97 to Rs. 22 crore in 1999-2000 and have recorded an average growth rate of around 12 per cent in the post-reform period which was considerably lower than the pre-reform period average of 58 per cent. On the other hand, the amount of operating profits earned by the RRBs has been Rs. 3.52 crore, Rs. 4.51 crore and Rs. 4.62 crore in 1997-98, 1998-99 and 1999-2000 respectively. The accumulated losses have witnessed a steadily declining growth rate from 38.68 per cent in 1996-97 to 5.94 per cent in 1999-2000.

7.5.3. Besides the quantitative progress in the performance of RRBs in the State as outlined above, it is noteworthy to highlight the qualitative achievements in their operations. The performance of these banks in the recovery front has been consistently improving from a mere 40 per cent in 1986 to 66 per cent in 1999-2000. C-D Ratios and percentage of recovery to demand in the State have been always higher than those at the all-India level. The RRBs have shown better average I-D Ratios in the post-reform period both in absolute terms and in terms of growth rate. The prudential norms were made applicable to RRBs during 1995-96 and since then, the asset quality of RRBs has shown perceptible improvement. The share of standard assets to total advances of RRBs has steadily increased from 49.28 per cent in 1995-96 to 78.40 per cent in 1999-2000. Assets per Staff, Branch and Employee Productivity of the RRBs have not only recorded steadily rising trend throughout the period of study, but also have registered more than two times higher average growth rates in the post-reform period. Some other key indicators of performance used in the study viz., accumulated losses to total assets ratio, salary to income ratio and interest-paid to interest-received ratio have also shown symptoms of improvement reflected in terms of their lower average growth rates in the post-reform period.

7.5.4. The trend of the all important indices of profitability reveals that the RRBs are on the right path of recovery. The financial margin, misc. income to working funds ratio have shown continuous improvement during the last 3 to 4 years of the study period. Similarly, the transaction cost to working funds ratio and risk costs to working funds ratio have also shown improvement which is indicated by their declining trend during these years in the post-reform period. This has led to a sharp reduction in the negative net margins of RRBs from a high of -8.71 per cent in 1996-97 to a low of -1.31 per cent in 1999-2000. The above findings show that the reform measures initiated by the NABARD, RBI and GOI on RRBs have started yielding results especially towards the last 3 to 4 years of the study period.

7.5.5. The RRBs in Orissa have exhibited phenomenal progress in their growth and performance during the post-reform period both in quantitative as well as in qualitative terms. However, it is also worthwhile to throw some light on the negative aspects of their performance. The emphasis of RRBs on farm sector advances seems to have been reducing in course of time, as the percentage shares of their advances to this sector has been declining during the post-reform period. The overdues have mounted from Rs. 62 crore in 1993-94 to Rs. 125 crore in 1999-2000 which constitutes about 17 per cent of their total outstanding advances as in March 2000. High proportion of term deposits in these banks leads to high debt-servicing cost which directly affects the banks' profitability. The ever increasing and huge amount of accumulated losses (to the tune of nearly Rs. 385 crore as on 31 March 2000) have been a cause of concern for these banks. Another disquieting feature is the continuous decline in the C-D ratios from a high of 173 per cent in 1988 to a low of 51 per cent in 1999-2000. It was further observed that the rate of decline in the C-D ratio was faster in the post-reform period. The NPA level of RRBs for the State as a whole was 22 per cent and is still high in comparison to the internationally accepted standards. These banks have witnessed higher average of accumulated losses to total assets ratio and salary to income ratio (in absolute terms) during the post-reform period. Interest paid to interest received ratio has remained more than cent per cent in 11 out of the 15 years of the study period.

Analysis of the Progress and Performance of RRBs in Orissa (Variable-Wise)

7.6.1. Micro-analysis of the performance of the RRBs in Orissa was justified on account of the existence of a lot of diversities among them with regard to their age, size, area of operation etc. The analysis has been made for the period from 1992-93 to 1999-2000 because the data on RRBs relating to this period were expected to reflect the impact of banking sector reforms on the performance of the RRBs.

7.6.2. The structural growth in terms of number of branches was concentrated in the eighties in cases of all RRBs except Koraput GB. However, the functional growth of all the RRBs in terms of volume of business took place mainly in the nineties. The functioning of the 9 RRBs in Orissa over the said period has shown signs of visible improvement especially after their coverage under the restructuring programme from 1994-95 till 2000. The number of RRBs posting operating profits has gone up to 5 at the end of March 2000 as against none in 1995-96. These RRBs are Puri GB, Koraput GB, Kalahandi GB, Rushikulya GB and Dhenkanal GB. These 5 banks have also shown gradual reduction in their accumulated losses. The remaining 4 RRBs have recorded declining growth rate of accumulated losses. Thus, though there are 5 RRBs in the State, attaining current viability, but none of them have attained sustainable viability up to the end of March 2000.

7.6.3. The variable-wise analysis of performance of RRBs in terms of 19 variables used in the study during the post-reform period reveals that all the 9 RRBs in the State have shown improving trend in respect of 5 variables viz. accumulated losses, assets per staff ratio, branch and employee productivity ratios and transaction cost to WFs ratios. Majority of the RRBs numbering 6 to 8 out of 9, have registered favourable trend with regard to 9 variables such as working results, I-D ratios, percentage of recovery to demand, NPAs to total advances, accumulated losses to total assets ratios, salary to income ratios, risk cost to WFs ratios, miscellaneous income to WFs ratios and net margins. However, majority of the RRBs in Orissa have witnessed unfavourable trend with regard to the remaining 5 variables like C-D ratios, interest-paid to interest-received ratios, average return on funds, average cost of funds and financial margins. Thus, majority of the RRBs in Orissa have shown improvement in their performance in respect of 14 out of 19 parameters used in the study during the post-reform period, i.e., 1992-93 to 1999-2000. The reform measures have positive impact on the performance of majority of the RRBs in Orissa. It is further observed that as per the yardstick adopted in the study, Dhenkanal GB is the best performing RRB in Orissa closely followed by Rushikulya GB, Koraput GB and Kalahandi GB. On the other hand, Balasore GB, Bolangir GB and Cuttack are the three worst performing RRBs in the State. The Puri GB and Baitarani GB remain in between these two extreme positions during the period under review. The declining C-D ratios of all RRBs in Orissa and the performance in all basic areas of operations of Balasore GB and Bolangir GB, deserve the attention of all concerned namely, the management of these banks, their sponsor banks, the State Government, NABARD, RBI and GOI.

Testing of Hypotheses

Hypothesis I

Rural credit gets more and more institutionalised with the passage of time.

7.7.1. It is found in the study that the percentage share of the institutional sources of credit inclusive of cooperatives, government and CBs in the total outstanding cash debts of rural households in 1951 was a meagre 7.1 per cent. This share increased to 17.3 per cent in 1961, to 29 per cent in 1971 and further to 61.2 per cent in 1981. At the end of June 1991, it has reached an impressive level of 64 per cent. The share of the cooperatives in the rural credit has increased from 2.9 per cent in 1951 to 20.1 per cent in 1971, to 28.6 per cent in 1981. But there has been a decline in the pace of increase in the outreach of cooperatives from 28.6 per cent in 1981 to 21.6 per cent in 1991. The share of the CBs in the rural credit has increased from 1.1 per cent in 1951 to 2.2 per cent in 1971. The outreach of the CBs to the rural sector improved considerably between 1971 and 1991, i.e., from a mere 2.2 per cent in 1971 to 28 per cent and 33.7 per cent in 1981 and 1991 respectively. This increase in the share of CBs in the rural credit can be attributed to bank nationalisation and the consequent stress on social banking. The corresponding decline in the importance of non-institutional sources is also to be observed during these years from a high of 92.9 per cent in 1951 to 81.6 per cent in 1961, to 70.8 per cent in 1971, 38.8 per cent in 1981 and finally to 36 per cent in 1991. The share of moneylenders in the non-institutional sources of rural credit has fallen from 68.6 per cent in 1951 to 62.9 per cent in 1961 to 36.9 per cent in 1971, and further to 16.9 per cent in 1981. The share of moneylenders has registered a small increase from 16.9 per cent in 1981 to 17.5 per cent, despite the measures taken by the GOI, RBI and NABARD for institutionalisation the rural credit with a view to curbing the exploitative practices of the moneylenders.

7.7.2. The rural credit policy of the GOI ever since independence has been to displace moneylender and to build and strengthen formal credit institutions. The Reserve Bank of India was established in 1935 with a separate agricultural credit department to monitor the flow of institutional credit for rural and agricultural sector. The foundations of the building of a broad credit infrastructure for rural credit were laid by the Report of the AIRCSC of 1954. The imposition of social control on banks in 1967, the nationalisation of CBs in 1969 and 1980, establishment of RRBs in 1975, creation of NABARD in 1981 and thereby imparting a multi-agency character to rural banking are all the efforts of the GOI directed towards the institutionalisation of rural credit. As a result of this, the rural credit is getting more and more institutionalised with the passage of time.

Hypothesis II

RRBs operate mainly in rural areas. RRBs in Orissa stay ahead of those at the all-India level so far as coverage of rural areas in terms of rural branch network, deposit mobilisation from and credit deployment in rural areas are concerned.

7.7.3. As on 31 March 2000, out of the total 843 branches of RRBs in Orissa, 764 or 90.63 per cent are operating in rural areas. RRBs' deposit mobilisation from rural area is Rs. 1138.39 crore which is 76.30 per cent of the total deposits of RRBs in the State. Similarly, out of the total advances of Rs. 761.71 crore, Rs.625.41 crore which accounts for 82.11 per cent of the total, is deployed in the rural areas of the State. RRBs' total number of branches, quantum of deposits and rural credits at all-India level are 14517, Rs. 32197.68 crore and Rs.13178.58 crore, out of which 12178, Rs. 22404.99 crore and Rs.9592.91 crore, relate to the rural area constituting 83.89 per cent, 69.59 per cent and 72.79 per cent respectively as on the said date. Thus, RRBs' coverage of rural area in terms of branch network, rural deposit mobilisation and credit deployment in rural areas are 90.63 per cent, 76.30 per cent and 82.11 per cent against 83.89 per cent, 69.59 per cent and 72.79 per cent at the all-India level respectively. Thus, RRBs operation in terms of branch network, deposit mobilisation and credit deployment, is concentrated mainly in rural areas of the State and is better than those at the all-India level.

7.7.4. In Orissa, there are 1614 rural branches of all Scheduled CBs out of which the rural branches of RRBs are 764 representing 47.34 per cent of the total number of rural branches of all Scheduled CBs. In India, there are 32,719 rural branches of all Scheduled CBs out of which those of RRBs are 12,178 which is 37.22 per cent of the total number of rural branches of all Scheduled CBs. RRBs' share in the total rural deposits of Rs. 4174.29 crore of all Scheduled CBs in Orissa is Rs. 1138.39 crore which is 27.27 per cent of the total rural deposits. Whereas out of the total rural deposits of Rs. 120446.75 crore mobilised by all the Scheduled CBs in the country, the share of RRBs is Rs. 22404.99 crore which is 18.60 per cent of the total. Similarly, in Orissa RRBs' share of rural credit is Rs. 625.41 crore in the total rural credit of Rs. 1837.20 crore of all Scheduled CBs in the State. RRBs, thus, share 34.04 per cent of the total rural credit deployment of all Scheduled CBs in the State. Whereas, the total credit deployed by all the Scheduled CBs in the rural areas of the country is Rs. 47396.02 crore out of which RRBs' share of rural credit is Rs. 9592.91 crore, i.e., 20.24 per cent of the total.

Thus, RRBs in Orissa stay ahead of those at the all-India level with regard to coverage of rural areas. RRBs' shares constitute 47.34 per cent of the rural branch network, 27.27 per cent of the total rural deposits and 34.04 per cent of the total rural credit of all Scheduled CBs in the State against 37.22 per cent, 18.60 per cent and 20.24 per cent respectively at the all-India level. The hypothesis is proved.

Hypothesis III

Structural growth of RRBs in terms of branch expansion was concentrated in the eighties (1981 to 1990) whereas, the functional growth, in terms of deposits, advances or volume of business was concentrated in the nineties (1991 to 2000).

7.7.5. The macro level study shows that out of the 843 branches of RRBs in the State as on 31 March 2000, number of branches established during the period from 1976 to 1980, from 1981 to 1990 and from 1991 to 2000 were 228, 591 and 24 respectively. Thus, 70.11 per cent of the total RRBs' branches were established during eighties. The micro level study shows that all RRBs except Koraput GB have witnessed the highest number of branches coming into existence during the period of 1981 to 1990. Whereas, Koraput GB showing deviation from the general trend has set up 55 (61 per cent) in the seventies against 35 branches (38.89 per cent) in the eighties respectively.

7.7.6. The macro level study also reveals that out of the total deposits of Rs. 1492.10 crore of RRBs, the amounts mobilised during seventies, eighties and nineties were Rs. 16.72 crore, Rs. 138.60 crore and Rs. 1336.78 crore respectively. These amounts constitute 1.12 per cent, 9.29 per cent and 89.59 per cent of the total deposits respectively. Similarly, the volume of advances sanctioned during the three decades were Rs. 28.84 crore, Rs. 194.06 crore and Rs. 538.81 crore constituting 3.81 per cent, 25.46 per cent and 70.73 per cent of the total advances of Rs. 761.71 crore of RRBs as on 31 March 2000. Further, it was found that out of the total volume of business of Rs. 2253 crore of RRBs as on the said date, Rs. 538.81 crore, i.e., 70.73 per cent was transacted only in the nineties. The micro level analysis reveals that all the individual RRBs in Orissa have transacted largest proportion of their business ranging from 74.27 per cent of Cuttack GB to 89.93 per cent of Rushikulya GB, during the 10 years period from 1991 to 2000.

7.7.7. The branch licensing policy of the RRBs for the period from 1985 to 1990 laid emphasis on consolidation of the business with the existing RRB structure and going slow in the expansion of the branch network due to increase in the number of loss incurring branches. This policy resulted in the rapid growth of the volume of business of RRBs in the State. This became possible due to the existence of a vast branch network of RRBs which was built up during the period from 1976 to mid-eighties. This policy led to the concentration of the structural growth of RRBs in the form of branch expansion in the eighties and of the functional growth in terms of volume of business in the nineties. Thus, the hypothesis is proved for the total sample as well as for the individual RRBs in the State.

Hypothesis IV

RRBs in Orissa have depended for their resources much more on deposits than on other resources available to them. Their dependence on borrowing has been gradually declining over the years. Thus, the trend of self-reliance can be looked upon as a welcome sign.

7.7.8. The resource base of the RRBs is comprised of 3 components: owned funds, deposits and borrowings. It is found from the analysis of the pattern of the resource composition that deposits constitute the major resource component and represent 61.98 per cent of the total resources in comparison to 35.21 per cent of the borrowing and 2.81 per cent of the owned fund for the entire study period from 1986 to 1999-2000. The share of deposits has been consistently rising from 44.30 per cent in December 1986 to 78.10 per cent in March 2000. Besides this, deposits registered an overall average growth rate of 24.46 per cent per annum which is more than 3 times higher than that of the borrowings during the same period. On the other hand, the shares of borrowings in the total resource base of RRBs have been steadily declining from a high of 53.20 per cent in 1986 to a mere 12.97 per cent in 2000. The micro-analysis shows that, deposits are the major resource components for all RRBs with average percentage shares thereof varying in the range of 54.49 per cent of Kalahandi GB and 69.88 per cent of Balasore GB during the study period. Deposits have recorded higher average growth rates and percentage shares in the post-reform period than their respective pre-reform period averages in cases of all RRBs implying upward trend. On the other hand, borrowings have shown downward trend both in terms of lower average percentage shares in cases of all RRBs and lower growth rates in cases of all but 3 RRBs viz. Puri GB, Baitarani GB and Dhenkanal GB in the post-reform period than their respective pre-reform period averages. Owned funds, both at the macro as well as micro level, though reveal the highest growth rate, constitute a very small proportion of the total resources of the RRBs.

7.7.9. The above findings lead to the conclusion that RRBs depend more on the deposits for their resources. Their dependence on borrowings is gradually declining over the years. It is certainly a welcome trend to involve more of internal resources in the form of deposits and owned funds in the business leading towards self-reliance on the part of the RRBs. The declining trend in C-D ratio further confirms the fact that RRBs have depended much more on deposits and their C-D ratios could have been much higher if they had used other resources to a great extent. Thus, the hypothesis is tested for the RRBs collectively as well as individually.

Hypothesis V

Term deposits constitute the major part of total deposits followed by savings bank deposits and current deposits of RRBs in Orissa.

7.7.10. The analysis of the pattern of deposit composition of RRBs for the period of study from 1986 to 1999-2000 shows that term deposits constitute the highest overall percentage share of 47.67 per cent followed by 43.41 per cent of savings bank deposits and 8.92 per cent of current deposits. Similarly, the term deposits also have registered the highest overall growth rate of 27.50 per cent followed by 19.84 per cent and 17.45 per cent of savings deposits and current deposits respectively during the study period. The trend analysis of the pattern of deposits reveals that the share of term deposits displays a continuously upward trend from 46.05 per cent in 1994-95 to 58.88 per cent in 1999-2000. On the other hand the share of savings deposits has registered a significant decline from 43.58 per cent to 37.44 per cent and that of current account deposits from 10.37 per cent to a mere 3.68 per cent respectively during the same period. This type of trend has been observed also in absolute terms since 1991-92 onwards. Thus, term deposits constitute the major part of total deposits in absolute terms, in terms of percentage share and growth rates. Savings bank deposits and current deposits follow the term deposits during the period under review. The hypothesis is proved.

Hypothesis VI

In terms of composition of credit structure of RRBs, there is a tendency towards diversification of the credit portfolio with specific emphasis being laid on giving credit support to the non-farm sector in addition to meeting the credit needs of the farm sector.

7.7.11. The very approach of RRBs to rural credit is sectoral i.e. lending to specified categories of rural poor. The priority sector discipline became effective on RRBs from the financial year 1997-98. These banks were brought on par with the CBs in this regard.

Therefore, the advances of RRBs can be broadly divided into two categories - priority sector and non-priority sector advances. Each of these sectors are further sub-divided into 5 sub-sectors. These are :

(i) Short-term Crop-loan finance (Short-term)

(ii) Agricultural Term loans (For Agricultural Investments and Allied Activities).

(iii) Advances for Rural Artisans, Village and Cottage Industries.

(iv) Advances for Retail-Trade, Small-Business and Self-employed Persons etc.

(v) Advances for miscellaneous purposes which include advances for small scale industries, small road transport operators, professionals, loans to self-help groups (SHGs) and nongovernmental organisations (NGOs), housing loans, staff loans, consumer advances etc.

7.7.12. The sector-wise classification of the advances of RRBs in Orissa as on 31 March 2000 shows that 36.09 per cent and 63.91 per cent of the total outstanding advances of Rs. 761.71 crore have been deployed in the agricultural and non-agricultural sectors respectively. In the agricultural sector, 16.10 per cent and 19.99 per cent of the total advances were earmarked for short-term crop loan and for long-term agricultural investments respectively. In the non-farm category, village, cottage industries and rural artisans get 5.69 per cent, retail trade, small business and self-employed persons get 24.51 per cent and miscellaneous categories of borrowers receive 33.71 per cent of the total advances in the year 1999-2000. The priority and non-priority sectors' shares in the total outstanding advances were 75.63 per cent and 24.37 per cent respectively. RRBs provide financial assistance under several government-sponsored anti-poverty programmes including IRDP to the weaker sections of the rural area for their economic upliftrnent. The distribution of advances under anti-poverty programmes was as follows: Small and Marginal farmers - 47.41 per cent, IRDP - 25.11 per cent, SC/ST borrowers - 18.74 per cent, Minorities Group - 1.44 per cent and loans under other government sponsored programmes - 7.30 per cent as on 31 March 2000.

These data confirm the fact that there has been a great deal of diversification in the advances sanctioned by the RRBs in the State.

7.7.13. RRBs' non-farm sector advances have been higher than their farm-sector advances in absolute terms in all the years from 1990-91 to 1999-2000 in Orissa. Further, the percentage shares of RRBs' advances to the farm sector in Orissa have declined sharply from 58.57 per cent in December 1986 to a mere 36.09 per cent in March 2000. As against this, the share of non-farm sector advances has increased from 41.13 per cent to 63.91 per cent in the same period. The overall average share of agricultural advances for the whole period of study was 47.70 per cent which was fairly lower than 52.30 per cent of non-agricultural advances. Similarly, the overall average growth rate of non-agricultural advances was 17.34 per cent which was higher than 10.14 per cent of agricultural advances during the study period. Thus, the non-agricultural advances of RRBs are higher than agricultural advances in absolute terms, in terms of growth rates and percentage shares especially from 1990-91 onwards up to 1999-2000.

The facts and figures presented above prove the hypothesis that there is a tendency towards diversification of the credit portfolio of RRBs with specific emphasis being laid on giving credit support to the non-farm sector in addition to meeting the credit needs of the farm sector.

Hypothesis VII

Though RRBs are providing credit to farm and non-farm sector, but are gradually shifting their priorities from farm sector to the non-farm sector lending. They are going away from their professed agenda of working in rural areas for the development of the rural economy in the post-reform period.

7.7.14. RRBs' non-farm sector advances have been higher than their advances to the farm sector in absolute terms in all the years during the period from 1990-91 to 1999-2000 in Orissa. The average percentage share of farm sector advances have decreased from 52.05 per cent in the pre-reform period to 42.44 per cent in the post-reform period. Whereas, the share of non-farm sector advances has gone up from a pre-reform period average of 47.95 per cent to a high post-reform period average of 57.56 per cent. Further, the average growth rate of non-agricultural advances of 19.67 per cent is considerably higher than that of 13.24 per cent of the agricultural advances in the post-reform period. This substantiates the fact that the RRBs are shifting their priorities from agriculture lending to the non-farm sector lending in the post-reform era.

7.7.15. There has been a steady decline in the C-D Ratios of RRBs in Orissa from 173 per cent in December, 1988 to 51 per cent in March 2000. All the individual RRBs also have witnessed fall in their C-D Ratios. This becomes evident from the overall negative growth rates thereof during the period from 1992-93 to 1999-2000, the highest and the lowest rates of decline of -11.96 per cent and -2.92 per cent being recorded by Balasore GB and Dhenkanal GB respectively. The C-D Ratio of RRBs declined from 66.70 per cent in 1994-95 to 50.48 per cent in

1999-2000. As against this, their I-D Ratio has increased from 42.45 per cent to 54.83 per cent in the same period. The 1-D Ratios of all RRBs except Puri GB in the State have shown upward trend during the period from 1992-93 to 1999-2000 especially towards last 3 to 4 years, which is evidenced by the positive overall growth rates ranging from 3.97 per cent in case of Baitarani GB to 19.47 per cent in case of Balasore GB.

7.7.16. The growth rates of RRBs' (total sample) I-D Ratios have been higher than those of their C-D Ratios in the State in 6 out of 8 years during the period from 1992-93 to 1999-2000 (vide Annexure I). In addition to this, a comparison between the average growth rates of C-D Ratios and I-D Ratios of RRBs for the said period shows that the average growth rate of C-D Ratios is far lower than that of I-D Ratio in cases of all the individual RRBs in Orissa (Vide Annexure - II). Thus, there has been a decrease in the C-D Ratios of RRBs and a corresponding increase in the I-D Ratios in absolute terms during the period. Further, the growth rates of C-D Ratios have been lower than those of the I-D Ratios in the same period. This reflects a trend of RRBs' preference for investment instead of improving credit portfolio through quality lending. This finding is disconcerting in view of the fact that the RRBs were set up primarily to develop rural economy. All these findings lead to the conclusion that RRBs have reduced their lending to the rural sector in general and the farm sector in particular especially during the post-reform period. Thus, the hypothesis is proved.

Hypothesis VIII

The revamping initiatives and other developmental measures taken by the NABARD, RBI and GOI have left positive impact on the working and financial health of the RRBs in the State.

7.7.17. The introduction of income recognition norms and asset classification norms in 1995-96 and provisioning norms in 1996-97, led the RRBs to adopt a more stringent and cautious approach to credit appraisal. Consequently, the growth rates of advances were restricted in the range of 9 per cent to 22 per cent during the period from 1992-93 to 1999-2000. On the other hand, the growth rates of deposits varied from 24 per cent to 30 per cent during the same period. This gave rise to increased short-term surpluses. Parking of these surplus funds in investment avenues was an easier option for the RRBs. Besides this the concessional refinance available to the RRBs, sponsor banks paying higher rate of interest, the low yield on loans and advances due to low recovery and high transaction cost and above all, the liberalised investment policy for the RRBs coming into effect since 1992-93 made the RRBs to prefer the investment route in their pursuit of improving profitability.

7.7.18. The above mentioned factors led to increase in the total investment of RRBs in Orissa from Rs. 141.67 crore in 1992-93 to Rs. 818.10 crore in 1999-2000 with an average growth rate of about 30 per cent per annum. Their I-D Ratio has remained above 50 per cent since 1996-97 and increased steadily from 50.50 per cent in 1997-98 to 54.83 per cent in 1999-2000. The I-D Ratios have shown higher average figure of 50.70 per cent in absolute terms and growth rate of 2.32 per cent in the post-reform period against their pre-reform period average of 37.82 per cent and 0.45 per cent respectively. Due to greater awareness among the RRBs about NPAs management, the level of NPAs against total outstanding advances decreased from 52 per cent in 1995-96 to 22 per cent in 1999-2000. This indicates the qualitative improvement in the NPAs management by the RRBs in the State. There has been steady improvement in the recovery percentage of RRBs as is evidenced by the increase in the recovery percentage from 48 per cent in 1992-93 to 66 per cent in 1999-2000. Increase in the number of RRBs reporting operating profits from 0 in 1995-96 to 5 in 1999-2000, the amount of their annual profits from nil to Rs. 4.62 crore in that period and decrease in the net operating losses from Rs.82.18 crore in 1996-97 to Rs. 21.50 crore in 1999-2000, reflect the improvement in the working results position of RRBs in the post-reform period. Further, the accumulated losses have shown continuous reduction in cases of 5 RRBs and declining growth rates in cases of rest 4 during the later half of the post-reform period.

7.7.19. The RRBs have shown symptoms of improvement in their financial position reflected in terms of steady improvement in their profitability ratios viz., financial margins from 0.48 per cent in 1995-96 to 1.64 per cent in 1999-2000, misc. income to WFs from 0.28 per cent in 1996-97 to 0.95 per cent in 1999-2000, transaction costs to WFs ratio has reduced from 7.03 per cent in 1994-95 to around 3 per cent in 1999-2000 and net margins have improved from -8.71 per cent in 1996-97 to

-1.31 per cent in 1999-2000. Thus, the banking sector reforms in general and the exercise of preparing DAP and execution of MoU with the sponsor banks in particular, for achieving a turn around in RRBs in a planned manner over three to five years seem to have started yielding results. Thus, the hypothesis is proved.

Conclusions

7.8.1. Since their inception RRBs have been serving the weaker sections of the society with outfits of cooperatives and commercial banks in rural areas of Orissa. By operating mainly in rural areas, they have provided access of banking services to the poor in hitherto unbanked and underbanked rural areas of the State. They have helped in creation of employment opportunities through provision of credit assistance to a large number of small borrowers in different capacities. Further, by sanctioning term loans for acquisition of productive assets, they have contributed directly to creation of assets. The RRBs have also helped in income generation in rural area through the financing of agriculture and allied activities, village and cottage industries and government-sponsored anti-poverty programmes in the State. Thus, considering the specific task assigned to the RRBs, these banks deserve credit for playing a very useful role in the socio-economic development of Orissa.

7.8.2. However, in the process of giving financial support to the poor, these banks themselves have become financially and operationally sick and could not do much to attain viability. Despite working with many odds like operating on low-margins, high cost of management, deteriorating financial position, etc., these banks have not lost their relevance till today. The RRBs have experienced far-reaching changes in their operation since the introduction of the banking sector reforms. These changes have brought about perceptible improvements in their performance both in quantitative as well as qualitative terms.

Limitations of the Study

7.9.1. The whole analysis is based on the secondary data collected from the financial statements published by the Central and Regional Office of NABARD, Annual Reports of Individual RRBs, Publications of the Bureau of Economics and Statistics, Orissa and RBI publications. Data were collected from different sources according to the need of the study and accessibility to the sources of data. Consequently, they are bound to show some variation even for the same bank for the same period. In spite of their limitations, secondary data constitute the major source of data for the study mainly due to scarcity of time and resources which are otherwise essential for collection of primary data. The average figures calculated in the study have been based on the principles and techniques of arithmetic mean which have their own limitations. Coverage of rural areas by individual RRBs could not be worked out due to non-availability of data. This constitutes another limitation of the study. The data used in the study have been analysed and interpreted keeping in view the above said limitations.

Practical Utility of the Study

7.10.1. The present study is primarily a fact-finding research work pertaining to the basic operations of RRBs in Orissa for the period from 1986 to 1999-2000. The study contains an analysis of the structural growth and progress of RRBs ever since their inception in 1976 in the State up to the year ended in March 2000. It also presents a comparative analysis of the basic operations of RRBs as a whole in the State between pre-reform and post-reform period. The study also seeks to bring into focus the strengths and weaknesses of the RRBs collectively and individually. The study, thus would help to know the quantitative an qualitative improvements in the performance of RRBs brought about by the banking sector reforms started in early nineties as a part of the financial sector reforms. In addition to this, the study will help initiating a policy shift as well as a conscious change in their mode of functioning by all concerned namely the GOI, RBI, NABARD, Sponsor Banks, State Governments with a view to enabling the RRBs to achieve steady progress towards sustained profitability and strength. They can use the findings of the study to take appropriate remedial measures where needed not only for the weak RRBs but also for other institutional financing agencies operating in rural areas viz. cooperatives and commercial banks to foster a sound rural banking environment in the State. The study would also serve useful purpose as a reference document to banks, the researchers and others concerned with rural banking.

Scope for Further Research

7.11.1. There are certain aspects of rural banking that came up in course of the study which provides scope for further research on the subject. An intensive study can be undertaken about the impact of RRBs' financing on the socio-economic development of the undivided KBK (Kalahandi, Bolangir and Koraput) districts, the perennially underdeveloped region of the State through an in-depth analysis of the operations of the three RRBs operating in that area. A study can also be initiated to ascertain the extent to which the borrowers of RRBs in real terms of money and income have improved their standards of living. A study pertaining to the extent to which RRBs could scale down or liquidate the debts of the poorest of the poor or the number of beneficiaries of RRBs who have gone above poverty line as a result of being financed by them. If the present study which is based entirely on the secondary data, is supplemented by the primary data relating to several issues as mentioned above, it will provide a better insight into the problem of rural banking in the State. It will also widen the scope of the study to a considerable extent and will provide a base for further extension of the research on the subject.

Annexure-I

Growth Rates of C-D Ratios and ID Ratios of RRBs in Orissa (Total Sample) (For the period from 1992-93 to 1999-2 000)

[Figures in per cent]

Sl. No,	*Year*	*Growth Rates*		*Remarks*
		CD-Ratio	*I-D Ratio*	
1.	1992-93	–13.39	6.61	(4) > (3)
2.	1993-94	–18.50	1.62	(4) > (3)
3.	1994-95	-7.82	-18.55	(4) < (3)
4.	1995-96	-4.33	7.54	(4) > (3)
5.	1996-97	-7.80	23.13	(4) > (3)
6.	1997-98	-4.96	-10.16	(4) < (3)
7.	1998-99	-7.01	4.12	(4) > (3)
8.	1999-2000	-3.02	4.28	(4) > (3)
9.	Average	-8.35	2.32	(4) > (3)

Source : The figures in Col. (3) and (4) are taken from Table - 5.13 and Table 5.16 respectively.

Annexure-II

Average Growth Rate of C-D Ratios and I-D Ratios of RRBs in Orissa

(Individual RRBs) (For the period from 1992-93 to 1999-2000)

[Figures in per cent]

Sl. No.	*RRBs*	*Average Growth Rates of C-D Ratios*	*Average Growth Rates of I-D Ratios*	*Remarks*
1.	Puri GB	-5.94	12.06	Av. Growth of C-D Ratio < I-D Ratio
2.	Bolangir GB	-10.89	-0.50	-Ditto-
3.	Cuttack GB	-9.22	5.53	-Ditto-
4.	Koraput GB	-3.18	-2.76	-Ditto-
5.	Kalahandi GB	-11.89	6.41	-Ditto-
6.	Baitarani GB	-8.12	3.97	-Ditto-
7.	Balasore GB	-11.96	19.47	-Ditto-
8.	Rushikulya GB	-10.18	6.15	-Ditto-
9.	Dhenkanal GB	-2.92	5.17	-Ditto-
10.	All RRBs in Orissa	-8.35	2.32	-Ditto-

Source : The figures in Col. 3 and Col. 4 are taken from Table - 6.10 and Table 6.14.

Bibliography

Books

Bapna, M.S.; *Regional Rural Banks in Rajasthan : A Case Study of their Working and Growth*, Himalaya (1989), Delhi.

Das, V.B.M., Rao, J.V.P. and Rao, P.H.K.; *Rural Banks and Rural Credit*, Discovery, New Delhi.

Government of Orissa; *Economic Surveys of Orissa, Bureau of Economics and Statistics*, Bhubaneswar, 1985-86 to 1999-2000.

Government of Orissa; *Statistical Abstracts of Orissa, Bureau of Economics and Statistics*, Bhubaneswar, 1996.

Government of India; *The Regional Rural Banks Act, 1976* (As amended up to Act 66 of 1988), Ministry of Law, Justice and Company Affairs, GOI, New Delhi.

Government of India; *Statistical Abstracts of India (1997)*, Central Statistical Organisation, Ministry of Planning and Programme Implementation, GOI, New Delhi.

Kumar, S., *RRBs and Rural Development*, Deep and Deep (1990), New Delhi.

NABARD Publication; *Annual Reports, 1998-99, 1999-2000*, Central Office, Mumbai.

NABARD Publication; *Financial Statements of RRBs in India, 1998-99 & 1999-2000*, Central Office, Mumbai.

NABARD Publication; *Institutional Development Role of National Bank*, Central Office, Mumbai.

NABARD Publication; *Review of Performance of RRBs in India*, 1995-96 and 1998-99, Central Office, Mumbai.

NABARD Publication; *Review of the Performance of RRBs in Orissa*; 1996-97, 1997-98, 1998-99, 1999-2000, Regional Office, Bhubaneswar.

NABARD Publication; *Statistics on RRBs (1986 to 1997-98)*, Central Office, Mumbai

Parikh, Kirti S.; *India Development Report (1999-2000)*, Indira Gandhi Institute of Development Research (IGIDR), Mumbai.

Reserve Bank of India (RBI), *Annual Report, 1999*, Mumbai.

RBI, *Banking Statistics, Quarterly Handout*, March 2000, Mumbai.

RBI, *Basic Statistical Returns*, Vol. 26, 27, 28, March 1996, March 1997, March 1998, Mumbai.

RBI Bulletin, May 1999, Mumbai.

RBI and Rural Credit (1985), Rural Planning and Credit Cell, RBI, Bombay.

RBI Statistical Statements Relating to Cooperative Movement in India, 1975-76, Part - I, Bombay (1977).

Sinha Roy, B.P., *RRBs in West Bengal,* Mittal (1994), New Delhi.

Vyas, M.R., *Evolution and Management of RRBs*, Arihant (1991), Jaipur.

Wadhva, CD., *Rural Banks for Rural Development*, Macmillan (1988), Madras.

Articles

Amannaya, K.K., "RRBs and Rural Economic Development", *Southern Economist*, Vol. 34, No. 23, 24, April 1-15, 1996, Bangalore.

Basu, S.K., "Creditworthiness of Purpose - A Study of RRBs", *Kurukshetra*, Vol. 36, No. 8, May 1988, New Delhi.

Bhatia, C.L., "Imperatives and Impediments of Rural Banking", *The Financial Express*, 6 October 1993, Mumbai.

Bhuleskar, A.V., "Rural Lending; Recovery System needs a boost", *Business Standard*, 20 November 1992, Mumbai.

Binswanger, H. and Khandeker, S., "The Impact of Formal Finance on the Rural Economy of India", *Policy Research Working Papers*, The World Bank, 1992.

Chadha, B.L., "Toning up the Rural Credit System to Improve Viability", *The Financial Express*, 23 April 1995, Mumbai.

"Centre may Take up Fresh Set of RRBs for Restructuring", *The Economic Times*, 22 March 1995.

Dadhich, C.L. and Srivastava, B.P., "RRBs Subsuming the Self to Survive", *The Economic Times*, 28 April 1994, Mumbai.

Dubey, J.P., "RRBs Loans must be need-based", *The Financial Express*, 9 December 1993, Mumbai.

Dubhasi, P.R., "Changing Profile of Banks in Rural Financing", *Kurukshetra*, Vol. 49, No. 1 (Annual Issue), October 2000, New Delhi.

Ghosh, B.K. and Patel, K.V., "Role of Banks in the Promotion of Agriculture and Rural Development - Indian Experience", NIBM (1995), Pune.

Goswami, S.N., "RRBs; Landmark in Rural Banking", *Kurukshetra*, July 1992.

Gulati, Ashok, "Agriculture and Rural Development", *Economic and Political Weekly (EPW)*, Vol. 35, No. 14, April 2000, Mumbai.

Gupta, S.K. and Sadhu, A.N., "Economic Liberalisation and Rural Credit System", *Kurukshetra*, Vol. XLIII, No. 10, July 1995, New Delhi.

Gupta, K.G. and Singh, R., "A new look to regional rural banking", *Khadi Gramodyog*, Vol. 37, No. 12, September, 1991, New Delhi.

Hundekar, S.G., "Performance of RRBs in Karnataka", *Khadi Gramodyog*, Vol. 38, No. 3, December 1991, New Delhi.

"IBRD Team to study rural credit opportunities in India", *The Economic Times*, 6 December 1996, Mumbai.

Jain, S.C., "Rural Financing in Transition", *Kurukshetra*, Vol. 49, No. 1 (Annual Issue), October 2000, New Delhi.

Kalia, S.K., "How Viable is Rural Credit?", *Observer of Business and Politics*, 3 February 1995, CMIE, Bombay.

Kaushik, C.B. and Gangwar, A.C., "An Appraisal of the Working of RRBs in Haryana", *Kautilya*, Vol. 3 No. 1-2, June-December, 1982.

Khuntia, Natabar, "Field Problems in Orissa", *The Economic Times* (Supplement), 1 December 1988, Mumbai.

Krishna, C., "RRBs and Rural Development", *Yojana*, Vol. 33, No. 24, 1 January 1990, pp.32-34, New Delhi.

Kumar, B.P., "RRBs, An analysis with reference to Andhra Pradesh vis-à-vis India", *Kurukshetra*, Vol. XLIII, No. 10 to 14, July 1995, New Delhi.

Majumdar, N.A., "Reviving Rural Credit", *EPW*, August 14-20, 1999, Mumbai.

Majumdar, N.A., "Overhauling the Somnolent Rural Credit System", *EPW*, Vol. 32, No. 42, 15 October 1997, Mumbai.

Menon, S., "Government to infuse Rs. 12.50 Cr. fresh share capital into RRBs", *The Economic Times*, 30 October 1994, Mumbai.

Menon, S., "RRBs allowed to invest extra funds in listed UTI Schemes", *The Economic Times*, 18 January 1995, Mumbai.

Menon, S., "Will mere recapitalisation benefit RRBs?", *The Economic Times*, 7 March 1996, Mumbai.

Mishra, B.N., "RRBs and Rural Development", *Kurukshetra*, Vol. XLIV, No. 10, July 1996, New Delhi.

Mishra, B.N., "Banking and Rural Development, with special reference to Orissa", *Kurukshetra*, Vol. XLIII, No. 10 to 14, July 1995, New Delhi.

Mishra, S.N., and Ramesh Chand, "Public and Private Capital Formation in Agriculture: Comments on Complementarity Hypothesis and Others", *EPW*, Vol. 30, No. 25, June 24, 1995, Mumbai.

"Myth and Reality of Rural Credit", Financial Express Research Bureau, *The Financial Express*, 5 March 1996, Mumbai.

Nair, A., "RRBs stage a turnaround after signing MoU - says RBI study", *The Financial Express*, 20 July 1995, Mumbai.

Nair, S.T., "Rural Financial Intermediation and Commercial Banks; Review of Recent Trends", *EPW*, 29 January 2001, Mumbai.

Patel, A.R., "Rural Credit System, Evolution, Innovation, Progress and Problems", *Kurukshetra*, Vol. 36, No. 8, May 1988, New Delhi.

Patel, A.R., "Rural Credit: Need for Banks' Initiatives", *Kurukshetra*, Vol. 48, No. 12, September 2000, New Delhi.

Patel, A.R., "Rural Credit System; Need for Restructuring", *Kurukshetra*, Vol. 49, No. 4, January 2001, New Delhi.

Patel, K.V., "On the Viability of Rural Banking", *Prajnan*, Vol. 23, No. 1, 1994-95, NIBM, Pune.

Patel, K.V., "Rural Development: Strategies and Experiences", *Pigmy Economic Review*, Diamond Jubilee Year, November 1984, Manipal.

Patel, K.V. and Shete, N.B., "RRBs: Performance and prospects", *Prajnan*, NIBM, Pune, January-March 1980.

Pattnaik, N., "Navin demands special category status for Orissa", *The Economic Times*, 7 June 2001, Kolkata.

"Poverty estimates for 1999-2000", *Kurukshetra*, Vol. 49, No. 7, IInd Cover Page, April 2001, New Delhi.

"Prudential norms for RRBs", Banking Bureau, *Business Standard*, 30 September 1995, Mumbai.

Raj, K.N., "RRBs Some issues", *Kurukshetra*, Vol. XLIV, No. 10, July 1996, New Delhi.

Raja Rao, A., "Impact of the RRBs on Income and Employment of Weaker Sections (with reference to Andhra Pradesh), *Kurukshetra*, Vol. XLIV, No. 10, July 1996, New Delhi.

Rangarajan, C, "Rural Credit Scenario in India", *Banking Finance*, Vol. 3, No. 7, July 1995.

Rangarajan, C, "Rural India: The Role of Credit", *The Banker*, 15 March 1996.

Rangarajan, C, "Some Issues Relating to Rural Finance", Abstracts of the First Ram Mathai Memorial Lecture at IIM, Ahmedabad, 8 March 1996. As cited in *RBI Bulletin*, May 1996, Mumbai.

Rao, P.S.M., "RRBs— Compulsions for restructuring", *Business Standard*, 7 January 1994, Mumbai.

"RBI asks RRBs to relocate sick branches", *The Business Age: The Asian Age*, 9 August 1995, Calcutta.

"Rural Branches and Rural Credit", *The Observer of Business and Politics*, 14 August 1995, Mumbai.

"Rural Credit during 7th and 8th Plans - Major issues", *The Financial Express*, 8 October 1992, Mumbai.

Sangwan, S.S., "Viability of Rural Credit Structure", *Prajnan*, Vol. 18, No. 2, April-June 1989, NIBM, Pune.

Sharma, H.L., "RRBs in Himachal Pradesh", *Kurukshetra*, Vol. XLIV, No. 10, July 1996, New Delhi.

Sharma, R., "Rural Credit: View from the field", *The Economic Times*, 18 October 1996, Mumbai.

Shete, N.B. and Karkal, G.L., "RRBs. Problems and Perspectives of Rural Credit", *Prajnan*, Vol. 18, No. 2, April-June 1989, NIBM, Pune.

Shivamaggi, H.B., "Reforms in Rural Banking; Need for bolder approach", *EPW*, Vol. 35, No. 20, May 13-19, 2000, Mumbai.

Singha, K., "A case for rural banking subsidiaries", *Kurukshetra*, Vol. 40, No. 10, July 1992, New Delhi.

Srinivasan, G., "Union Budget 2001-02: Thrust to Rural Development", *Kurukshetra*, Vol. 49, No. 7, April 2001, New Delhi.

"Statement referred to in reply to paras (a), (b), (c) and (d) of Rajya Sabha Starred Question No. 4 for 14 February 1995 regarding losses incurred by RRBs", New Delhi.

Toluyemi, T., "Operations of Rural Financial Institutions (RFIs): A Comparative Review of Indian and Nigerian Experience", *Journal of Rural Development*, Vol. 15, No. 3, 1996, NIRD, Hyderabad.

Thamarajakshi, R., "Agriculture and Economic Reforms", *EPW*, August 14-20, 1999, Mumbai.

Thingalaya, N.K., "Concretising rural banking through Gram Vikas Kendras", *The Financial Express*, 9 April 1995, Mumbai.

Varde, V.S. and Singh, S.P., "Profitability Performance of RRBs", *Prajnan*, October-December, 1982, NIBM, Pune.

Velayudham, T.K. and Sankaranarayanan, V., "RRBs and Rural Credit: Some issues", *EPW*, September 22, 1990, Mumbai.

Yaron, Jacob, "Successful Rural Financial Institutions", *World Bank Discussion Papers*, 1992.

Reports

Report of the Committee on Cooperation (1915) RBI; [As cited in "RRBs : Problems and Perspectives of Rural Credit", Shete and Karkal, *Prajnan,* 18 (2), NIBM, Pune, 1989].

Report of the Rural Banking Enquiry Committee (1949), GOI, New Delhi.

All India Rural Credit Survey, *The Survey Report*, Vol. I, Part - 2, (1951), RBI, Bombay.

Report of the Committee of Direction, All India Rural Credit Survey (AIRCS); RBI (1954), Bombay.

Report of the All India Rural Credit Review Committee (AIRCRC) (1969), RBI, Bombay.

Report of the National Commission on Agriculture (1969), GOI, New Delhi.

Report of the Committee on Differential Interest Rates (1971), RBI, Bombay.

Report of the Banking Commission (1972), GOI, New Delhi.

Reports of the All-India Debt and Investment Surveys, 1981-82, RBI (1987), Bombay.

Report of the Working Group on Rural Banks (1975), GOI, New Delhi.

Report of the Working Group on Operational and Accounting Procedures for RRBs (1976), RBI, Bombay.

Report of Review Committee on RRBs (1978), RBI, Bombay.

Report of the Committee on Control over RRB Branches (1980), RRB, Bombay.

A Study on the Viability of RRBs (1981), RBI Bulletin, March 1981.

Report of the Committee to Review the Arrangements for Institutional Credit for Agriculture and Rural Development (CRAFICARD) (1981), RBI, Bombay.

Report of the Kelkar Working Group on RRBs (1986), GOI, New Delhi.

Report of the Khushro Agricultural Credit Review Committee (1989), RBI, Bombay.

Report of the Narasimham Committee on the Financial Sector Reforms (1991), RBI, Bombay.

All India Debts and Investment Survey (1991-92): Salient Features: *RBI Bulletin*, May 1999, Mumbai.

Report on the Trend and Progress of Banking in India (1998-99), December 1999, RBI, Mumbai.

India Development Report (1999-2000), Edited by Kirti S. Parikh, IG1DR, Mumbai.

Report of the Expert Group on Estimation of Proportion and Number of Poor (Lakdawala Committee) (1999-2000), National Sample Survey Organisation (NSSO), GOI, New Delhi. (As quoted in IInd Cover Page - *Kurukshetra*, Vol. 49, No. 7, April 2001, New Delhi.)

Index

A

20-Points Economic Programme, 55
Advanced States, 92
- Bihar, 92
- Haryana, 92
- Punjab, 92
- Tamil Nadu, 92
- Uttar Pradesh, 92

Agricultural
- Finance, 29
- Price, 22, 246
- Refinance Corporation (ARC), 31

Agriculture, 24-25, 27, 29, 31, 39, 42, 44-45, 49, 52-53, 90-91, 96-97, 116, 142, 246-47, 249, 254, 271
- and Rural Development, 28
- Credit Department (ACD), 29, 32
- Credit Review Committee, 62, 250
- Credit System, 31
- Finance Sub-Committee (Gadgil), 29
- Growth, 99
- Infrastructure, 25
- Labourers, 22, 51, 60, 99
- Refinance and Development Corporation, 31

Agro-Climatic Conditions, 97
Agro-Climatic Zones, 88
All India Mineral Resources Estimate, 93
All India Rural Credit Review Committee (AIRCRC), (Venmkatappiah), 22, 26, 30-31, 54, 246-47, 249
All India Rural Credit Survey Report, 50
Allahabad Bank, 124, 257
Andhra Bank, 124, 181, 257
Andhra Pradesh, 88, 98
Anti-Poverty Programme, 11, 100, 111-13, 118
- ERRP, 11
- IRDP, 11, 100, 111-12, 118
- JRY, 11
- RLEGP, 11

Aquaculture, 24
Assam—West Bengal, 90
Asset Classification Norms, 142, 180, 202, 207

B

Baitarni GB, 186-87, 189-95, 197, 199, 202-04, 207, 211, 216, 218, 221-22, 226, 229, 232, 236, 239, 241-44, 257, 265, 269

Balasore GB, 131, 186-87, 189-97, 199, 202-04, 207, 211, 213, 216, 229, 257, 261, 265, 268-69
Bandh and Deogarh, 124
Bank Credit, 257
Bank Nationalization, 41
Bank of India, 181
Banking Commission (Saraiya), 54-55, 250
- Proposals, 55
Banking Sector in Orissa, 98
Banking Sector Reforms, 8, 129, 240, 252
Banking System, 33, 83, 251
Basu, K, 62
Bay of Bengal, 88
Below Poverty Line (BPL), 21, 254
Bhandari Committee, 251
Bhandari, MC, 62
Bihar, 78, 84, 88
Bihar—West Bengal, 253
Bolangir District, 124
Bolangir GB, 124, 186-87, 190-97, 199, 202-04, 211, 213, 216, 218, 221-22, 226, 229, 232, 236, 239, 241-44, 257, 261
British Colonial Rules, 29

C

Cash Crops, 91
Commercial Banks (CBs), 7, 10, 15, 29, 31-33, 35, 38-39, 44-45, 50-52, 54-55, 57, 60-61, 63, 65, 82, 99-100, 247-51, 261-62, 272
- System, 31
Central Bank, 28
Central Banking Inquiry Committee, 29
Central Ground Water Board, 91
Centre for Monitoring Indian Economy (CMIE), 12
Chhattisgarh, 88
Civil Courts, 29
Coal Reserve, 93
Commercial Crops, 24
Committee on Cooperative Credit (Mehta), 54
Committee on—Regional Rural Banks, 61
Committee to Review—Rural Development (CRAFICARD), 61, 250
Communication—Insurance Facilities, 94
Cooperative
- Banking System, 28
- Banks, 34-55
- Credit Institute, 36
- Credit Movement, 29, 54
- Credit Societies, 44
- Credit Structure, 55
- Credit System, 7, 10
- Societies Act, 1904, 29
- Societies, 32, 39, 60
Cooperatives, 36, 51-52, 248, 250, 261
Cottage Industries, 93
Credit Delivery System, 31
Credit Deposit Ration (CD Ration), 94, 98, 105, 159, 183, 184, 202, 232, 251, 253, 255-56, 258-61, 265, 269
Crop Loan System, 34
Crops, 272
Customer Services, 171

Cuttack GB, 124, 186-97, 199, 202-04, 207, 211, 216, 229, 260, 264

D

Dairy Farming, 24
Dantwala Committee, 61, 250
Dantwala, Prof. ML, 15, 60
DCCB (District Central Cooperative Banks), 36, 38, 248
Deposit Insurance and Credit Guarantee Cooperative (DICGC), 171, 232
Deposit Mobilization, 11, 84, 180, 253, 272
Depression of 1930, 346
Development Action Plans (DAPs), 64, 83, 252
Dhenkanal GB, 122, 124, 189-95, 197, 199, 202-04, 211, 213, 216, 218, 221-22, 226, 229, 232, 236, 239, 241-44, 257, 260, 265, 268

E

Eastern Ghats, 88
Economic
- and State Bureau of-, 13
- Development, 21, 35, 94, 99
- Infrastructure, 116
- Liberalization, 62, 142
- Survey of Orissa, 12

Economy, 11, 87, 94, 115-16, 254-55
- Indian, 22, 42
- National, 29
- Orissa, 11
- Rural and Agriculture, 255

Electronic and Telecommunication Revolution, 9
Employment Opportunities, 11, 53, 98, 116, 118, 257, 271
Expert Group on Policy Issues of Regional Rural Banks, 62

F

Farm and Rural Development, 21
Farm Development Policy, 10
Farm Sector Development, 246-254
Farming Community, 52
Fibre Crops, 91
Financial Institutions in India, 44, 82
Financial Sector Reforms (FSR), 34, 49, 62-63, 251
Five Year Plan (8th), 24
Floriculture, 24
Food Policy Research Institute (Washington), 9

G

Gadgil, DR, 30
General Line of Credit (GLC), 28
Gorwala, AD, 30
Green Revolution, 25
Gujarat, 76, 98

H

Haryana, 76, 98
Himachal Pradesh, 76
Horticulture, 24, 97

I

Imperial Bank of India, 31, 247
Income Distribution Pattern, 53
India's Development Strategy, 9
Indian
- Agriculture, 25
- Banking System, 28
- Council of Social Science Research, 12
- Economy, 246
- Economy, Rural and Agrarian, 246, 255
- Overseas Bank (IOB), 124, 181
- Public Policy, 26

Indira Gandhi Institute of Development Research, (IGIDR), 12
Institutional Credit, 185, 248
Institutional Finance System, 29
Integrated Scheme of Rural Credit, 30
Investment-Deposit Ratio (ID Ratio), 164
IRDP, 256, 267
Iron Ore, 93
Irrigation Canals, 88

J

Jawahar Lal Nehru University, 12
Jharkhand, 88

K

Kalahandi Anchalika GB—Balasore GB, 122
Kalahandi GB, 186-87, 189-95, 197, 199, 202-04, 207, 211, 216, 218, 221-22, 226, 229, 232, 236, 239, 241-44, 257, 260, 265, 260
Kalahandi—Koraput, 124
Karnataka, 76, 98
Kelkar Committee, 83
Kelkar Working Group, 61, 250
Kelkar, SM, 61
Kerala, 76, 84, 98
Khanna, PN, 61
Khusro Committee, 171, 173, 221
Khusro, AM, 62, 250
Kisan Credit Cards (KCC), 34, 247
Koraput GB, 188, 194-97, 199, 202-04, 207, 211, 216, 218, 221-22, 226, 229, 232, 236, 239-44, 257, 260, 263

L

LAB (Local Area Banks), 32, 33, 44-45, 247
Land Laws, 25
Land Reforms, 25
Landless Agriculture Labourers, 53, 111
Lead Bank Scheme, 31, 249
Legislation, 21
Liberalization and Globalization, 8, 11

M

Maclagan Committee, 29
Madhya Pradesh, 78, 84
Maharashtra, 98
Maharashtra—Karnataka, 33
Marine Resources, 98

Market Conditions, 167
Medicinal Herbs, 97
Micro Finance Scheme, 32
Mineral and Forest Wealth, 38
Mineral Deposits, 93
Mishra, Baidyanath, 17
Monetary Policy Measures, 171
MPCE, 96
Mysore Resettlement and Dev. Agency (MYRADA), 32

N

NABARD (National Bank for Agriculture and Rural Development), 9, 13, 15, 28, 31-35, 44-45, 49, 59-65, 69, 83, 132, 136, 139, 181, 184, 239, 247, 252, 259, 261-62, 269, 271-72.
Nagaland, 66
Narasimham Committee on Financial System, 60, 63, 250
Narasimham Working Group on Reg. Rural Banks, 31, 33-35, 57, 249-50
Narasimham, M, 56, 62, 82
NASSDOC (National Social Science Documentation Centre), 12
National
- Credit Commercial Study Group, 54
- Industrial Tribunal (NIT), 63, 152, 170, 242
  – Award, 151
- Institute of Bank Management (NIBM), Pune, 16
- Rural Credit Fund (NRCF), 28
- Sample Survey Organization (NSSO), 90

Nationalization, 31
Nationalization of Commercial Banks, 38, 248-49
Nationalized Banks, 105, 117, 247-48, 256
Natural Calamities, 11
New Economic
- Policy, 13, 62, 129
- Programme, 56

NGO, 32, 45, 107, 267
Non-Banking Finance Corporation (NBFC), 33-34
Non-Performing Assets (NPA), 64, 76, 162, 164, 183-84, 207, 236, 253, 259
Non-Target Group (NTG), 63, 146, 149, 182, 252
North-Eastern States, 66, 76, 84
- Assam, 76
- Tripura, 76

NSDP (State's Net Domestic Product), 11, 91, 96

O

Orissa, 7-8, 11-12, 17, 78, 84, 87, 89, 91
- Agricultural Pattern, 88
- Crop Pattern, 91
- Demographic Profile, 88
- Economic Development of-, 17, 99
- Economic Profiles, 87, 115
- Economy, 89, 91, 96, 99
- Employment Situation, 89
- GSDP, 90

- Industry, 93
- Infrastructural Facilities, 94-95, 98
- Irrigation, 91
- Mineral and Financial Resources, 93
- Rainfall, 88
- Regional Rural Banks in-, 94

P

PACs, 51, 248

Patel and Shete, Profs., 16

Pisciculture, 24

Planning Commission, 7, 11, 66, 89, 254

Plantations Corps, 97

Poultry Farming, 24

Poverty Alleviation Programmes, 7, 9, 26

Poverty Line, 7, 11

Preferencial Refinance Scheme, 27

Primary Cooperative Agriculture and Rural Dev. Banks (PCARDBs), 38

Priority Sector Landing, 27

Public Sector Banks (PSBs), 34, 56, 63, 126

Public Sector Commercial Banks, 248

Punjab, 76

Puri GB, 121, 124, 180, 186, 188-89, 194-95, 197, 199, 202-04, 207, 211, 216, 218, 221-22, 226, 229, 232, 236, 239, 241-44, 257, 265, 269

Puri GB—Panchbati GB, 122

R

Rajasthan, 84, 98

Recapitalization Programme, 64

Reforms Measures, 8

Regional Rural Banks, 7-8, 10-13, 15-18, 28-35, 38-39, 44, 49, 50, 54, 56-67, 69-72, 76, 78, 80, 82-84, 87, 94, 99-100, 103, 105, 107, 109, 111-12, 116-118, 121-22, 124, 126, 128-29, 131-32, 136, 139, 142, 146, 149, 152, 159, 162, 164, 167, 170-72, 178, 180-86, 188, 245, 247-48

- Act, 1976, 57
- Amendment Act, 57, 61, 82
- Amendment Act, 250
- Branches in States, 66
- Coverage, 122
- Credit Structure, 15
- Deposit Mobilization, 69
- Establishment in Orissa, 50, 121-22
- Growth and Development, 14
- Location Policy, 59
- Loss Incurring RRBs, 76, 80, 152, 186, 258
- Management and Capital Structure, 59
- Objectives, 58
- Operations, 60
- Performance, 185, 258-59
- Productivity, 12
- Resources, 69
- Setting of Banks in Five States, 57
- Special Features, 58
- Sponsorship, 58
- Structural Growth in Orissa, 12, 14

- Structural Growth, 240, 263
- System, 188
- System in India, 8

Reserve Bank of India (RBI), 14-16, 184, 247, 252, 261-62, 271
Resource Mobility, 188
Return on Advances (ROA), 173
Return on Investments (ROI), 173
Review Committee on Regional Rural Banks, 15-16, 60-61.
Rotating Savings and Credit Asscciation (ROSCA), 35, 248
Roy, BP Sinha, 17
Rural
- Agriculture Economy, 142
- Artisans, 99, 146, 182, 266-67
- Bank in India, 14
- Banking
  - Enquiry Committee, 1949, 30, 54, 249
  - in India, 21, 28, 245-46
  - Infrastructure, 10
  - System in India, 247
  - System, 7, 10, 35
- Banking, 7, 13, 34, 35, 50, 52, 55-56, 247, 249, 272
  - Working Group on-, 56
- Credit, 10, 14, 21-22, 26, 28, 30, 32, 36, 44, 49, 50, 57, 66, 82, 245-46, 248-49, 250
  - Cooperative, 242
  - Delivery System, 249
  - in India, 34
  - Institutions in India, 9, 10
  - Policy, 14, 26, 33, 246
  - Sources, 35, 36
  - Structure, 13
  - Survey, 30
  - System, 21, 41, 44, 49, 61
- Development, 9, 11, 15-17, 21, 24-25, 53, 99, 116, 121, 246
- Economy, 7, 9, 116
  - Development of-, 7
- Educated Youth, 56
- Finance, 21
- Finance System, 35
- Financial Institutions, 8
- Infrastructure, 7, 9
- Infrastructure Development Fund (RIDF), 25, 32-33, 45, 247
- Planning and Credit Cell, (RPCC), 32
- Population, 7, 9, 11, 21, 30, 35, 38, 96, 246, 249

Rushikulya GB, 122, 186-87, 189-97, 199, 203-04, 207, 211, 213, 216, 218, 221-22, 226, 229, 232, 236, 239, 241-44, 257, 260

S

Saving Bank Deposit, 15
SC/ST, 111-12, 118, 254, 256, 267
SCB (State Cooperative Banks), 36, 38, 248
Scheduled Commercial Banks, 52, 53, 60, 66, 99-100, 105-07, 117, 248-49, 254-56, 263
Scientific Methods, 24
Sector,
- Agriculture, 8, 24, 55, 71
- Banking, 82
- Commercial Banks, 31
- Cooperative Banking, 55
- Cooperative, 22, 25, 247
- Farm, 52-54, 253, 256
- Financial, 35
- Industrial, 98

- Mineral, 98
- Non-Agriculture, 39
- Non-Farm, 182
- Private, 94
- Rural, 1, 55, 96

Self Employment Programme, 21
Self-Help Groups (SHGs), 32, 45, 107, 267
Sericulture, 24
Service Area Approach, 249
SIDBI, 69
Sir Malcolm Darling Report, 1934, 29
Sivaraman, V, 61
SLR, 182
Small Scale Industries, 107
Social Banking, 41
Society, 121
- Rural, 25, 246

Socio-Economic Development, 96, 116
Special Credit Programme, 27
Spices, 97
Sponsor Banks, 63-65, 83, 136
State Bank of India (SBI), 31, 105, 117, 124, 247, 256
State Cooperative Agriculture and Rural Dev. Banks (SCARDBs), 38
State Electricity Boards, 39
State Land Development Banks (SLDB), 32
State Level Bankers Committee (SLBC), Bhubneshwar, 13
Storage and Warehousing, 31
Subsidised Credits, 27
Sundaravaradam, R, 61
Super Cyclone, 96, 254

T

Tamil Nadu, 76, 98
Term Deposits, 15
Thakurdas, Sir Purushottamdas, 30, 54
Thingalaya, NK, 62
Thingalaya Expert Group on Policy Issues, 251
Traditional Methods, 24
Traditional Rural Artisans, 53

U

UCO, 124, 181
University of Bombay, 12
UTI Schemes, 63

V

Village and Cottage Industries, 71, 73, 98, 100, 107, 113, 116, 257, 266-67, 271

W

Wadhva, CD, 16
West Bengal, 17, 84, 88, 98
Working Funds (WFs), 171, 178, 180, 221, 226, 229, 236, 270
Ratio, 260
Working Group on Rural Banks, 60, 82